A HISTORY OF AMERICAN GIFTED EDUCATION

A History of American Gifted Education provides the first comprehensive history of the field of gifted education, which is essential to recognizing its contribution to the overall American educational landscape. The text relies heavily on primary documents and artifacts as well as essential secondary documents such as the disparate historical texts and relevant biographies that already exist. This book commences its investigation of American gifted education with the founding of the field of psychology and, subsequently, of gifted education at the early part of the 20th century and concludes just over a century later with the passage of the No Child Left Behind Act in 2001.

Jennifer L. Jolly is Associate Professor of Gifted Education at the University of Alabama, USA.

A HISTORY OF AMERICAN GIFTED EDUCATION

Jennifer L. Jolly

NEW YORK AND LONDON

First published 2018
by Routledge
711 Third Avenue, New York, NY 10017

and by Routledge
2 Park Square, Milton Park, Abingdon, Oxon, OX14 4RN

Routledge is an imprint of the Taylor & Francis Group, an Informa business

© 2018 Taylor & Francis

The right of Jennifer L. Jolly to be identified as author of this work has been asserted by her in accordance with sections 77 and 78 of the Copyright, Designs and Patents Act 1988.

All rights reserved. No part of this book may be reprinted or reproduced or utilized in any form or by any electronic, mechanical, or other means, now known or hereafter invented, including photocopying and recording, or in any information storage or retrieval system, without permission in writing from the publishers.

Trademark notice: Product or corporate names may be trademarks or registered trademarks, and are used only for identification and explanation without intent to infringe.

Library of Congress Cataloging-in-Publication Data
A catalog record for this title has been requested

ISBN: 978-1-138-92427-7 (hbk)
ISBN: 978-1-138-92429-1 (pbk)
ISBN: 978-1-315-68445-1 (ebk)

Typeset in Bembo
by Deanta Global Publishing Services, Chennai, India

CONTENTS

Introduction   *1*

SECTION I   5

1 The Foundational Underpinnings of a Field   7

2 Early Empirical Influence, High Ability, and Individual Difference   11

3 A *New* Psychology   15

4 Individual Difference and Its Measurement   22

5 The Proliferation of Psychological Study   29

6 Progressive Era of Education   34

SECTION II   39

7 A Field of Their Own   41

8 Preliminary Studies of High Ability and Eminence   46

9 Staggered Attempts at Meeting the Educational Needs of Bright Children   52

10	Father of Gifted Education	61
11	Mother of Gifted Education	73
12	The Residue of Eugenics	82
13	Challenging the Status Quo	84

SECTION III — 89
By Jennifer L. Jolly and Jennifer H. Robins

14	The Growth of Gifted Education	91
15	Legislative Initiatives	96
16	Technology and Science Driven Reform: Searching for Talent	106
17	Identification, Educational Practices, and Considerations	115
18	Recognizing the Need and Establishing Advocacy Organizations	122
19	Creativity as an Empirical Investigation	132

SECTION IV — 135

20	Building and Sustaining Capacity	137
21	Continued Growth, Creativity Research, and Implementation	140
22	The Marland Report	145
23	Capacity Building	155
24	Acknowledged Neglect and Competing Priorities	162
25	Gifted Education's Failings: Underserved Populations	169
26	Competing Conceptions and Definitions of Giftedness	174

Epilogue — *181*
References — *185*
Index — *208*

INTRODUCTION

> History requires a world of time and bitter hard work when your "education" is no further advanced than the cat's; when you are merely stuffing yourself with a mixed-up mess of empty names and random incidents and elusive dates, which no one teaches you how to interpret, and which, uninterpreted, pay you not a farthing's value for your waste of time.
> —*Mark Twain*

This survey of the history of gifted education attempts to present the development of a field over the past century and a half and uses history as the method of understanding the evolution of the field. Scholars in the field of gifted education have recorded brief histories (Robinson & Jolly, 2014; Tannenbaum, 1983) to provide perspective, and these have typically appeared in chapter or article form, leaving the reader with an introduction to its historical past. The significance of the history presented in this text is understood through the lens in which we live today and no way is it a definitive account, as there are always individuals, places, ideas, and events that will be missed, remain unknown, or are yet to be discovered. As gifted education advanced as a field, it evolved and was informed by a number of other fields such as psychology, creativity, and educational policy—these too could have separate volumes of their own.

This historical analysis allows the opportunity to consider changes over time, the causality of an individual's contributions, action, or an event, and the context in which all of this occurs (Wineburg, 2001). Historical analysis is also important because "if we refuse to listen to history, we will find ourselves fabricating a past that reinforces our understanding of current problems" (Crabtree, 1993, para. 57). Depending on the point in time, the field of gifted education has been pushed along and galvanized by different forces, progress and shifts have been led by great men and women, and forces that have worked in sync or collided to further along the research and practice of gifted education or subdued its progress.

Parallel to the historical analysis is an evaluation to trace the development of the field—what hallmarks signify the structural rendering of an empirically driven discipline. Fensham (2004) argued that these indicators include (1) academic recognition by other fields of study, (2) the establishment of research journals specific to the discipline, (3) professional associations devoted to the advancement of the field, (4) research conferences focused on the advancement of empirical knowledge, (5) the creation of research centers, and (6) the concerted effort to train new researchers. This historical survey reveals that the contemporary field of gifted education in the United States required approximately 50 years to accumulate these features, which is revealed in the following chapters.

This text is also a contemporary history of gifted education as educational opportunities for those with extraordinary ability can trace their origins to the earliest civilizations. The continued existence of these civilizations and societies were dependent on their most able citizens making contributions for progress and growth. The Western origins of gifted education are often charted back to ancient Greek and Roman empires. In these societies military leadership and acumen was highly prized as the advancement of their civilization depended on those individuals whose talent who had been cultivated. In Sparta, military skills and leadership were highly prized and valued and were cultivated in those young people who exhibited early promise and talent. These specially selected students received instruction focused on leadership, warfare, mathematics, politics, and combat (Colangelo & Davis, 2003; Tannenbaum, 1983). Plato described children and/or adults who were singled out based on their abilities to one day strategize on the battlefields or as leaders in government. These highly selective groups were chosen from the uppermost echelons of society and labeled the "Patricians." To be among the Patricians was a right earned by birth and thus the nature of their ability was hereditary. The plebs, free citizens of Rome, were not included within this educated class, as they were not afforded this right by birth. In Plato's *Republic*, he noted that natural ability and training could determine one's class, and early training was paramount in moving one out of his birth rank (Colangelo & Davis, 2003; Kaufman, Kaufman, & Plucker, 2013; Moyers, 1996).

Feudal China (AD 587–AD 1904) implemented the Imperial Examination System (IES) over a 1,300-year period to identify a class of elite government officials (Gan, 2008). This exam was executed to aid in discovering the best and brightest males in Chinese society. The exam system was only open to males from families of means, those who had wealthy sponsors, or who had shown exceptional promise. Performance on the IES was further leveled and dictated the type of leadership position or government service an examinee would undertake. The highest level, *jinshi*, provided membership to the Chinese bureaucracy. The provincial level, *juren*, allowed those who achieved this degree to wield particular powers in the provinces throughout China. The most common degree was that at the prefectoral level, *xiucai*. These degree holders became teachers or village leaders. Regardless of level achieved, due to the relatively small number of males who were eligible to sit for the examination, some type of social mobility was guaranteed. The level of mobility could only be dampened by the degree achieved by the test taker (Smith, 1994).

Circumvent the globe and fast-forward to the foundational years of the United States in the late 18th century. Thomas Jefferson hoped to secure the future of the fledging country with an educated citizenry. He outlined his plan in the Bill for the More General Diffusion of Knowledge (1779) and in *Notes on the State of Virginia* (1801). The plan included three years of free schooling in each district of approximately five or six square miles. Twenty boys deemed geniuses of their school and unable to afford any further schooling were eligible for a free grammar school education with the expectation that these young men would eventually attend William and Mary College (Jefferson, 1801).

These systems were designed on developing the talents of recognized individuals in order for them to support and contribute to society, not necessarily for the goals of personal or individual fulfillment or growth. The arguments for gifted persons' societal contributions continue to drive contemporary gifted education but now include individual potential and promise. The needs of changing societies have also brought about amendments to the way talent is cultivated. This is also true for the United States as it has grappled with challenges caused by societal, political, economic, and scientific changes.

The contemporary study of gifted children emerged in the United States as a result of the foundational work conducted in the areas of experimental psychology, the investigation of individual differences, and the measurement of intelligence (Chapman, 1988) and was influenced by four distinct "strains of scientific development: German, French, English, and American" (Young, 1924, p. 4). There is a general agreement that the contemporary seeds of gifted education largely influenced by the works of Sir Francis Galton, an Englishman, and his first studies of eminent men approximately 150 years ago.

This book opens with the founding of the field of psychology, the initial interest in precocious children, and the changing landscape of American schools. These elements produced the conditions that led to the establishment of the contemporary field of gifted education. Section II provides an insight into the dominant personalities who led to the establishment of the field of gifted education and the resulting research agendas. Section III explores the contextual issues that forced the contraction and then eventual growth of the field. Finally, Section IV examines the capacity building the field undertook in the face of yet another cycle of retrenchment and expansion imposed on it by contextual forces.

SECTION I

1
THE FOUNDATIONAL UNDERPINNINGS OF A FIELD

The field of gifted education emerged in the midst of the American progressive education movement. During the late 19th and early 20th centuries, progressive education represented a segment of America and its societal views: "Progressive education was an attempt by educational reformers, psychologists, and philosophers to develop a school experience that would benefit the whole child's intellectual, social, artistic, and moral development" (Berube, 1994, p. 14). The movement was based on the scientific findings of evolutionary concepts and the rising field of "new" psychology in conjunction with child-centered schools, which fostered creativity, self-expression, critical thinking, and individualism (Benjamin, 2006; Berube, 1994; Green, Shore, & Teo, 2001). During this time, America's public schools faced considerable challenges. These complications included an exponentially growing student population due to the mandating of compulsory education, including the influx of a sizable immigrant population, escalating operating costs, and changing curricular objectives (Berube, 1994; Chapman, 1988). Some in the Progressive Education community identified the newly developed tests of intelligence as a panacea for these challenges in public schools (Chapman, 1988; Gamson, 2009). The beginnings of gifted education are inextricably intertwined with this time period, the science and scientific methods that drove the development of the emerging field of psychology, and the select group of men who founded the empirically driven field of psychology and then turned their attentions to the study of individual differences and the quantification of intelligence.

Shaping a Diversifying and Expanding School Population

Beginning in the 1830s, education reformers in the United States advocated for publically funded school systems throughout the country. Education in the

19th century was solely a function and responsibility of individual states, and because of this, the implementation and institution of compulsory schooling across the country required over half a century to complete. Massachusetts was the first in 1852 to institute the practice and Mississippi trailed behind in 1917, with the bulk of compulsory school laws being passed toward the end of the 19th century (Richardson, 1980; Tyack, 1976).

These laws also paralleled the enactment of state child labor laws. Child labor largely reflected the socioeconomic means of families. Rather than children being sent to school they were sent to work out of economic need. This labor included work in textile mills, as shoeshine boys, in garment production, or in agricultural work on the family farm. The work was most often dangerous, low paying, and offered few protections from employers. In the late 1800s and early 1900s, shifts began to occur in how child labor was conceptualized, which included mandatory schooling. A growing antagonism to child labor in the northern United States caused many businesses to move their factories to the South, which correlated to the implementation of both compulsory schooling and child labor laws in both regions. Northern states were the first to enact both types of laws (George Meany Center for Labor Studies, 2000). Massachusetts enacted the first Child Labor Law in 1836, requiring at least three months of schooling, and by 1899, 28 states had passed laws regulating child labor. The federal government, however, did not pass the Fair Labor Standards Act until 1938, setting the minimum age for work during school hours to 16 years of age. There was also a greater understanding that child labor pushed down adult wages and as children were receiving little to no formal education, thus continued the child's prospects of remaining in poverty (Mayer, 2013).

Apart from compulsory school laws, which gradually pushed school attendance upwards, an additional influx of school children resulted from a massive migration wave from Europe. Seeking to enhance their circumstances in life, the initial surge of immigrants were from Germany, Ireland, and England and a second inundation from Southern and Eastern Europe which totaled approximately 23.5 million men, women, and children from 1881 to 1920 (Martin & Duignan, 2003; U.S. Citizenship and Immigration Service, 2012). These immigrants could not help but contribute to the changing demography of schools. Southern and Eastern European immigrants tended to settle in metropolitan and urban centers, significantly impacting schools in these areas. In addition to the growth in numbers, immigrants brought languages and customs that were appreciably different from those of early English and Irish settlers. Until the Immigration Act of 1917, immigrants were not required to read and write in their home language, thus schools were presented with a large range of literacy issues, in addition to the multitude of social milieus, religions, and customs (Chapman, 1988; Martin & Duignan, 2003; U.S. Citizenship and Immigration Service, 2012).

As a result, school attendance increased and a logical outgrowth was the steep historical upsurge in public school enrollments, particularly in urban centers.

This diversity in student populations was a direct reflection of the waves of European immigration, compulsory school laws, and the introduction of child labor laws. Schools then "became, above all, a way of managing the new society, and the schools became necessarily social organizations which would direct and define: direct the mass toward responsible behavior and define the individual's role in society" (Fass, 1980, p. 437).

A steady stream of rural families migrating to cities sought employment in factories and other industries. This influx of farmer workers into the cities to fill assembly line jobs in the factories and newly arrived immigrants also changed the demography of cities and urban centers in the United States (Sherman & Theobald, 2001). For example, between 1860 and 1920, the population of New York grew by 300%, Chicago by 400%, and Detroit by 700%. Los Angeles by and large experienced the most sizable growth of approximately 1000%. By 1920, populations in cities outnumbered those in rural areas for the first time in America's history, thus irrevocably changing the social, political, economic, and educational landscape of the nation (Chapman, 1988).

The 1909 play *The Melting Pot* by Israel Zangwill illustrated societal changes being undertaken in the United States at the time, particularly in metropolitan areas. The concept of disparate peoples immigrating to America to be "God's Crucible, the great Melting Pot, where all the races of Europe are melting and reforming!" was the central theme of the play (Zangwill, 1909, p. 53). However, the "melting pot" emerging in America's schools presented real challenges for school administrators and teachers. In 1860, approximately 4 million students attended schools; 40 years later in 1900 nearly 11 million students were recorded in attendance in American schools. Only two decades would elapse before another approximate doubling of the school population. In 1920 nearly 18,500,000 students attended public schools, overwhelmingly concentrated in the nation's growing metropolitan hubs (NCES, 1993). Progressive Era reformers would seek tools and strategies to untangle these perceived and real challenges present in American schools.

Educating children en masse was not a new phenomenon; however, the large diversity in learning abilities and readiness levels were not ones that teachers and school administrators had encountered previously (Chapman, 1988). Unraveling the myriad of readiness levels, learning difficulties, and cacophony of languages that students arrived at school with would require explicit, novel, and targeted policies and approaches.

Coinciding with the exponential growth in school populations was the emergence of the field of psychology. With its theories and methodologies, psychologists inserted themselves into the challenges of addressing the needs of these diverse student bodies. These tools included a growing corpus of assessments to evaluate, classify, and sort students. The confluence of these factors gave rise to a new field of inquiry, educational psychology, and eventually to the subfield of gifted education as students of exceptional and advanced abilities were noticed in the sorting and classifying procedures by the individuals who would aid in establishing what would eventually become the field of gifted education.

Before an exploration of the field of gifted education can be undertaken, an understanding of the newly emerging field of psychology at the turn of the 20th century should be explored. This exploration considers context and the forces of the various personalities that catapulted this field into a reputable and viable expanse of inquiry and discarded the earlier pseudo-scientific conclusions regarding mental traits and the brain's inner workings, which had previously explained intelligence, thinking, and learning.

2
EARLY EMPIRICAL INFLUENCE, HIGH ABILITY, AND INDIVIDUAL DIFFERENCE

Unusual intellectual prowess in young people had long captured the imagination of the general public as chronicled in the stories of young boys and men such as Christian Heineken, John Stuart Mill, and William Sidis (and will be discussed in greater detail in Chapter 7). Sir Francis Galton would be the first to provide systematic investigations into individuals who had achieved eminence and exhibited evidence of high intellectual ability (Beineke, 1987; Burt, 1962), thus positioning the foundation for the field of gifted education to emerge and assembling an alternative narrative to the pervasive and traditional stories told about sickly and unstable precocious children.

Sir Francis Galton

Francis Galton and Charles Darwin shared a common grandfather, Dr. Erasmus Darwin. Their extended family included a number of successful and eminent bankers and men of science and considered among Britain's elite. Born in 1862, Galton was an intelligent child himself and grew up in a home that valued and encouraged education. In fact, Lewis Terman had estimated his IQ in childhood at "not far from 200" (Terman, 1917a, p. 209). His older sister Adele appointed herself Francis' tutor and introduced him to his first serious novels (Terman, 1917a; VanTassel-Baska, 2014). He would go on to study at King's College and eventually graduate from Cambridge University. In 1844, when Galton was 22 years old, his father died, bequeathing him an annual income, which allowed him to discontinue the pursuit of medicine as a profession (this was serendipitous, as he had lost any real motivation toward the subject or profession; Beineke, 1987; Gillham, 2001). Instead of falling into a life of a leisured dilettante, Galton committed his life to one of scientific inquiry and travel, writing about a number of scientific topics, and is remembered as one of the "men of high native ability and independent fortune, who devote[d] themselves to the advancement of knowledge and its application in the public service from an intrinsic interest and a keen sense of public duty" (Baldwin, 1910, p. 150).

Although Galton and Darwin were not in close physical contact, they communicated and deeply influenced each other's work (Young, 1924). Darwin's work piqued Galton's curiosity toward variabilities and his exiting interests in the methods of biologists and demographers. Interestingly, he was not influenced by psychological perceptions and only interested in the "quantitative measurement of character traits, mental imagery, associative processes in reference to the needs of the man on the street and practical social controls" (Young, 1924, p. 25). Yet Galton's work would clearly help to define and influence psychology through the statistical methods he introduced and theories that influenced individual differences.

Galton seized upon the ideas laid out in Darwin's *Origin of Species* (1859). In 1865, Galton published "Hereditary Character and Talent" in *Macmillan's Magazine*, which provided an indication of what would be fully addressed in *Hereditary Genius* (1869), challenging some of the most pervasive ideas of the time regarding intelligence. Galton (1865, p. 157) wrote, "It is commonly asserted that the children of eminent men are stupid; that, where great power of intellect seems to have been inherited, it has descended through the mother's side; and that one son commonly runs away with the talent of a whole family." He also noted the "popular belief that men of great eminence, are usually of feeble constitution and of a dry and cold disposition. There may be such instances, but I believe the general rule to be exactly the opposite" (Galton, 1865, p. 164). In *English Men of Science: Their Nature and Nurture*, Galton for the first time highlighted the distinction between nature and nurture as each component brought something distinct to an individual's development. Drawing on this belief, Galton amassed a body of evidence to support this theory and developed statistical techniques to illustrate the tendencies to average and individual differences (Gillham, 2001).

His body of work also highlighted the exceptional character of eminence and the role of individual difference in performance (VanTassel-Baska, 2014) and "emphasized the need of statistical treatment by the methods of averages, measures of dispersion and correlation" (Young, 1924, p. 26). The biographical methodology and statistical procedures he developed were also distinctive and groundbreaking. This combination of biographical studies and statistical analysis illustrated how superior ability could be found throughout families and attributed to hereditability (Hankins, 1925). Biographic study remains a contemporary method of inquiry and the statistical method of correlational coefficients to illustrate the relationship and variation between phenomena continue as a central statistical tenet.

Galton also advanced "his formulation of the Ancestral Law—the characters of the individual are derived one-fourth from each parent, one-sixteenth from each one of the four grandparents, and so on" (No author, 1911, p. 149). This changed how heredity was considered as a scientific study, which also encompassed the study of eugenics, a term which Galton framed to describe the cultivation of a race. Galton described eugenics as

> a brief work to express the science of improving stock, which is by no means confined to questions of judicious mating, but which, especially in the case of man, takes cognizance of all influences that tend in however remote a degree to blood a better change of prevailing speedily over the less suitable than they otherwise would have had.
>
> *(Galton, 1883, p. 17)*

Galton's work has also been identified as the "main fountain-head for the varied streams of statistical measurements of individual differences in ... education" (Hankins, 1925, p. 275). Guiding Galton's work was his belief that if scientific rank was to be applied to a field, measurement must be employed (Tomlinson, 1997). Galton was "caught in the Zeigeist which demanded quantitative measurement in all the sciences" (Young, 1924, p. 25). He would also incorporate the work of Adolph Quetelet, a Belgian statistician and biologist. Using Quetelet's calculations for normal distribution Galton first attempted to apply them to mental aptitude by examining the admission scores of the Royal Military College at Sandhurt in 1868 (Gillham, 2001).

Galton's Influence on Gifted Education

Francis Galton's influence on the pioneers of gifted education, Lewis Terman and Leta Hollingworth, cannot be understated. Galton's work, encountered early on in their graduate school readings, made an indelible impression upon both Terman and Hollingworth. Working separately, they applied Galton's conclusions and unanswered questions to their own lines of inquiry. These conclusions included that (1) intelligence ranged widely across the general population (according to the general laws of distribution) and that (2) a certain segment of the population was endowed with a significantly higher degree of intelligence (Jolly, 2004). Hollingworth (1942, p. 5) recognized the ineffaceable impact that Galton had on the foundations of her own scientific inquiry:

> Galton was the first to place the study of genius on the basis on the quantitative statement, so that comparisons might be made and verifications be effected. Galton formulated the theory that genius (great natural ability) is nothing more nor less than a very extreme degree in the distribution of a combination of traits—intellect, zeal, and power of working .... Galton applied for the first time in human thought the mathematical concepts of probability to the definition of genius.

Terman also understood the implications of Galton's findings and noted them in his dissertation where he quoted Galton (1906, p. 311): "One of the most important objects of measurement ... is to obtain general knowledge of the capabilities of a man by sinking shafts, as it were, at a few critical points." Several of Galton's conclusions would appear again in Terman's longitudinal studies: (1) that a high degree of eminence required being highly gifted with matching abilities, and (2) possession of such abilities all but guaranteed eminence for these individuals (Cox, 1926).

Galton developed many of the statistical procedures that rendered modern psychology possible, including the concept of regression, correlation coefficients, mean, and medians, using Quetelet's mathematical concepts, and in collaboration with Karl Pearson (Walsh, Teo, & Baydala, 2014). Eugenics would eventuate in a contentious movement in the early half of the 20th century in which Hollingworth and Terman both participated. Their motivations were much like Galton's, based in improving mankind through the procreation of the couples who showed the best matching across a number of criteria. Eugenic societies in America were often instrumental in removing the reproductive rights of the most vulnerable people in their communities. Contemporary educators and psychologists would largely reject Galton's exclusive hereditarian views of talent and eminence as a robust understanding of the influence of environment and psychosocial factors have developed during the past 150 years, including those from gifted education.

3
A *NEW* PSYCHOLOGY

As psychology sundered itself from philosophy and focused on mental functions and structures, the consequences and implications for education came into focus (Green et al., 2001; Lagemann, 2002). The architects of gifted education, Lewis Terman and Leta Hollingworth, were part of a greater psychological familial tree, finding themselves only two degrees of separation from the first contemporary psychologists in the United States (see Figure 3.1).

The "new" or experimental psychology that emerged in America toward the later part of the 19th century was deeply influenced by several central figures who would also directly influence the field of gifted education. Although the work of Gustav Theodor Fechner and Wilhelm Weber preceded Wilhelm Wundt in the German context in the use of modern or new/scientific psychology, Wundt provided what were to be the experimental methodologies, focus, manipulation, and measurability of a phenomenon—"Wundt clarified the concept of the term 'experimental' as follows: 'In an experiment we produce the phenomenon artificially from the conditions we manipulate. By changing these conditions we change the phenomenon in a measurable way'" (Sinatra, 2006, p. 93). These first men of the new psychology were shaped by the theories of evolution, their work was empirical and scientific in nature, experimental, and incorporated the statistical procedures developed by Galton, which differed significantly from the earlier work and theories that focused on the inner workings of the mind (Green et al., 2001; Walsh et al., 2014; Wertheimer, 1970).

This new psychology begins with Wilhelm Wundt, a German professor, and William James, an American, each contributing to the burgeoning field of American psychology. This new psychology extended to mental testing as a form of applied psychology and from this the fields of educational psychology and

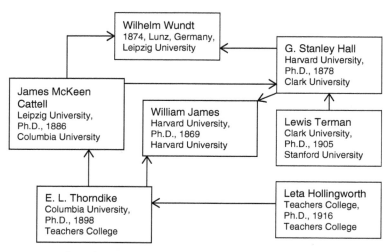

Direction of arrow indicates links back to Ph.D. advisor

FIGURE 3.1 Gifted education and psychological familial tree

gifted education would eventually emerge. Before catapulting straight to the trajectory that belongs to gifted education, a brief exploration of these men, their work, and the newly emerging field is necessary.

Wilhelm Wundt

As one of the organizers of this new psychology, Wilhelm Wundt contributed to American psychology through his methodologies. Despite his enduring methodological influence, his theories, principles, and writings never developed a substantial following in American psychology (Benjamin, 2006). These influences migrated via America's first psychologist who traveled through Wundt's lab and brought back his methodologies and lab techniques to the United States.

Little is known about Wundt's early life other than that he was the son of a Lutheran pastor and born in Necharau in Baden, Germany, on August 16, 1832. How these formative years may have shaped his career path and eventual choice to pursue psychology are unknown (Titchener, 1921). Wundt derived much inspiration and provocation from John Stuart Mill's *Logic*. Mill, too, described psychology as a science of observation and experimentation. Wundt would enact upon Mill's description of experimentation as Titchner (1921, p. 173) described in his memoir of Wundt, "Where John Mill theorised, Wundt performed; and the spirit of his performance has spread over the civilised world." Wundt studied medicine, eventually abandoning the profession as a practicing physician when he grew weary of seeing patients and once again entered university, emerging as a professor of philosophy of inductive logic in 1874.

In 1875, he found himself at the University of Leipzig. Leipzig University offered an atmosphere that supported its academics and allowed for innovation. The city itself was also an important crossroads in Europe for commerce and industry. It was here Wundt established a demonstration space or laboratory, which eventually became the Psychologische Institut—a destination for early American psychologists (Cattell, 1888; Hall, 2003; Wertheimer, 1970). The psychological laboratory at Leipzig would serve as a model for those established at Johns Hopkins, Harvard, and the University of Pennsylvania (Cattell, 1888). An 1891 description of the Leipzig laboratory illustrates the influence it had on the future of American laboratories and researchers:

> The value of their new experimental method so impressed these students that it was soon carried into effect in other institutions, and happily this new movement early found its way to America. To President G. Stanley Hall and Dr. J McK. Cattell, Wundt's first American students, belongs the credit of introducing the experimental methods of treating psychology into the American college; the first laboratory being that of Johns Hopkins University at Baltimore, in which laboratory so many of the teachers of experimental and comparative psychology in the various colleges of the United States received their training.
> *(as cited in Ruckmich, 1912, p. 517)*

Wundt's determination to move psychology from the science of the mind or the soul to the science of the consciousness and the immediate experience initiated development of methods to test and observe these structuralist theories (Hilgard, 1987). These methods would become his enduring contribution to the field of psychology as he introduced experimentation and observations that were practiced in his lab—methods that remain a part of the fabric of contemporary psychological research and practice. Wundt used these methods to study his own brand of psychology known as structuralism or the analysis of the basic elements that constitute the mind (Titchener, 1921). As Titchener (1921, p. 175) recalled,

> Wundt was the first psychologist to bring demonstrational apparatus into the lecture-room. ... He came to see the real purpose of a demonstration: the provision namely, of conditions under which the audience may observe for themselves the fundamental phenomena of the subject-matter of discussion.

His students would include several in the first wave of American psychologists, many who would go on to have influential and eminent careers of their own. Included in this exclusive group are G. Stanley Hall, James McKeen Cattell, and E. B. Titchener who through their sojourns at Wundt's Leipzig Psychologische Institut brought his methods to America. These men "helped to define and to start work on many of the questions of interest to the psychologist of the second half of the twentieth century" (Wertheimer, 1970, p. 65).

William James

Wundt's American contemporary, William James, was considered to be the first American psychologist. He developed his own unique type of psychology. With no one mentor or guide, James instead drew on the influences of multiple individuals including those from the fields of evolutionary biology, physiology, and associationism. Over time, he would develop functionalist psychology. Functionalism, as opposed to Wundt's structuralism, studied how a person adapted to his environment through his senses (Wertheimer, 1970).

James hailed from an intellectual family of some financial means. His education was rather haphazard in nature and provided forays into art, anatomy, chemistry, and physiology. At the close of the Civil War, aged 23, James was invited by Louis Agassi, one of the founders of the American scientific establishment, to travel on the Thayer Expedition (1865–1866) of the Amazon Basin to collect new species. From there he made his way to Germany in 1867 to study physiology but in the end decided not to pursue a career as a naturalist. Eventually he returned to the United States and earned an M.D., like Wundt, but never practiced medicine. Up until this point had been described as a man with plenty of talent and no vocation (McDermind, n.d., para. 4). He finally found his way to Harvard where he would spend his entire academic career (1872–1907) and began giving lectures on psychology (Baldwin, 1911). His *Principles of Psychology* (1890) was considered the first general textbook on the subject, which expounded on his ideas regarding consciousness, attention, memory, habits, and emotions, and where he conceived of the term *stream of consciousness* (Hilgard, 1987).

In 1891 James was the first psychologist to seriously engage with classroom teachers with psychological concepts applied to school settings during his series of 12 lectures to teachers delivered at Harvard University. James defined education as "the organization of acquired habits of conduct and tendencies to behavior" (as cited in Baldwin, 1911, p. 375). These lectures were distributed widely and appeared serially in the *Atlantic Monthly* and were later published as a collection in *Talks to Teachers on Psychology and to Students on Some of Life's Ideals*. James (1899/1962, p. 3) addressed the teachers on a number of topics, including their role in the application of psychological principles to the classroom:

> I say moreover that you make a great, a very great mistake, if you think that psychology, being the science of the mind's laws, is something from which you can deduce definite programmes and schemes and methods of instruction for immediate schoolroom use. Psychology is a science, and teaching is an art; and sciences never generate arts directly out of themselves. An intermediary inventive mind must make the application, by using its originality.

James envisioned himself as the intermediary, believing teachers could not consume the psychological concepts. He approached the lectures by providing the most practical of suggestions and foregoing what he considered their dense psychological underpinnings. *Talks to Teachers*, along with the *Principles*, were the first texts "to bring modern psychology into the schoolroom and apply it to the everyday problems of the aim of education" (Baldwin, 1911, p. 373). James attempted to provide a framework for teachers in order to "be aware of the child's native interests, bring material in a straightforward and clear manner, and carefully connect the new knowledge to the existing knowledge and to the native interests in a natural, logical, systematic, and telling way" (Pajares, 2003, para. 53). This practical approach was both appealing and popular with teachers as it provided one of the first that was based in science and a scaffold and framework to understanding student behaviors and preferences.

Despite the parallel nature of Wundt's and James's work, even establishing demonstration laboratories the same year, Wundtian psychology never achieved the same level of popularity or academic application that James's work in the United States achieved. There are several possible reasons for this. American universities housed departments of psychology and acknowledged the interdisciplinary nature of the field, while in Europe psychology evolved in special technological institutions, which did not allow for the ease of interdisciplinary outreach and application (Wertheimer, 1970). Wundt's and James's personalities also aided in the spread of their own brand of psychology. Wundt rarely attended conferences and opposed traveling. Students and interested scholars traveled to Wundt, while James spoke extensively and published with equal measure. Even those Americans who studied with Wundt applied an American flavor to his psychological approaches. Wundt's and James's students would be the next generation of psychologists to build the field and firmly establish its scientific usefulness across a number of fields, including education, advertising, and workforce development just to name a few. James McKeen Cattell and G. Stanley Hall would be the next generation of psychologists to establish a cadre of psychologists and build their own psychology empires.

G. Stanley Hall

If Williams James was acknowledged as the first preeminent psychologist in the United States, G. Stanley Hall was the presumptive heir, at least in Hall's estimation. Hall had studied with James at Harvard earning the first American Ph.D. in psychology in 1878 with James being Hall's senior by only two years. Hall's Ph.D. began a succession of firsts for him. He was the first American to study with Wundt; established the first laboratory explicitly founded for psychological pursuits in America (1883); established the first psychological journal, *American Journal of Psychology* (1887); was named the first president of Clark University (1888); and was voted the first president of the American Psychological Association

(APA; 1892). His boundless energy, which he channeled into a number of interests and lines of inquiry (Roback, 1952), combined with his academic positions, helped him to influence and advance the burgeoning field of psychology like no other contemporary of his time (Berliner, 1993).

Unlike many of his academic contemporaries, Hall's life began simply enough on a New England farm in 1846 (some reports give his birth as 1844) (Berliner, 1993; Lepore, 2011; Thorndike, 1925). His father managed to secure a substitute for him during the Civil War and a life as a theologian was planned for him, even attending Williston Seminary and Union Theological Seminaries (Thorndike, 1925). Hall instead went on to earn a Ph.D. in psychology and then extended his studies abroad, mostly in Germany where he spent some time in Wundt's lab. In 1882, after languishing upon his return from the Continent for several years, he eventually found a permanent position at Johns Hopkins University and in 1884 was made professor of Psychology and Pedagogics. While at Hopkins, Hall would establish the first psychological laboratory (Berliner, 1993), and "from this one comparatively small laboratory at Johns Hopkins the number rapidly increased to fifteen new in actual use while no less than ten other institutions took steps to secure lab facilities within a year" (Ruckmich, 1912, p. 517). The more successful psychology programs included those with laboratories, which allowed them to attract the most talented students and produce leading graduates. As the number of psychology programs increased, so too did the graduates trained in psychological methodologies. The quick successions in which laboratories were established and the sharp increase in graduates secured the continued expansion and advancement of the "new" psychology. This could be considered a successful blueprint for academic empire building (Roback, 1952).

During Hall's six-year tenure at Johns Hopkins, students such as John Dewey, James McKeen Cattell, Edmund Sanford, Joseph Jastrow, and W. H. Burnham obtained their Ph.D.s under Hall (Thorndike, 1925). Based on his success at Hopkins, Hall's next major professional milestone would be as the first president of Clark University in 1888. At Clark, another group of students and future influential psychologists would pass under his tutelage, including H. H. Goddard, Arnold Gesell, and the contemporary cofounder of gifted education, Lewis M. Terman (Hall, 2003; Thorndike, 1925).

Hall masterfully promoted and coordinated the still fledgling field of psychology, leaving him to be characterized more as "an initiator, mentor, and founder than a scientist" (Hall, 2003, p. 32). Evidence of this influence could be illustrated in the sheer number of students he produced: "In 1893, 11 of the first 14 Ph.D.s awarded in American psychology were to Hall's students. By 1915, Hall's students numbered well over half of all Ph.D.s in American psychology … whom profoundly influenced general, development, and educational psychology" (Berliner, 1993, p. 43). Hall also imbued a sense of curiosity and interest in his students (Thorndike, 1925) that would underpin the inquiry of individual difference, mental testing, and a host of other psychological questions during the first half of the 20th century.

Despite Hall's influence, his approach to science, especially in the later part of his career, began to suffer criticism for numerous and varied methodological flaws. Hall's efforts to extend psychology often sacrificed quality for quantity. He favored questionnaires as a method of data collection, a technique he had originally observed in Germany. However, his use of questionnaires often lacked standardization and he would use untrained persons to collect data, and the analysis of this data was suspect (Hall, 2003). In 1904, fellow psychologist E. L. Thorndike offered a critical summation of Hall after reading *Adolescence* and noted that the text was "chock full of errors, masturbation and Jesus. He is a mad man" (as cited in Lagemann, 2002, p. 57). Regardless of Hall's brand of science, the growth of the field of psychology would not have been possible without his efforts.

4
INDIVIDUAL DIFFERENCE AND ITS MEASUREMENT

Alfred Binet

Working on the European continent, but propelled by quite another purpose, Frenchman Alfred Binet would provide the materials for what would eventually become the American instrument responsible for the classification and sorting, and the tool that was central in the establishment of gifted education. Binet's father was a physician and his mother an artist. Born in Nice, France (when it was still part of the Kingdom of Piedmont-Sardinia) on July 11, 1857, Binet's family wealth meant a career was not absolutely required and perhaps made choosing one more difficult. Having completed law school in 1877, his first career choice as a lawyer was short-lived (Jarvin & Sternberg, 2003): "It appears that this professional choice was only a stopgap, for he did not follow this profession" (Wolf, 1964, p. 763). Binet lamented, "As for the law, it is the career of those without any [yet] chosen vocation" (as cited in Wolf, 1964, p. 763).

In 1880, Binet began his tenure at the Sorbonne's psychological laboratory in experimental research (Nicolas & Santitioso, 2011). While there he founded the first French psychology journal, *L'Anée Pscyhologique*, in 1895. In contrast to the United States, French psychology grew from medicine with an original focus on psychopathology. From these abnormal exemplars grew a better understanding of normal psychology (Jarvin & Sternberg, 2003). Binet's first psychological studies focused on atypical adults. He would then turn his attention to the study of atypical or elite children in 1900 (Nicolas & Santitioso, 2011). He initially hypothesized that anthropometric measures could explicate differences in mental capacity. When those experiments proved inadequate, Binet turned to experimental and individual psychology seeking to identify which abilities best represented intellectual prowess and also ways in which to best develop those abilities (Howard, 2009).

Despite Hall's influence, his approach to science, especially in the later part of his career, began to suffer criticism for numerous and varied methodological flaws. Hall's efforts to extend psychology often sacrificed quality for quantity. He favored questionnaires as a method of data collection, a technique he had originally observed in Germany. However, his use of questionnaires often lacked standardization and he would use untrained persons to collect data, and the analysis of this data was suspect (Hall, 2003). In 1904, fellow psychologist E. L. Thorndike offered a critical summation of Hall after reading *Adolescence* and noted that the text was "chock full of errors, masturbation and Jesus. He is a mad man" (as cited in Lagemann, 2002, p. 57). Regardless of Hall's brand of science, the growth of the field of psychology would not have been possible without his efforts.

4
INDIVIDUAL DIFFERENCE AND ITS MEASUREMENT

Alfred Binet

Working on the European continent, but propelled by quite another purpose, Frenchman Alfred Binet would provide the materials for what would eventually become the American instrument responsible for the classification and sorting, and the tool that was central in the establishment of gifted education. Binet's father was a physician and his mother an artist. Born in Nice, France (when it was still part of the Kingdom of Piedmont-Sardinia) on July 11, 1857, Binet's family wealth meant a career was not absolutely required and perhaps made choosing one more difficult. Having completed law school in 1877, his first career choice as a lawyer was short-lived (Jarvin & Sternberg, 2003): "It appears that this professional choice was only a stopgap, for he did not follow this profession" (Wolf, 1964, p. 763). Binet lamented, "As for the law, it is the career of those without any [yet] chosen vocation" (as cited in Wolf, 1964, p. 763).

In 1880, Binet began his tenure at the Sorbonne's psychological laboratory in experimental research (Nicolas & Santitioso, 2011). While there he founded the first French psychology journal, *L'Anée Pscyhologique*, in 1895. In contrast to the United States, French psychology grew from medicine with an original focus on psychopathology. From these abnormal exemplars grew a better understanding of normal psychology (Jarvin & Sternberg, 2003). Binet's first psychological studies focused on atypical adults. He would then turn his attention to the study of atypical or elite children in 1900 (Nicolas & Santitioso, 2011). He initially hypothesized that anthropometric measures could explicate differences in mental capacity. When those experiments proved inadequate, Binet turned to experimental and individual psychology seeking to identify which abilities best represented intellectual prowess and also ways in which to best develop those abilities (Howard, 2009).

Binet referred to abilities as *spirits* and classified these as literary, scientific, and artistic, which were to be developed globally and to their highest potential (Da Costa, Zenasi, Nicolas, & Lubart, 2014).

Binet's development of a mental test for retarded and feebleminded (terminology used at that time) children seems to have overshadowed his overall contribution to psychological testing and his intelligence test is recognized as his most lasting international contribution. In actuality, Binet was interested in children of all abilities (Da Costa et al., 2014; Howard, 2009; Nicolas & Santitioso, 2011). The Binet–Simon Metric Scale of Intelligence (1905) was developed in order to identify children who would profit from instruction in regular classrooms and those who would receive specific instruction provided in special schools. The test items became increasingly more difficult and sought to measure "visual coordination, execution of simple orders, knowledge of objects, repetition of sentences, giving differences between pairs of familiar objects, repetition of sentences, giving differences between pairs of familiar objects, repetition of digits, and making distinctions between abstract forms" (Watson, 1961, p. 217). To Binet, the development of a theory of intelligence was not paramount and instead he worked toward the identification and assessment of behaviors that evoked intelligence or specific spirits (Boake, 2002).

The 1908 revision of the Scale was markedly different, retaining only 30% of the original content and providing more structured and detailed directions and clarifications in terms of answers. The norming sample was also more representative, taking in greater ranges of intellectual capacity and those from different socioeconomic backgrounds (Da Costa et al., 2014). The 1908 version also included year scales, which allowed age levels to be assigned that corresponded to a child's intellectual level (Boake, 2002). Binet began to acknowledge that intelligence and school learning intersected and that environment and language attainment impacted intelligence (Zenderland, 1998). Binet's scales would go on to deeply alter how the intellectual capabilities of youngsters would be captured and quantified, particularly in the United States. Over the next two decades, American psychologists would apply their own interpretation of Binet's work to educational and social problems in the United States, most significantly Lewis M. Terman and H. H. Goddard (Boake, 2002; Sternberg, 1991).

Terman (1930a, p. 331) was especially taken with Binet, describing him as, "My favorite of all psychologists … not because of his intelligence test, which was only a by-product of his life work, but because of his originality, insight, openmindedness, and because of the rare charm of personality that shines through all of his writings."

Unlike Binet, who recognized the connections among school learning, environment, and language attainment, Goddard and Terman adapted and applied Binet's work to the American context failing to recognize that other variables could play in the development of intelligence. They believed intelligence was solely inherent (Richardson & Johanningmeiera, 1998; Zenderland, 1998). Terman sensed the

Binet–Simon "was only [a] point of departure for something better" to capture and provide a numerical score to intelligence (Terman, 1917b, p. 287).

James McKeen Cattell

Born on the eve of the Civil War in Easton, PA, in 1860, James McKeen Cattell was the son of a college president (Pillsbury, 1947). His travels through Europe after graduating with his undergraduate degree exposed him to the new psychology emerging in Europe. After a brief return to the United States to study at Johns Hopkins under Hall, Cattell returned to Europe and became the first American to earn a Ph.D. in psychology with Wundt in 1886 (Benjamin, Durkin, Link, Vestal, & Acord, 1992). Before returning to the United States, he interrupted his journey to study individual differences with Galton in 1888, an idea that was discouraged in Wundt's lab as Wundt focused on establishing the bounds of the entire adult mind (York, 2011). The combination of Galton's and Wundt's work would be significant in Cattell's future academic development.

Cattell extended and enhanced Galton's anthropometric measures, introducing the measurement of individual qualities as an elemental function of psychological study in his laboratories at the University of Pennsylvania. This stream of research became the centerpiece of the work done in his next laboratory at Columbia University (Sokal, 1971; Thorndike, 1914). As a result of this trajectory, "What Galton cried of in the wilderness ... Cattell took pains to prove [which] is now codified in text-books like Whipple's, a familiar feature of school surveys and children's courts, sought after by bureaus of vocational guidance" (Thorndike, 1914, p. 93).

Cattell's initial research sought to establish the link between "psychophysical methods to mental tests" (Sokal, 1971, p. 629), even introducing the term *mental test* (Boake, 2002; Cattell, 1890). Cattell also sought to distinguish between men of genius, greatness, and eminence, aspiring to provide a greater scientific nuance and meaning behind the terminology. He provided the following examples to illustrate this logic,

> Thus many a genius has [lacked] the character of the circumstance for the accomplishment of his task. Washington was scarcely a genius, but was a truly great man. Napoleon III was neither a genius nor a great man, but was eminent to an usual degree.
>
> *(Cattell, 1903, p. 361)*

Cattell realized the possession of genius, greatness, or eminence did not guarantee the achievement of an additional status. He hypothesized that science could reveal the amount of genius an individual possessed and worked to devise instruments to illustrate the amount that individuals held (Cattell, 1903).

Alfred Binet's work on psychological tests of intelligence would prove superior to Cattell's (Sokal, 1971). However, his influence on America's new psychology includes his importation of the Wundtian iteration of German psychology and its methodology, establishment of laboratories at several universities, and his editorial contributions to several scientific journals (Capshew, 1992; Pillsbury, 1947).

Despite Cattell's professional success, his personal convictions sometimes hindered his professional progress, and his relationships with others have been described as difficult, which led to some fractured associations, including his dismissal from Columbia University in 1917 for his vocal opposition to America's entry into World War I (Sokal, 1971). This would also explain his absence from the influential committee that developed intelligence tests and other measures to assess World War I recruits' abilities. Cattell penned a letter to members of Congress stating,

> The letter that I wrote on Aug. 23 to members of the Congress, on account of which I have been dismissed from the chair of psychology at Columbia University, asked support for a measure then before the Senate and the House to prohibit sending conscripts "to fight in Europe against their will." ... To do this would be contrary to the intent of the constitution and to the uniform policy of the nation. It would provide a less efficient army and might cause disorder and possible revolution at home. Surely this should not be done without careful consideration by the Congress after efforts to learn the will of the people. I have done nothing except exercise the constitutional right and fulfill the duty of a citizen to petition the Government to enact legislation which I believe to be in the interest of the nation. For this I am dismissed from the Division of Philosophy, Psychology and Anthropology of Columbia University, which I have made the strongest of any university in the world. Professors of every university are terrorized, so that they dare not exert their influence for peace and goodwill.
> *(New York Times, 1917)*

After 26 years of service to the university and a four-year legal battle with Columbia, Cattell was awarded pension and the charges of encouraging disloyalty were dismissed. After leaving Columbia, Cattell went on to edit *Science, School and Science*, and the *American Naturalist* (*New York Times*, 1922).

In addition to providing foundational work on individual differences from which the field of gifted education would evolve, Cattell inadvertently contributed to the growth of gifted education on a much more human and personal level. In 1909, the United States government charged the Coca-Cola Company with selling a product that was harmful and damaging to consumers' health, based on the levels of caffeine contained in the beverage. The Coca-Cola Company needed expert testimony to challenge the government's claims regarding caffeine levels. Cattell had originally been approached but felt that the work would impinge on his scientific integrity (Benjamin, 2013).

When Cattell passed on the offer, Harry Hollingworth, a former graduate student of Cattell's, was approached. At the time, Hollingworth was an instructor at Barnard College. Young and struggling financially, he did not object about the possible questions of scientific integrity, given the early stage of his career. He had never shied away from hard work. Before entering academia, Hollingworth had been a grave digger, part-time preacher, church janitor, and school teacher (Poffenberger, 1957). Harry hired his wife, Leta Hollingworth, to manage the double-blind studies. Leta used the income from Coca-Cola to fund the entirety of her own Ph.D. studies in psychology at Teachers College studying under E. L. Thorndike—thus setting the course for her entry into gifted education (Benjamin, Rogers, & Rosenbaum, 1991).

H. H. Goddard

Henry H. Goddard, born in Maine just two years after the close of the Civil War, was the only boy born to his parents, who were advancing in years at the time of his birth in 1866. He went on to graduate from Haverford College in 1889 and spent a year at the University of Southern California as an instructor (1887–1888) and incidentally was their first head football coach before heading back to Haverford to earn his M.A. in 1889. He then set off to Clark University to pursue a Ph.D. under G. Stanley Hall in 1896. His last academic position at The Ohio State University, which he began in 1922, was his longest academic appointment. However, his work from 1906 to 1918 at Vineland, NJ, established him as one of the nation's leading psychologists (Benjamin, 2009; Goddard, n.d.; Zenderland, 1998).

Goddard's position as superintendent of the New Jersey Training School for Feeble-Minded Girls and Boys in Vineland required him to study feebleminded (accepted terminology of the time period) children. He was very interested in "measuring their degree of *feeble-mindedness,* but was most clueless about how to do it" (Benjamin, 2009, para. 4). After unsuccessful trials with Cattell's measures of intelligence, he set off for Europe in 1908 in hopes of finding new inspiration for his own work. Goddard had initially dismissed the work of Binet as he had received poor reports about its use. However, upon further inspection and once translated to English from French, he realized their usefulness in the American context (Benjamin, 2009; Zenderland, 1998). From this work he was the first "to classify mental defectives as idiots, imbeciles, and morons. He even invented the word moron to identify that particular kind of feeble-minded person" (Goddard, n.d.).

His most well-known publication, *The Kallikak Family: A Study in the Heredity of Feeble-mindedness,* illustrated how he believed hereditary feeble-mindedness caused generations of "an appalling amount of defectiveness" (Goddard, 1912, p. 16; Kevles, 1985). This publication reinforced the popular eugenic ideas of the era, even suggesting female sterilization as one way to combat further "social consequence" (Benjamin, 2009; Goddard, 1912, p. 109).

Goddard also contributed to the psychological testing efforts during World War I, with the focus on identifying those soldiers who were feeble-minded and potentially undermining the security and safety of themselves and those around them. Findings from the approximately 1.7 million soldiers tested supported Goddard's earlier intention of wanting to develop a measure that would distribute a population over a single bell curve. Goddard's collective work represented yet another application of the IQ test to classify and organize society for efficiency and the betterment of society (Fancher, 1985; Zenderland, 1998).

E. L. Thorndike

Edward Lee Thorndike, the son of a Methodist preacher was born in Massachusetts in 1874. Thorndike commenced university studies at Wesleyan University in 1891, where he studied literature, and he planned to extend his studies at Harvard. However, he encountered James's *Principles of Psychology* at Wesleyan in his junior year, which immediately piqued his interest in the subject. Once at Harvard he sought out James's lectures and eventually changed his major from literature to psychology in his second year (Mayer, 2003; Woodworth, 1952). Thorndike eventually transferred to Columbia University's psychology department and under the guidance of James McKeen Cattell commenced his doctoral studies. At Columbia, Thorndike conducted experiments on feline and canine problem-solving abilities, applying quantitative analysis. Thorndike's doctoral studies extended the psychological paradigm by offering a "science of human engineering" based on animal behavior (Tomlinson, 1997, p. 368), eventually publishing *Animal Intelligence* which would become a foundational text in learning theory. Thorndike subscribed to Galton's theories and studies, noting the hereditary nature of individual differences (Lagemann, 2000).

Thorndike was one of the first psychologists who highlighted the field's interdisciplinary nature and application to education. In his 1910 article in the *Journal of Educational Psychology*'s first issue, "The Contribution of Psychology to Education," his manifesto outlined the type of work that educational psychologists would engage in, in order to improve the educational outcomes of students by applying the science of psychology, which Thorndike (1910, p. 5) described as "the science of the intellects, characters and behavior of animals including man." By employing psychological principles and methods, researchers and practitioners could ascertain which teaching strategies would be most successful with particular groups of students.

Thorndike's theories of intelligence and learning challenged the late 19th century rule of learning, which accepted the transfer of training. It was thought that by properly developing "habits of the mind," these would transfer across subject and content areas (Mayer, 2003). For example, learning subjects such as Latin or Greek and geometry would promote certain exercises for the mind. By applying the psychological methods of a controlled study, Thorndike (1906, p. 237) illustrated that this was in fact not necessarily the case and "that learning to attend to Latin forms will make one not only attend but remember, reason and observe better than he did before. The observation of facts proves this answer to be false." Only when subjects were closely related did this principle have merit. Thorndike (1906, p. 248) remarked, "Improvement of any one mental function or activity will improve others only in so far as they possess elements common to it also."

Thorndike's appointment to Teachers College in 1899 placed him in a fortuitous position to influence educational practices with the principles of psychology for the next 50 years at the university (Mayer, 2003). Thorndike was a man who firmly believed that all could be quantified and noted, "Whatever exists at all exists in some amount. To know it thoroughly involves knowing its quantity as well as its quality" (Thorndike, 1918, p. 16). This unflagging belief, combined with his belief that inherited traits were explained by individual differences, drove the brand of educational psychology practiced at Teachers College under his leadership. It was also under his guidance that Leta Hollingworth would obtain her Ph.D. in 1916.

5
THE PROLIFERATION OF PSYCHOLOGICAL STUDY

The founding of the American Psychological Association in 1892 with 31 of the most prominent members in the field including Williams James (Harvard), James McKeen Cattell (Columbia), Joseph Jastrow (Wisconsin), and George Ladd (Yale) with G. Stanley Hall (Clark) elected as its first president (Fernberger, 1932; Roback, 1952) only helped to legitimatize and institutionalize the field. The establishment of peer-reviewed journals such as the *Journal of Educational Psychology*, *American Journal of Psychology*, *Pedagogical Seminary*, *Psychological Bulletin*, and *Psychological Review* also facilitated the dissemination of research in the field and further extended its legitimacy (Fensham, 2004).

Eager to popularize psychology and gain mainstream appeal, Jastrow and Hugo Munsterberg of Harvard took advantage of the 1893 World's Fair in Chicago to exhibit psychological apparatus to fair attendees. For a small fee, members of the general public could participate in a testing laboratory (Benjamin, 2004; Roback, 1952). The exhibit provided researchers the opportunity to introduce the public to the new science of psychology and distance itself from the distinctly non-empirical practices of phrenology, psychic readings, and séances (Benjamin, 2004). Psychology's exponential growth was due to its immediate application to other disciplines, especially education and the social sciences (Ruckmich, 1912).

Hall and Thorndike extended the fundamental work of James and Wundt, envisioning ways in which psychology would replace philosophy as a way to understand educational theory and practice. As the number of school children rapidly expanded due to the introduction of child labor laws, large numbers of non-English-speaking immigrant children entering American schools, and the introduction of compulsory schooling presented varied challenges for public schools, schools became a natural extension of the psychological laboratory furthering the growth of the field and enhancing the field's value (Hall, 2003). However, the application of psychological methods and instruments to the United States' war machine during World War I helped solidify its permanence and utility to stakeholders and constituents beyond academia.

World War I and the Army Alpha and Beta

Before World War I, the large-scale use of IQ tests was not a widespread practice. They were employed in school districts across the country but not as a matter of convention. In 1914, Goddard had unsuccessfully tried to persuade the New York City School Board to adopt the Binet-Simon test. However, World War I presented the occasion for psychologists to apply intelligence tests as a tool to organize the human resources in aid of the war effort (Spring, 1972; Zenderland, 1998).

When Congress voted to declare war on April 6, 1917, the U.S. Army numbered only 200,000 men with nearly half of this count consisting of members from National Guard units. Approximately 3 million (2.7 million draftees and 300,000 enlistees) men joined the U.S. Army to fight in World War I (Yockelson, 1998). America's late entry into the war forced the quick mobilization of a large fighting force. In 1917 the United States was wholly ill-equipped to enter a global conflict that had already been ongoing for three years. Psychologists seized the opportunity to apply their expertise to a national security interest while simultaneously advancing their own research agenda. The U.S. Department of Defense inadvertently funded and provided research participants for the largest study using intelligence tests during this time period (Chapman, 1988; Hilgard, 1965).

The APA led the efforts to develop a measure to classify and organize Army recruits after its president, Robert Yerkes, compelled organization members to employ their expertise and join in the war effort—after all, it was in the nation's best interest and a member's patriotic duty (Yerkes, 1921). In a letter to the Council of the APA he outlined two main objectives:

> In the present perilous situation, it is obviously desirable that the psychologists of the country act unitedly in the interest of defense. Our knowledge and our methods are of importance to the military service of our country, and it is our duty to the efficiency of our Army and Navy .... We should act at once as a professional group as well as individually.
>
> *(Yerkes, 1918, p. 86)*

Yerkes assembled a group of psychologists who would be known as the Committee on the Psychological Examination of Recruits. The committee's psychologists included Yerkes, Lewis Terman, Henry H. Goddard, Walter Bingham, Guy M. Whipple, Thomas Haines, and Frederick Wells, all leading psychologists and researchers of the time working in the space of intelligence and individual differences and ascribing to a hereditarian view of intelligence. One notable exception, James McKeen Cattell, had already raised his very public objections to America's involvement in the war. Terman's membership on the committee was due to his recent successful experience with a grouped, scored version of Binet's intelligence test that would eventually became the Stanford-Binet (Jolly, 2004; Lagemann, 2000; Minton, 1988). Between April and July of 1917 the committee constructed, piloted, and developed testing procedures for a group examination "to discover mentally inferior recruits as soon as they arrived in camp and to make suitable recommendation concerning them" (Yerkes, 1921, p. 103). Their work on these instruments became the model for future group intelligence tests and illustrated how these tests could be significant in defining social efficiency (Richardson & Johanningmeiera, 1998; Spring, 1972).

In collaboration with the newly established School of Military Psychology, a staggering 1,726,999 recruits and enlistees were administered psychological examinations at 35 different Army training camps between September of 1917 and January of 1919 (Yerkes, 1921). The examinations, the Army Alpha and Army Beta, tested the *native intellectual ability* of recruits. The Alpha, designed for literate recruits, and the Beta, for illiterate recruits, were reported to be free of cultural and educational bias. Army Alpha test items included problem solving and multiple-choice items, while Army Beta items included pictures and recruits were asked to identify the missing item from each picture (ASVAB, n.d.; see Figure 5.1). Although the committee thought that prior schooling did have some influence, Yerkes, a hereditarian at heart, still insisted that "in the main the soldier's inborn intelligence and the not the accidents of the environment determined his mental rating or grade" (Yoakum & Yerkes, 1920, p. 33).

The Committee far exceeded its original goals and purpose, conceived at the outset of the project. Seven key outcomes were achieved including (1) the intelligence rating assigned to every soldier, (2) the identification of men of "superior intelligence" who should be considered for special assignment, (3) the identification of the "mentally inferior" for battalions not used in regular battle, (4) the matching of ability with specific assignments, (5) the selection of recruits for military training schools, (6) the use of data to drive specialized instruction, and (7) the removal of men deemed unfit for service due to their "inferior" intelligence (Yerkes, 1921). Yerkes, serving as editor, would publish the findings of the Army testing program in what would be known in short as the *Army Report* (Pastore, 1978). The amount of data produced by the Committee and actually used by the U.S. Department of Defense remains imprecise. The data appear to have been far more useful to the fields of psychology and testing and measurement than to the U.S. Army or Department of Defense.

The results garnered from the test administration did give the committee pause, but only momentarily. Given the concerns regarding immigrants at the time and what Goddard termed "hereditary defect," he was surprised to learn that many of the soldiers taking the Beta were native born and not immigrants. Also challenging the ideas of hereditarian beliefs as they related to intelligence was the strong correlation between years of schooling and test scores. Just over a quarter of the soldiers were not able to read or write and were administered the Army Beta. Terman discounted this influence of environment or schooling by arguing that smarter people merely attained more education (Pastore, 1978; Zenderland, 1998).

The scope and success of the administration of the Army Alpha and Army Beta imbued those who worked in the province of intelligence test construction with an even greater sense of their use and of what subsequent results could mean for society at large, especially America's schools and school children. Lewis Terman, who had already adapted Binet's scales in the form of the Stanford-Binet IQ scales, immediately recognized the practical application for schools and his

Army Alpha Items

1. A company advanced 6 miles and retreated 2 miles. How far was it then from its first position?
2. A dealer bought some mules for $1,200. He sold them for $1,500, making $50 on each mule. How many mules were there?
3. Thermometers are useful because
    They regulate temperature
    They tell us how warm it is
    They contain mercury
4. A machine gun is more deadly than a rifle, because it
    Was invented more recently
    Fires more rapidly
    Can be used with less training

For these next two items, examinees first had to unscramble the words to form a sentence, and then indicate if the sentence was true or false.
5. happy is man sick always a
6. day it snow does every not

The next two items required examinees to determine the next two numbers in each sequence.
7. 3 4 5 6 7 8
8. 18 14 17 13 16 12

A portion of the Army Alpha required examinees to solve analogies.
9. shoe — foot. hat — kitten, head, knife, penny
10. eye — head. window — key, floor, room, door

In these next two examples, examinees were required to complete the sentence by selecting one of the four possible answers.
11. The apple grows on a shrub, vine, bush, tree
12. Denim is a dance, food, fabric, drink

FIGURE 5.1 Examples from Army Alpha and Beta (ASVAB, n.d.)

Army Beta Items

FIGURE 5.1 (*Continued*)

work on children with high ability (Gottfredson & Saklofske, 2009; Spring, 1972). Terman's membership on this committee would only strengthen his portfolio of experiences with intelligence tests and enabled his longitudinal study on gifted children, which would begin only two years after the end of World War I (Hilgard, 1957; Jolly, 2004).

6
PROGRESSIVE ERA OF EDUCATION

It is suggested that Progressive Reformers identified with one of two ideologies: pedagogical progressives and administrative progressives. These two groups were at disparate odds with how to approach school reform. The centrality of the pedagogues' efforts focused on the learning experiences and learning needs of children. They worked with teachers to transform classroom practices, developing from children's naturalistic inquiry. Pedagogues did not embrace IQ testing and its intended applications of sorting and grouping of students, unlike their counterparts the administrative progressives (Labaree, 2005).

The Progressive Era in education (circa 1890–1930) sought educational reforms in America to counter the constricting curriculum and pedagogy traditionally practiced during this time period and to also address the rapidly altering society presented by industrialism, changing child labor laws, and a growing, diverse immigrant population in urban centers that collectively impacted schools and schooling (Beauvais, 2016; Chapman, 1988; Cremin, 1959; Fass, 1980). Psychology's development and rise paralleled this reform era and presented an opportune occasion to advance the newly established field of psychology by applying psychological theories and methods to solve America's educational challenges.

In the midst of this reform movement, E. L. Thorndike and John Dewey became central and competing scholars during the Progressive Era (Lagemann, 1989). Lagemann (1989, p. 185) argued that, "One cannot understand the history of education in the United States during the twentieth century unless one realizes that Edward L. Thorndike won and John Dewey lost." This is fundamental to recognizing psychology and educational psychology's ability to influence educational systems and procedures. Thorndike was a psychologist and empiricist to his core and aligned with administrative progressives. Dewey is best remembered as an educational philosopher rather than a psychologist and one of the most influential American progressive educational reformers of the 20th century (Dreier, 2012).

John Dewey

John Dewey, born in 1859 near the New England town of Burlington, VT, was the third of four boys. His parents' 20-year age difference exacerbated their vastly different personalities. Dewey spent most of his youth attempting to facilitate his father's laid back nature and his mother's intense religious fervor (Bredo, 2003). It is suggested that his work later in life always carried a hallmark of "adopting a mediating a role between polarized positions" most likely developed during his childhood (Bredo, 2003, p. 83).

His formative years were years spent in a one-room elementary school with 54 students with children ranging in age from 7 to 19. His high school years were decidedly better and he graduated at the age of 16 and went on to the University of Vermont. He taught high school after graduation but found classroom management difficult. Dewey eventually made his way to Johns Hopkins University, where he earned a Ph.D. in psychology (studying in part with G. Stanley Hall). He was part of first wave of "new" psychologists and his style of psychology concentrated on the individual development embedded in the social and cultural context (Bredo, 2003; Pillsbury, 1957), eventually becoming president of the APA in 1899. Dewey, too, recognized schools as places of scientific study:

> The school is an especially favorable place in which to study the availability of psychology for social practice; because in the school the formation of a certain type of social personality, with a certain attitude and equipment of working powers, is the express aim.
>
> *(Dewey, 1900, p. 120)*

His first academic position had been at the University of Michigan for ten years followed by another decade-long tenure at the University of Chicago, where he established a laboratory school and carried out his ideas of progressive education (Bredo, 2003; Mayhew & Edwards, 1936). Schools were integral in the promotion of a democratic society, in tandem with moral and intellectual development (Cremin, 1959; Dewey, 1916). Despite Dewey's career as a psychologist he is more often identified as an educational philosopher and this can be partly attributed to his appointment to the philosophy department at Columbia in 1904 (Pillsbury, 1957), where he remained until he retirement in 1930.

The Measuring of Intelligence—IQ

Those involved in the measurement of intelligence, namely educational psychologists, joined forces with administrative progressives to implement individualized instruction through the execution of widespread of IQ testing (Chapman, 1988; Zenderland, 1998). American psychologists were keenly interested in quantifying the amount of intelligence held and exploring the consequence of differing levels of intelligence. The successful large-scale testing of recruits during World War I provided evidence for the scales' utility in classifying and sorting of any number of populations, including school children. For the first time, "American designers and promulgators of intelligence tests proposed ... an absolute measure of potential not merely a relative way of discriminating among individual abilities" (Fass, 1980, p. 440). In keeping with hereditarian positions, IQ was considered fixed, providing a perpetual measure of a child's intelligence. The IQ test provided an apparently infallible approach to sorting and categorizing students with the greatest efficiency possible (Chapman, 1988; Fass, 1980). Terman (1916b, p. 4) argued that the IQ test would and should guide classroom instruction:

> Before an engineer constructs a railroad bridge or trestle, he studies the materials to be used, and learns by means of tests exactly the amount of strain per unit of size his materials will be able to withstand. He does not work empirically, and count upon patching up the mistakes which may later appear under the stress of actual use. The educational engineer should emulate this example. Tests and forethought must take the place of failure and patchwork. Our efforts have been too long directed by "trial and error." It is time to leave off guessing and to acquire a scientific knowledge of the material with which we have to deal.

With the progressive reform era's emphasis on the individual, the IQ provided what was thought to be an accurate measure of an individual's capacity. The IQ score was thought to provide a direct window into an individual's capacity,

> For the schools needed to first, to find a means for discovering each individual's potential, and second, to develop, organize, and systematize a learning process which could educate that potential. They needed, in short, to find a mechanism for selection and a basis for curriculum development .... The IQ was just the organizing principle needed to fulfill all these goals.
> *(Fass, 1980, p. 447)*

IQ tests were not embraced blindly, and certain critics were vocal regarding their use. Walter Lippmann, a journalist for the *New Republic*, raised objections to the wholesale acceptance of a measure. After reading the *Army Report*, he found the result of the average mental age of recruits reported at 13 from the *Report* "nonsense" (Pastore, 1978). Similar measures to those used during World War I were now to be deployed on American school children, and this caused great pause and concern for Lippmann. Lippmann and Terman would engage in a particularly public and heated debate in the *New Republic* during 1922 and 1923 over the use and relative merits of intelligence tests. Lippmann also questioned the IQ test as a valid measure of intelligence, as intelligence had been poorly defined by the test constructors. He argued that the potential use of the IQ test was an "abuse of scientific method" proffered by the creators of these measures (Lippmann, 1923, p. 146) and lamented that some teachers "will stop when they have classified and forget that their duty is to educate" (Lippmann, 1922, p. 298). The most salient and central point of Lippmann's argument was not how the IQ tests would be used but how they would be misused. William Bagley was one of a number of psychologists who raised concerns over the *Army Report*, the value of intelligence tests, and their implications for education. He argued:

> The proposal to apply the intelligence tests in selecting at an early age those who are to be the later leaders of the nation has received a sanction, and in my humble judgment a most specious sanction, from the unquestioned success of the tests in the Army. In picking out the men who are better able than their fellows to learn new duties quickly, tests which measure this capacity have an obvious value. In how far these men owed their superiority to innate traits and how far to education, we have now no certain means of knowing, although the determinist is usual cocksure that education has nothing to do with it.
>
> *(Bagley, 1922, p. 380)*

Dewey (1928) also questioned the efficacy of IQ testing:

> It would not be hard to show that the need for classification underlies the importance of testing for IQs. The aim is to establish a norm. The norm, omitting statistical refinements, is essentially an average found, any given child can be rated. He comes up to it, falls below it, or exceeds it, by any assignable quantity. Thus the application makes possible a more precise classification than did older methods which were by comparison hit and miss. But what has this to with schools where individuality is a primary object of consideration, and wherein the so-called "class" becomes a grouping for social purposes and wherein diversity of ability and experience rather than uniformity is prized?
>
> *(as cited in Rudnitski, 1996, p. 2)*

These criticisms did not dissuade psychologists, such as Terman and Goddard, who were deeply invested in the testing movement, nor those school personnel who valued their utility and applied them in schools. Administrative progressives pinpointed social efficiency and utilitarianism as the main drivers of reform (Labaree, 2005) as well as a control of the curriculum—a curriculum that would prepare students for their eventual role in society. These were concrete ideals that government, school officials, and the general public could readily support.

The platform of administrative progressives presented the solving of real and perceived problems and as a part of this solution was the rise of the IQ test as a tool to achieve social efficiency (Chapman, 1988).

Administrative progressives began with the inherent differences students possessed, which objectively could be measured through a host of aptitude and achievement measures, then addressed within the school by a systematic approach (Benjamin, 2009; Chapman, 1988). In the end, the administrative progressives prevailed and their legacy remains evident in contemporary federal, state, and local school policy and practice (Lagemann, 2000; Stoskopf, 2002).

Summary

The "new" psychology established during closing decades of the 19th century and the earliest parts of 20th century provided the bedrock for the establishment of numerous subfields of psychology, including educational psychology and the tangential field of gifted education in the proceeding decades. This group of predominantly male psychologists also illustrated their impact and usefulness to a range of societal issues and challenges by employing the field's methodologies and tools (particularly the IQ test), allowing for a rapid proliferation of their ideas and theories, especially as they applied to children and schools. Gifted education would be indissolubly fashioned to these early tools, practices, and theories.

SECTION II

7
A FIELD OF THEIR OWN

The establishment of the field of psychology and the impact of psychological constructs and methodologies on disciplines such as education was nearly immediate. This led particular psychologists to undertake the study of individual differences and the expression of intelligence in educational environments. These avenues of research were accelerated by societal events—such as an expanded interest in science, changes in school populations, and the United States' entry into World War I. The growth of psychology and its subfields, chiefly educational psychology, coupled with the events of World War I, hastened the establishment of gifted education and the emergence of researchers who would commence in earnest the study of gifted children with measured IQs (Jolly, 2004; Robins, 2010). Included in this contextual milieu were the Progressive Era educational reforms aimed at providing the "freest and fullest development of the individual, based upon the scientific study of his physical, mental, spiritual, and social characteristics and needs" (Kliebard, 1995, p. 164). Building on the foundations as described by Julian Stanley (1976, p. 39), the lineage of gifted education was established with "Galton was the grandfather of the gifted-child movement and Binet its midwife, Terman must qualify as the father [and] ... Hollingworth may be considered the nurturant mother of the movement" and thus the familial tree of gifted education has flourished or withered depending on the changing educational climate and societal backdrop (Davis & Rimm, 1989; Tannenbaum, 1983).

Early Fascination and Development of Exceptional Youth

An interest in children with exceptional mental abilities existed long before the formal field of gifted education was established or compulsory schooling enacted.

In fact, many of the earliest examples of schooling for children with extraordinary mental abilities were cases of schooling at home. These illustrated cases appeared as articles in popular publications or recorded in royal court chronicles and thus the public's preoccupation with precocious youth, who were often interpreted as defective and troubled. However, not all recorded narratives reveal ruinous inevitabilities. These overt displays of mental gymnastics caused interminable conjecture about the origins of the children's abilities, their mental stability, and the permanence of said ability. These were typically extreme examples of children who had burned brightly then faded into obscurity, succumbing to a mental illness or an early death. If they did live to adulthood, they were sensationalized as extreme underachievers who entered into careers that did not match their abilities or mental aptitude. Many myths and misunderstandings endured regarding prodigious youth, and these misconceptions provided a wealth of speculation and eventually contributed to the first research questions in a new field of empirical study.

Initial Examples

One of the first widely published accounts of a child prodigy was that of Christian Heinrich Heineken, described as a profoundly gifted child born in Lubeck, Germany, in 1721. Heineken had impressed his parents with his keen sense of speech, displayed at the tender age of ten months. Sensing that his educational development might be unusual based on this behavior, they solicited the help of a tutor to work with Christian. While still maturing from infant to toddler, he was known to recite Bible stories from memory, and eventually accumulated a knowledge base that included world history, mathematics, and anatomy. At the age of four, he could read, write, and speak in his native German, speak colloquial French, and recite approximately 1,500 Latin proverbs (*Scot's Magazine*, 1780; Whipple, 1924).

With printed materials broadly available throughout Europe by this time, Heineken's parents decided to publicize and display their son's extraordinary talents. This provided widespread exposure and demand to know more about Christian—he quickly gained fame throughout the Europe, drawing large crowds to watch him demonstrate his abilities and once entertaining the King of Denmark during a royal visit to Germany. Heineken died at four years four months of an undiagnosed illness, raising many questions as to his physical fortitude, which helped feed the mythology that would build surrounding the physical frailty of the so-called *wunderkind* (Whipple, 1924), especially as examples of similar children emerged over time. Nearly 60 years after Christian's death, stories about his extraordinary abilities remained in the public's fascination. *Scot's Magazine* (1780, p. 9) published an account of the "infant scholar" in 1780 going so far as to suggest that his parents were to blame for his early death by "exhausting his strength and shortening his life." Stories such as this emerged periodically over time, including those of a young American boy and girl during the early 20th century.

William James Sidis, who was the child of Russian immigrants, was born in 1898. Nearly 200 years after the stories of Christian circulated, the public consumption of stories regarding precocious youth remained in demand. Reports often concentrated on their extraordinary academic accomplishments and sensationalized details about each child's early prodigious behavior. William's father, Boris, had attended Harvard and worked in medical psychology (Montour, 1977). Using John Stuart Mill's childhood as a model and unhappy with American public schools, Boris sought to apply the same type of homeschooling education to William that had been instituted by Mill's father. The news story recounted, "Dr. Sidis discounts the idea that his son is a genius or that his ability to grasp abstruse and difficult subjects is inherited or abnormal. He attributes it, on the contrary, to his own system of education" ("Cultured Boston," 1910, p. 11), contrary to prominent hereditarian views of the day. Boris argued the special education he had designed for his son's great capabilities, not his genetic material, provided "an education having as its chief purpose the training of the child to make facile, habitual, and profitable use of his hidden energies" (Bruce, 1910, p. 692).

As a small boy, William was educated in the skills of reasoning and observation and by age three could read and spell and by age four write (Bruce, 1910). By age five, he had mastered reading in Russian, French, and German and possessed medical student knowledge of anatomy (Montour, 1977). Completing seven grades of school in six months, William was kept at home so his father could continue to provide content and work that met his son's unique abilities, including high levels of mathematics. Boris outlined his thoughts about education, railing especially against the shortcomings of America's public school treatment of precocious children during the early decades of the 20th century. His tome to parents, *Philistine and Genius* (1911), was dedicated to "the fathers and mothers of the United States" and intended to provide guidance to other parents with children of advanced abilities. He vociferated:

> The goody-goody schoolma'am, the madarnin-schoolmaster, the philistine-pedagogue, the pedant-administrator with his business capacities, have proved themselves incompetent to deal with the education of the young. They stifle talent, they stupefy the intellect, they suppress genius, they benumb the facilities of our children. The educator, with this pseudo-scientific, pseudo-psychological pseudogogics, can only bring up a set of philistines with firm, set habits,—marionettes,—dolls.
>
> (Sidis, 1911, pp. 42–43)

Boris orchestrated the media's documentation of William's progress, evidenced by the various newspaper and magazine articles, which the younger Sidis despised (Montour, 1977). His father advocated for his admittance to Harvard at the age of nine but the university required him to wait until William turned 11, much to Boris's frustration and disappointment. However, at Harvard, William's abilities in mathematics and science were finally able to flourish. And due to his father's continued promotion, the media remained actively interested in William's progress. William would remain in the spotlight's glare for the remainder of his childhood.

With few like-minded peers, William found adult life as difficult but for different reasons and the media continued to document his life, except misfortune now seemed to plague him, including an arrest in 1919. Eventually, he found seclusion to be an easier life path. Adulthood included estrangement from his father and chronic underemployment. He died in 1944 with the press declaring his life a failure—as an adult he never achieved the promise that his childhood had suggested (Montour, 1977).

A contemporary of Sidis, Winifred Stoner Jr., also found herself in the media spotlight based on her precocious behaviors and abilities. Winifred Stoner, Winifred Jr.'s mother, also played a central role in shaping and exploiting her child's exceptional abilities. Winifred Jr. spoke in full sentences by age one and read in English and French by age three, the same year a tour of Europe was arranged to display her unusual talents. Her mother even taught her how to type so that Winifred Jr. could put her thoughts to paper before her fine motor skills had developed (O'Shea, 1911). Similar to Boris Sidis, Winifred Stoner devised an entire educational regime, which she thought produced these advanced abilities in her daughter and published them in *Natural Education* (1914). Winifred Jr.'s adult life was wayward and marked by unfortunate marriages. Her great potential as a child was never realized into an adult career or occupation especially when careers for women remained very limited (*Time*, 1937).

Not all prodigious youth were fated to doom and despair—John Stuart Mill was a prime example, even though he certainly could have found himself on this path. In a time where the contemporary concept of gifted children and best practices for their education did not exist, John Stuart Mill, the renowned English philosopher and political theorist, was subjected to a rigorous educational regime created and instituted by his father. This homeschooling arrangement allowed Mill to advance at his own rate, yet prevented him from understanding how his abilities compared to his peers and isolated him from other children ("Autobiography," n.d.). Given that Mill's father exerted complete control over his academic studies for his entire childhood, he had much trouble adjusting in adulthood, which led to a deep depression in his 20s. Mill recalled,

> My education, which was wholly his work, had been conducted without any regard to the possibility of its ending in this result; and I saw no use in giving him the pain of thinking that his plans had failed, when the failure was probably irremediable, and, at all events, beyond the power of his remedies. Of other friends, I had at that time none to whom I had any hope of

making my condition intelligible. It was, however, abundantly intelligible to myself; and the more I dwelt upon it, the more hopeless it appeared.

("Autobiography," n.d., para. 58)

Unlike Heineken or Sidis, Mill's father did not exploit him, though his education was strict and kept him sequestered from his peers. Once Mill emerged from his depression, he found value and purpose becoming one of the world's most prominent thinkers in the fields of philosophy, political theory, and economics ("Autobiography," n.d.). His life remains a rich and valuable source of study for those concerned with the education of child prodigies, particularly the pitfalls of neglecting basic social and environmental needs of the gifted, both of which have been well-established as important factors in a child's holistic development (Jolly & Bruno, 2010).

In addition to Mill, examples of prodigious youth who went on to have successful adult careers exist throughout the historical literature, rather than just the ill-fated futures such as those of Heineken and Sidis. These include Juan Caramel y Lobkowitz, a 17th-century Spanish priest and philosopher; Johann Carl Friedrich Gauss, 19th-century German mathematician; and Norbert Wiener, an MIT mathematician. However, misfortune and the sensational stories of precocious youth burning bright and fading out appear to capture the public's attention more readily and helped to reinforce the negative myth-building surrounding gifted children of exceptional intellect (Bell, 1937; Galileo Project, n.d.; Hardesty, 2011).

8
PRELIMINARY STUDIES OF HIGH ABILITY AND EMINENCE

To say that Hollingworth and Terman were the first to investigate individuals of advanced intellect is inaccurate. The work of individuals such as Sir Francis Galton, Henry Yoder, Cesare Lombroso, and Guy M. Whipple—to name just a few—had begun initial investigations but lacked the sophisticated instruments and/or sustained research agendas. Lombroso's studies, flawed in their design, resulted in individuals with great intellectual prowess to be characterized as sickly, mentally imbalanced, and/or ostracized (Hollingworth, 1926; Jolly & Bruno, 2010; Tannenbaum, 1983).

Cesare Lombroso

Cesare Lombroso established the most misleading portrayal of gifted persons. Better known for his research in criminology, his studies resulted in some of the utmost negative stereotypes being lodged against gifted children (Hollingworth, 1926). In his 1901 text *Man of Genius*, he proposed a link between genius and mental neurosis. Lombroso presented a collection of men who were considered geniuses but also suffered from mental health issues. These portrayals included Isaac Newton, Jean Jacques Rousseau, and Arthur Shopenhauer. These sensational and one-sided examples of genius and insanity captured the attention of the mainstream public and became accepted as the norm, rather than the exception, despite the contradictory findings offered by Francis Galton and Henry Yoder (Jolly, 2005). Umbrage was taken with the methodological approaches used by Lombroso, as they were characterized as unscientific. Hollingworth (1926, p. 14) noted, "Lombroso started with a theory and ... then looked for illustrative examples, selected to prove it." Terman (1924a, p. 360) directly linked Lombroso's findings to the treatment and education of gifted children, lamenting,

> Another circumstance that has blocked the educational progress of gifted children is the superstition given currency by Lombroso and others, that intellectual precocity is pathological; that bright children are prone to die young, become insane, or develop post-adolescent stupidity. So thoroughly has this superstition become imbedded in popular thought that even prominent educators are likely to assume that the child of high intelligence quotient must, ipso facto, be anemic, nervous, conceited, eccentric, non-social, and a stranger to play.

Sir Francis Galton

Not all studies of eminence began from a biased vantage point; there were certainly other individuals who sought to combine the methods of psychology, principles of individual differences, and/or educational ideologies. Francis Galton's revolutionary studies of intelligence, which measured mental capability and individual differences by gathering evidence regarding adults recognized as having notably contributed to fields such as the arts, science, politics, and scholarship (Burt, 1962), heavily influenced both Terman and Hollingworth. "He studied these facts with a view to determining degrees of eminence, the frequency of persons in the various degrees, and why some persons become eminent while others do not" (Hollingworth, 1926, p. 4). His conclusions featured heavily in her 1926 text:

> Hence we arrive at the undeniable but unexpected conclusion that eminently gifted men are raised as much above mediocrity as idiots are depressed below it; a fact that is calculated to enlarge considerably our ideas of the enormous difference of intellectual gifts between man and man.
> *(Galton, 1869, p. 36)*

Galton was not the first to suggest that genius was inherited; however, he was the first to use statistical methods to provide numerical interpretations (Burt, 1962). Galton proposed using the normal distribution to map intellectual range. By dividing the entire population "into 18 classes, and mak[ing] the subdivisions between each approximately equal to the so-called 'probable error.' The term 'genius' is defined as covering the top three classes, that is to say, the brightest 248 in a million" (Burt, 1962, p. 17).

> Galton (1865, p. 318) also used the life histories of men of high ability to illustrate, that intellectual capacity is so largely transmitted by descent that, out of every hundred sons of men distinguished in the open professions, no less than eight are found to have rivaled their fathers in eminence. It must

be recollected that success of this kind implies the simultaneous inheritance of many points of character, in addition to mere intellectual capacity.

He recorded his findings in *English Men of Science: Their Nature and Nurture* (Galton, 1874). Galton's conclusions would feature prominently in Terman's own research as he tried to link previous familial eminence to current high ability and that high ability or genius to guaranteed eminence later in life (Jolly, 2005). Hollingworth felt equally encouraged by Galton's methods and findings. These advances provided the opportunity to begin measuring intelligence and dismiss the persistent acceptance that "at the beginning of life all children of the nation are equally well endowed with capacity for learning" (Hollingworth, 1924a, p. 277).

Galton's investigations provided foundational sources for the greater systematics and rigorous investigations that were still to occur, while Lombroso's damaging studies would be the impetus for a collection of smaller studies at the turn of the 20th century.

Alfred Yoder

In 1894, using the methodology of biographic study established by Galton, Alfred Yoder, another Clark University graduate, undertook a study of the boyhoods of 50 great men in order to help better understand how to educate bright children (Hearst & Capshew, 1988). Collecting the biographies, memoirs, and other available documents, this research provided the first preview into the early lives of men such as Charles Darwin, Thomas Edison, Abraham Lincoln, and Edgar Allan Poe. Yoder (1894, p. 135) was motivated out of concern for

> the modern teacher['s] need to recognize and treat talent in the child. Our methods of mass education have almost destroyed this faculty in public schools. Every day in every school unnamed crimes are committed against the soul, the best children suffering most; not only is their talent undetected and unaided, but often positively discouraged or even blighted.

Terman and Hollingworth found Yoder's methodology instructive but sought to improve its execution and expand its application (Jolly, 2005).

Guy M. Whipple

Guy M. Whipple was an early psychologist whose research interests were varied, including mental testing, reading instruction, vocational education, and gifted education. He had collaborated with Terman during their work on the APA's Committee on the Psychological Examination of Recruits during World War I, and Whipple's seminal two-volume *Manual of Mental and Physical Tests* (1910) was the standard reference for psychological test administrators for approximately two decades (Jolly, 2007a). Whipple also recognized the early application of psychology to education and the study of individual differences. In 1919 he published *Classes for Gifted Children*, arguing that a common pace of instruction for all children was impossible, so much so that special classes for "extra dull" students had been established, producing an extensive evidence base and pedagogy for this particular group of students. Whipple proposed that bright children could also profit from such specialized instruction (Whipple, 1919a). In 1920 Whipple is credited with "[having] done much to further the interest in special educational facilities for bright children ... [and it is to him] we owe the term 'gifted' as the standard designation of children of supernormal ability" (Henry, 1920, p. 9). Whipple's adoption of the label "gifted" has proven to be a point of controversy for the field, "possibly because it seems to imply a desirable status that is mysteriously granted to some yet remains unavailable to others" (Matthews, Ritchotte, & Jolly, 2014, p. 372), while other contemporary researchers suggest that proper educational services for gifted students are more important than the label itself (Peters, Kaufman, Matthews, McBee, & McCoach, 2014).

Classes for Gifted Children chronicles Whipple's year-long investigation focused on not only mental testing and identification, but also classroom practices and organization. These included a curriculum centered on student interest, a classroom environment that promoted independent learning including moveable furniture, the reduction of drill and direct instruction, and the ability for the teacher to extend the latitude and adjust the curriculum to meet the needs of gifted students (Whipple, 1919a, 1919b). Whipple also observed that teachers and principals did a poor job of selecting students for gifted programs based on "school work, health, industry and application ... some pupils having been wrongly placed in the gifted group whereas gifted children had been held back" (Richards-Nash, 1924, p. 213). Given Whipple's background in mental testing, he observed that IQ tests were better identifiers and the selection process error had been reduced to near zero (Richards-Nash, 1924):

> With the improved means of mental measurement thus afforded by the intelligence scale it was possible for the psychologist to give a better rating of a child's mental ability than the teacher who had known the child for a year or more in close personal contact could give.
>
> *(Peterson, 1925, p. 255)*

Hollingworth noted Whipple's recommendations and would expand on many of them in her own subsequent students at both P.S. 165 and P.S. 500 in the New York City Public Schools.

W. E. B. DuBois

This early work on gifted students rarely included diverse populations of students as part of the participants researched, as social class and race were strongly linked to hereditarian viewpoints. The Talented Tenth, originally developed by Henry Morehouse in 1896, provided a framework that W. E. B. DuBois popularized for African American leaders (Mitchell & Jenkins, 2010). DuBois (1903, p. 45) suggested that

> The Talented Tenth rises and pulls all that are worth the saving up to their vantage ground. This is the history of human progress .... How then shall the leaders of a struggling people be trained and the hands of the risen few strengthened? There can be but one answer: The best and most capable of their youth must be schooled in the colleges and universities of the land.

This group in the 90th percentile would be in the best position to shepherd, lead, and advance African Americans' interests and needs. Historically Black colleges and universities were identified as the institutions to develop the talent of the top 10% (DuBois, 1903). One instrument in DuBois's efforts to propagate the Talented Tenth was the *Crisis*, the official magazine of the National Association for the Advancement of Colored People aimed at middle-class Black America (Reed, 1997). As its first editor, DuBois (1910, p. 10) outlined the publication's goal:

> The object of this publication is to set forth those facts and arguments which show the danger of race prejudice, particularly as manifested today toward colored people. It takes its name from the fact that the editors believe that this is a critical time in the history of the advancement of men.

DuBois easily qualified as a member of the Talented Tenth that he proposed, and his life foreshadowed the path that was laid for this percentage of the population.

DuBois was born in Great Barrington, MA, shortly after the end of the Civil War, in 1868. DuBois became the first African American to earn a Ph.D. from Harvard and also earned a fellowship from the John F. Slater Fund for the Education of Freedmen for study in Europe before his graduation in 1895 (Lewis, 2009). DuBois's educational journey beyond Great Barrington was made possible due to the intercession of benefactors in his hometown of Great Barrington, who thought that his intellectual talents required further educational opportunities (Worrell, 2013). Before attending Harvard, DuBois first attended Fisk University, a historically Black college, in Nashville, TN. Having grown up in small New England community, it was here that DuBois first encountered Southern segregation and racism. Despite earning a bachelor's degree at Fisk in 1888, he would be required to enter Harvard as an undergraduate and earned a second bachelor's degree in 1890 before beginning his doctoral studies (Lewis, 2009).

The concept of the Talented Tenth was not embraced by the mainstream gifted education community at large, as the foundational leaders held largely to hereditarian views of intelligence that were tied to race and class. This is important especially for African American students, as they were almost exclusively precluded from gifted identification, inclusion in research, and/or classroom programming based on their race alone (Jolly, 2008b; Valencia & Suzuki, 2001).

What separated the formal field of gifted education, under the watch of Terman and Hollingworth, from these previous investigations was the systematic and methodological nature of the research. The content of their research also grew in substance, identified questions, and included expanded methodologies systematically applied to address the problems of gifted children, eventuating in new concepts and hypotheses (Jolly, 2004; Kuhn, 1996). Their research on gifted children dominated the empirical literature in the 1920s and 1930s when compared to the previous decades, and the impact of their work was far-reaching with legacies that continue to impact contemporary gifted education and other fields of inquiry.

9

STAGGERED ATTEMPTS AT MEETING THE EDUCATIONAL NEEDS OF BRIGHT CHILDREN

The earliest formal educational practices initiated for the *gifted, bright children,* or those of *superior intellect* in public schools focused primarily on ability grouping, grade skipping, and subject acceleration; still, these were sporadic and no systemic or systematic provisions were implemented in schools across the United States (Jolly, 2004). The progressive education ideology of an individualized approach to schooling began to encroach on educators' practice and curricular changes began to emerge, including these for gifted students (Burk, 1913). Some schools introduced actual curricular modifications, but this was the exception rather than the rule. Curricular changes were often found to be too difficult, cumbersome, time consuming, and—the eventual determiner of their demise—costly (Washburne & Marland, 1963; Whipple, 1924). Ironically, these are some of the same pretexts advanced as to why curricular changes are not implemented in schools today. The empirical research to support or refute the effectiveness of curriculum changes to impact the learning of gifted students had yet to be undertaken.

School administrators made some of the first serious and systematic attempts to reach students of advanced academic ability under the direction of William Torrey Harris just after the end of the Civil War, in 1868. Considered an educational visionary for his time (he would be appointed United States Commissioner of Education in 1899), he established the first permanent kindergarten in United States public schools. These were based on the kindergartens begun in Germany and the teachings of Friedrich Frobels, which Harris recognized held potential educational benefits for young children (O'Connor, 1999). For academically advanced students in St. Louis schools, he developed a plan allowing students to advance every five weeks based on academic performance, and provided a promotion schedule and opportunities for children to rapidly advance through the school curriculum and successive grades (Hollingworth, 1926; Jolly, 2009a; Tannenbaum, 1983). Harris felt this approach, innovative for the period, would prevent lethargy encroaching on the work habits of bright young people.

The National Education Association (NEA), a highly influential organization in the early 20th century, endorsed a similar system of promotion "as short as five weeks in the lower grades—and gifted pupils in each section could, without much difficulty, be passed on to the section just above their own" (Whipple, 1924, p. 8). The NEA also called for an organization of curricular flexibility in schools. In their 1918 *Cardinal Principles of Secondary Education* it was stated that

> flexibility should be secured by 'election' of studies or curriculum, promotion by subjects from the beginning of junior high school, possible transfer from curriculum to curriculum, provision for maximum and minimum assignments for pupils of greater and less ability, and under certain conditions, for the rapid or slow progress of such pupils.
>
> *(NEA, 1918, p. 22)*

The NEA's endorsement of curricular flexibility also aligned with the Progressive Era reforms and focus on the individual student: "Individual differences in pupils and the varied needs of society alike demand that education be so varied as to touch the leading aspects of occupational, civic, and leisure life" (NEA, 1918, p. 17).

Over the next half century, school districts instituted some type of grouping, flexible promotion, and acceleration through curricular or grade skipping to meet the needs of gifted students, even if the implementation was haphazard, often arbitrary, and lacked permanence in its implementation. Districts representative of these practices included Woburn, MA, Denver, CO, Elizabeth, NJ, Santa Barbara, CA, and New York City, NY (Davis & Rimm, 1994; Ericson, 1985; Gallagher & Weiss, 1979; Tannenbaum, 1983). For example, the Elizabeth Plan (Elizabeth, NJ) provided

> three or four sections formed within each of the eight grades in such a way that pupils of nearly the same attainments were grouped together. Each section was allowed to do as much work as it could, and individual pupils were also promoted to sections above them, without formal examination, as soon as they demonstrated fitness for that work.
>
> *(Whipple, 1924, p. 9)*

The X-Y-Z plan also was a common approach used by districts across the United States to divide grades by ability and continued to be used as a means of tracking well into the mid-to-late 20th century (Hildebrand, 1981; Robins, 2010).

Special classes for gifted children gained particular momentum parallel to the implementation of special education services gradually granted to "children of subnormal intellect" in the early part of the 20th century (Van Sickle, 1910, p. 357). Some educationalists recognized how the lockstep system of schooling was limited in meeting students' needs and that providing curriculum and instruction for the "mythical average pupil" was the central source of the dissatisfaction. Although recognition was being given to children struggling in school, others sought to provide educational alternatives for gifted children in addition to efforts that were solely focused on acceleration (Burk, 1913; Van Sickle, 1910). In a speech given at a meeting of superintendents, J. H. Van Sickle, Superintendent of Schools in Baltimore, MD, addressed the difficulties that the uniformity of a graded school system posed and the significant disadvantages for all children:

> It is not easy to break … [what] fifty years of uniformity have created. … Adherence to fixed and unchangeable courses of study and to inflexible schemes of classification fall far short of furnishing equal opportunity to all in our schools.
>
> *(1910, pp. 358–359)*

The NEA at its annual meeting in 1907, building upon some of the earliest recommendations for grade promotion, convened a special committee to discuss the educational needs of gifted learners. The committee recommended that gifted students be grouped together in special classes to be led by teachers with a favorable disposition towards these precocious children using curricula designed to meet their advanced intellectual needs (Ericson, 1985). In a position statement, the NEA proclaimed:

> In our conception of what the gifted child should do, we are inclined to look too exclusively upon the shorter time in which he can accomplish the tasks of the conventional course of study. Until we comprehend that for the gifted child a somewhat different atmosphere should be provided, that, too, a different curriculum should be developed, we shall accomplish little.
>
> *(as cited in Van Sickle, 1910, p. 361)*

These special classes were often designated as "opportunity classes" and began to appear in school districts such as Los Angeles, Cincinnati, and New York City (Davis & Rimm, 1994; Jolly, 2004).

One proponent of an alternative educational approach to instruction was Dr. Frederic Burk, President of the San Francisco Normal School. He noted, "The class system does permanent violence to all types of pupils" (Burk, 1913, p. 10) and that "it does injury to the rapid and quick thinking pupils, because these must shackle their stride to keep pace with the rate of the mythical average." Burk's proposition allowed for student self-instruction, which included the elements of flexibility in the lesson length, student self-assessment, and the ability for students to move at their own rate of progress (Burk, 1913).

The Cleveland Major Works Program and the Winnetka Plan provided examples of how districts in the 1920s made more detailed provisions for gifted students. Roberta Holden Bole, an active and influential citizen in Cleveland, was following the progress of Terman's longitudinal study, which had just commenced. She approached Herbert Bixby, the assistant superintendent of the Cleveland School District, about the possibility of offering provisions for gifted students (Gold, 1984). The Major Works Program arranged classes on the basis of IQ scores of students who would participate in gifted classes at each grade level (Ericson, 1985; Gold, 1984). Also incorporating Progressive Education principles, the curriculum stressed and emphasized engaging in activities that would prepare students for their future roles in society (Whipple, 1924).

Carleton Washburne, superintendent of schools in Winnetka, IL, devised the Winnetka Plan in 1922, soon after his arrival in the school district. After receiving support from the Commonwealth Fund of New York (the same granting body that would fund Terman's longitudinal study), Washburne devised a plan to investigate a program that called for students to move through a common curriculum in mathematics and reading, working at their own individual pace (Washburne, 1924). He believed that "children [with] above normal intelligence should not be held but encouraged to do as much more than a year's work as they can" (Washburne & Marland, 1963, p. 23). Students who were capable of working ahead of the rest of the children should not be penalized by being made to work in sync with the other children if they were able to accelerate through the content. Washburne recognized the absurdity of this arrangement. He also recognized "the futility of attempting to group children by intelligence quotients and then treating each group as if it were homogeneous" (Washburne, 1924, p. 255), which would be echoed in the studies conducted by Hollingworth at P. S. 165 and P. S. 500.

Based on this rationale, he devised the individualized self-instruction adapted from the work of Dr. Frederic Burk, President of San Francisco State Normal School where Washburne had taught and conducted research at the Normal School's allied elementary school while attending the University of California, Berkeley, and before his appointment at Winnetka (Washburne, 1918). This self-instruction was based on "100 hours, 11 are given to class work, 42 are given to work at 'free choice' and to 'work in common,' 32 to individual work, and 15 to other categories of activity" (Corcoran, 1927, pp. 63–64). Washburne recognized that the preparation of the materials for self-instruction could be time-consuming for his staff but that this initial expenditure of effort and resources would eventually pay off for both teachers and students (Washburne & Marland, 1963), considering that "adaption to individual differences is made by allowing individuals to progress through the various subjects at their own natural rates" (Washburne, 1924, p. 259) and that

> [educators] must replace the lock step of class instruction because it is only teaching *individuals*, that the time and material of courses can be made to

fit those for whom they are intended. It is inconceivable that an inefficient, slow and harmful method of instruction should survive in the face of the proof of its evils. If the lock step is abolished, the only alternative is some form of individual teaching.

(Washburne, 1918, p. 391)

By 1920, two-thirds of public school districts in urban centers reported having some type of programming for gifted students (Davis & Rimm, 1994; Hildebrand, 1981); however, these reports included huge variances in quality and type of programming and services. Even as programming was initiated across the United States, there was poor or limited empirical evidence to support its implementation and impact on student achievement. This was all about to change as researchers like Leta Hollingworth, Lulu Stedman (in coordination with William Root), and Lewis Terman began to design studies to capture not only much needed demographic data to describe the population but enact intervention studies to begin to understand programs, services, and curriculum.

Lulu Stedman: Early Schooling Responses and Curricular Changes

Lulu Stedman, Organizer of Teacher Training at Los Angeles State Normal School, provided one of the earliest and most detailed school-based descriptions of classroom interventions for gifted children. She was also instrumental in establishing an "opportunity class" for gifted students at the Normal School. After a series of interactions with a highly gifted boy and encouragement from the Normal School faculty, Stedman felt the opportunity class was a needed addition to the Normal School's Training School, which provided a setting for pre-service teachers to gain practical experience (Jolly, 2006a).

While Stedman implemented pedagogical and curricular provisions, she collaborated with William T. Root of the University of Pittsburg, who carried out the social and psychological studies on the 53 students in Stedman's opportunity class (Root, 1921). The opportunity class opened in January 1918 just before the transition of the Normal School to the Southern Branch of the University of California system (now UCLA; Stedman, 1924). Stedman described the opportunity room's organizational and curricular progress in *Education for Gifted Children* (1924), which was published five years after its establishment. Her chronicle of the opportunity class never explicitly defined giftedness; however, entry to the opportunity room was clearly tied to a predetermined IQ cutoff score—age 7 to 12, IQ 135 and above; and age 13 to 15, IQ 120 and above (Root, 1921; Stedman, 1924).

The training school was an ideal environment to institute special provisions for gifted learners based on the progressive educational ideals of the time; after all, the purpose of school was to serve as a place to train pre-service in contemporary pedagogical practices. The young boy, N. W., who instigated Stedman's interest in gifted children, entered the training school in the third grade at seven years old in 1915. Not long after his arrival it became clear that the curriculum was inadequate and that the student teachers were ill equipped to cater for his intellectual needs. In fact, he "was not especially interested in talking with many of them [pre-service teachers], as he felt they seldom knew what they were talking about" (Stedman, 1924, p. 1). His peer interactions were equally as poor. Stedman (1924, p. 1) recalled:

> He was extremely non-social, lacking both inclination and ability to play. Soon a mutual antagonism developed between the other boys of the class and himself. So great was the animosity aroused that it was a common occurrence for the boys to waylay him after school, chase him home, and administer, when possible, vigorous physical discipline ... Obviously something had to be done.

Stedman's aim was to provide an environment that would meet the special educational needs of N.W. and other children with similar educational and social needs. The argument for the opportunity class grew out of special classes that progressive educators advocated and achieved for "subnormal" or "feeble-minded" children. She believed special education interventions were required for children to realize their potential and contribute to society. However, Stedman was resistant to focusing solely on rapid acceleration, such as grade skipping through school—often attributing this practice to overzealous parents: "Serious danger results from a mere speeding-up process, especially in the case of children of foolishly ambitious parents who take undue pride in rapid advancement" (Stedman, 1924, p. 11) and to avoid "the social ostracism which is the invariable fate of the 'high school baby'" (Stedman, 1924, p. 187). Instead she tried to balance content acceleration with enrichment, offering students opportunities to explore concepts and topics with depth and complexity.

The varying ability and interest levels within the opportunity class called for each child to have his or her own individual assignments. Group-based work proved woefully inadequate in addressing the varying advanced ability levels of students. Considerable emphasis was given to independent instruction, so children would not have to wait for one another in order to move on to the next set of content or activity. Stedman also understood that too great an emphasis on individual work could be isolating and incorporated group discussion of independent projects as a strategy so that "contributions are welded into a whole, amplified, and enriched" (Stedman, 1924, p. 12). Students practiced receiving specific training in accepting constructive criticism, so that sessions would be of utmost value to all participants (Stedman, 1924).

Many students up until this point had drifted through school with little challenge presented to their schoolwork, so the opportunity classes offered the first real intellectual peers, content, and pedagogy commensurate with their abilities.

The opportunity class was located within the larger training school, and interaction between students in the opportunity class and in the regular classes happened frequently. Stedman recognized their importance, noting, "Inter-class athletics activities, school plays, pageants, or projects of various kinds involving the entire school perpetuate a social relationship between the opportunity room and the school" (Stedman, 1924, p. 17).

Education of Gifted Children was one of the earliest texts to comprehensively detail the curricular needs of gifted children. Based on her five years of collective experience with this group of gifted students, Stedman constructed 19 curricular recommendations to guide educators and researchers who worked with this population. The 19 recommendations included strategies and activities that were holistically supportive and intended to provide for a well-rounded education (Table 9.1), many of which would be reflected in the practices and research over the next several decades.

Lewis Terman would write the editor's introduction for *Education for Gifted Children,* which was published in 1924, nearly a decade and a half after Terman's departure from the Los Angeles State Normal School, and he also served as one of the editors of William T. Root's monograph of the opportunity classroom study. One can only speculate if Lewis Terman interacted with Stedman during his tenure at the Normal School (1906–1910) (Jolly, 2006a), but given the size of the institution and the nature of the work, the interaction seems likely.

For a time, William T. Root served as an instructor of child psychology at Los Angeles State Normal School before becoming a professor of educational psychology at the University of Pittsburgh (Anderson, 2015). He must have remained in contact with colleagues from this period of employment, as it would be the only reasonable explanation for a professor in Pittsburgh to take up the study of 53 "supernormal" children in Los Angeles long before the advent of the Internet and email. Root's investigation of Stedman's opportunity classroom sought to establish a baseline for "supernormal" children.

Root (1921, p. 1) intended to "trace out some of the factors, both social and psychological, found with a group of children purported to be superior." He observed the raft of literature being generated on "subnormal and defectives," based on individualized instruction and reasoned that equal deliberation should be given to the supernormal student. Psychological data included the administration of a full battery of subtests, including the Stanford-Binet and a number of other measures of imagery, and associative and mnemonic devices. Social data collected encompassed a large variety home environment factors along with physical and health data. Seven case studies were also conducted (Root, 1921). He found the children under investigation exceeded the norm across all psychological and social measures and in social measures also found a degree of superiority. The final question concerned the occurrence of geniuses in the group. Root (1921, p. 134) felt that none of the sample supported this conclusion:

TABLE 9.1 Stedman's 19 Curricular Recommendations

1. A curtailment of the time allotment of the various subjects from one-half to two-thirds the time required in the average classroom.
2. Reduction of drill, explanation, and development.
3. Definite instruction in how to study independently.
4. Development in the child of a scientific attitude toward his own progress and of a scientific method of attacking problems.
5. Opportunities for all forms of creative work—the writing of plays, stories, and poems; publication of newspapers; organization and direction of literary and civic societies; presentation of plays, pageants, and pantomimes.
6. Instruction in foreign languages.
7. Opportunities to see especially good motion pictures and spoken plays.
8. Opportunities to hear eminent lecturers, political leaders, visiting consuls, travelers from foreign countries, or specialists in any line, such as musicians, artists, librarians, scientists, and others.
9. Trips into the country under the guidance of a specialist in nature lore for the purpose of studying birds, animals, or growing things.
10. An understanding of commercial and industrial life through visits to commercial and industrial institutions.
11. Opportunities to visit libraries, art galleries, and museums.
12. Provisions for symmetrical development by permitting the child to abandon for a time work in which he excels in order to concentrate on skills in which he is lacking.
13. Provisions for special exercises and definite instruction in body building for the child of delicate physique and for the bookish child who is disinclined to participate in play or physical activity.
14. Opportunities to work out social and civic projects for the purpose of developing group consciousness and quickening the child's awareness of his obligations to the school and the community.
15. Definite training in leadership through voluntary assumptions on the part of the child of responsibility for the successful culmination of school projects, and through the membership on committees concerned with governmental policies of the school.
16. Special courses in music, art, dramatics, and other special subjects, for the purpose of meeting the needs of children possessing aptitude for technical or aesthetic vocations.
17. Definite provision should be made and concessions granted regarding programs and school attendance of children highly gifted in music, dramatics, and art, in order that general education and preparation for a career may continue at the same time.
18. Special courses in all phases of manual work adapted to the physical development of the child should be provided.
19. The social subjects should stimulate the child to use the research method and to read widely in correlated subjects. They should ordinarily revolve around some central projects, creative in nature, with which the entire group is concerned. It is expedient that they create a need for efficient use of the tool subjects [research method].

Source: Stedman, 1924, pp. 188–189.

> The writer conceives genius as possessing but the same characteristics we all possess only in a markedly superior degree; and while it seems to him that the evidence warrants attributing some superior innate ability to a very great majority of the cases presented here, more than that he cannot say.

Here is where Root and Stedman's empirical work ends with gifted children and Stedman's published work in gifted education remained limited. She did publish one additional curricular text in 1935, but not specifically targeted for gifted children. By this time, she had been appointed Supervisor of Special Education in Elementary Education at UCLA. The book's content reflected a similar flavor to that revealed in the *Education of the Gifted* (Stedman, 1924). *Our Ancestors in the Ancient World* (Salisbury & Stedman, 1935, p. vii) offered readers

> the story of the evolution of western culture .... The task has been two fold: first the selection of vivid details and episodes which are of interest to children, and secondly the organization of such content to illustrate broad principles of the growth of civilization and to indicate great trends in human progress throughout ancient times.

Despite not being a text developed for gifted learners, the activities at the end of each section were typically open-ended with great latitude for learners of varying ability levels rather than concentrating on the memorization of dates, places, and people. For example, questions or activities were either framed as problems to solve or things to construct or prepare (Salisbury & Stedman, 1935).

As the field of gifted education was established and grew, so did the understandings of their characteristics, behaviors, and educational and emotional needs. These early efforts would be more fully developed as researchers began to investigate the intersection between theory and practice.

10
FATHER OF GIFTED EDUCATION

Lewis M. Terman

Lewis M. Terman often carries the moniker "father of gifted education" (Stanley, 1975; Tannenbaum, 1983). He helped to establish a formal field of inquiry and provided much-needed systematic and longitudinal evidence regarding the behaviors of advanced abilities. Within this line of research, he set in motion a legitimate subfield of educational psychology—gifted education.

Terman was a man of his times, shaped by his early influences and environment—reflecting and promoting a strict adherence to the then-contemporaneous hereditarian theory, which tied IQ to race, giving little attention or regard to environmental influence. Terman held the utmost belief in the science of psychology and its ability to improve the lives of all Americans, particularly children who exhibited superior levels of intelligence when compared to their chronological aged peers (Chapman, 1988; Jolly, 2004). An appreciation and knowledge of Terman's early influences and his life course provides a window into his approach to gifted education, the identification of gifted children, and approach to their education.

Not a Farm Boy Was He

Before Terman was known for the development of the Stanford–Binet IQ test, his expertise in the areas of intelligence and individual differences, and his longitudinal work with gifted children, his life began on an obscure farm in rural Johnson County, IN. Terman was born in 1877 after his parents had been married 22 years and was the twelfth of their 14 children (Boring, 1959). Near the end of the 19th century, the life of a farmer was far more likely than that of an intellectual for Terman, but at the age of 15 he began to sense that the monotony of an agrarian lifestyle was not going to be his chosen career path (Boring, 1959; Terman, 1930a). Terman (1930a, p. 299) reflected on his choice to teach: "Not to teach meant to continue forever ploughing the same fields, doing the same chores, and getting nowhere."

At the age of 15, having finished his formal elementary and secondary education in a one-room schoolhouse, his parents sent him to Central Normal College to prepare to be a teacher. After he finished taking a number of courses at Central and completed several degrees, Terman served as teacher and principal in one-room schoolhouses similar to the one he had attended in Johnson County (Terman, 1930a). In 1901, he entered Indiana University and would leave two years later with a master's degree in psychology, a wife, and two children (Feldhusen, 2003; Winkler & Jolly, 2014).

Psychology and Study of Individual Differences

Terman received his master's degree from Indiana University, where his views of psychological principles were largely forged by psychologists W. L. Bryan, E. H. Lindley, and J. A. Bergstrom. All three men were Clark men and had received their Ph.D.s under G. Stanley Hall (Hearst & Capshew, 1988). So Terman's decision to pursue his own doctoral studies at Clark was a natural extension of his studies and influences at Indiana. However, funds for his formal studies had always been limited and further study for Terman would only be possible with a fellowship. Bergstrom and Lindley both wrote letters to Hall in support of his fellowship. Lindley's description of Terman to Hall concluded with "a decidedly brilliant man. He has a remarkably incisive mind and great capacity for work. ... I think I have never recommended a man to you with more confidence than I do Mr. Terman" (E. H. Lindley, personal communication to G. S. Hall, June 13, 1903, in Hall, 1888–1920). Bergstrom was equally favorable in his estimation of Terman to Hall: "he [Terman] is worthy of much recognition. He is an excellent student. He has also considerable preliminary training to fit for the opportunities he will have with you and I therefore take pleasure in recommending him to you" (J. A. Bergstrom, personal communication to G. S. Hall, June 15, 1903; in Hall, 1888–1920). These letters of recommendation and Terman's own notable record of scholarship at Indiana were enough to secure Terman a Senior Fellowship with at $200 stipend awarded in Psychology at Clark in June 1904. A private loan in conjunction to his stipend provided Terman the financial means to embark on his new life in Worcester, MA, with his young family in tow (Terman, 1930a; Winkler & Jolly, 2014).

His interest in individual differences and bright children began during his graduate studies at Clark University, initially under the direction of G. Stanley Hall. Terman's time at Indiana and experience with Bryan, Lindley, and Bergstrom put him in good stead with Hall. This research pedigree also produced certain expectations regarding Terman's capabilities (Terman, 1930a). Terman remembered his studies at Clark with a particular fondness that challenged him intellectually—an environment where he could envelop himself in research and cerebral stimulation. He fully engaged with the unfettered access to the library and Hall's Monday evening seminars (Terman, 1930a). The seminars could be a showcase for students of ability where others would listen with intent; for less able students or those who were an unknown quantity, the seminar could be quite demoralizing and challenging, where peers could be quite critical (Terman, 1930a). Some seminars were also epic, beginning at 7:30 p.m. and lasting well past midnight. Nearly 40 years later Terman described the seminars in a letter: "To me it was intoxicating; often leaving me sleepless for hours after I got back from it. No other educational experience I ever had was comparable to his [Hall] seminar" (L. Terman, personal communication to H. Sheldon, August 27, 1945; in Terman, 1910–1992). This level of preparation that he applied at Clark served him throughout his life.

As a result of Terman's broad reading, he encountered the writings of Stern, Cattell, Thorndike, Galton, Jastrow, and Spearman—researchers focused on individual differences, statistics, and experimental psychology. These conceptions, theories, and methodologies would eventually lead him to pursue his dissertation topic on testing. Although Terman would have preferred Hall as his advisor, Hall was not supportive of a doctoral thesis topic on mental tests. Terman instead sought out Edmund Sanford as his supervisor. Sanford, a renowned psychologist in his own right, had earned his Ph.D. under Hall at Johns Hopkins and became the founding director of the psychological laboratory at Clark (E. B. T., 1925).

Terman's dissertation topic would guide the remainder of his life's work. He noted, "everything I have done since 1905 was foreshadowed in my interests at that time—in psychology of genius, the measurement of intelligence, the phenomena of individual differences" (Terman, 1930a, p. 301). The findings from Terman's dissertation "Genius and Stupidity: A Study of Some of the Intellectual Processes of Seven 'Bright' and Seven 'Stupid' Boys" far from advanced the knowledge base in regard to highly able children, but instead fueled his queries into the vast array of unanswered questions it generated in regard to children of advanced intelligence in comparison to those of average or below average intelligence (Seagoe, 1975; Terman, 1906).

Before Any Other in All the World

After leaving Clark, Terman spent the next several years moving between unrewarding and intellectually unstimulating positions in California—he would describe these years as his "fallow period," as they were professionally unfulfilling and uneventful. Despite the fellowship he was awarded at Clark, Terman had incurred personal loans to cover his living expenses, so immediate paid employment was essential upon graduation in order to repay his benefactors and support his family. It was also thought that his tuberculosis (which first appeared in 1899) would be more stable in the drier climate of the western United States (Winkler & Jolly, 2014).

His first position was as a principal at San Bernardino High School in California. In a letter to Hall, Terman described his predicament: "Blues seize me only when I think of the probability of delayed emancipation. It is very well now, but if long continued it will become a prison. ... I intend to make a desperate effort again this year to get into my chosen work [a university faculty position]" (L. M. Terman, personal communication to G. S. Hall, January 29, 1906; in Hall, 1888–1920). Six months later Terman managed to secure a position at Los Angeles State Normal School (present-day University of California, Los Angeles) despite being offered "very material inducements to stay with them [San Bernardino High School]" (L. M. Terman, personal communication to G. S. Hall, June 23, 1906; in Hall, 1888–1920). An academic position was finally within Terman's grasp and significant financial incentives that would have been beneficial in paying off his loan could not dissuade him from the intellectually challenging environment and opportunity to conduct research he had worked so hard and waited so patiently to secure.

Four years later, in 1910, Terman would garner an academic appointment at Stanford University, where he would remain until his retirement (Jolly, 2008a). After leaving Clark, Stanford was the type of institution that matched the mission and nature of work that Terman aspired to carry out—he felt like he had truly arrived at "the university I would have chosen before any other in the all the world" (Terman, 1930a, p. 324). Stanford University, only established in 1891, just two decades before Terman's arrival, was still a relatively young institution and continued to recruit talented academics and researchers to build on its already impressive portfolio. Terman fit the profile and prominence of academics the institution was seeking.

E. P. Cubberley, Dean of the School of Education at Stanford and a Teachers College graduate (and a former student of James McKeen Cattell and E. L. Thorndike), offered the position of Stanford Professor of Educational Psychology to Terman in 1910. Cubberley, in consultation with Thorndike, then moved Terman to the Department of Psychology and simultaneously named him head of the department in 1922. This appointment acknowledged Terman's growing national expertise and prominence in the field of psychology (Dahlstrom, 1985; Hastorf, 2011; Terman, 1930a).

While at Stanford, Terman had been recruited to work on the Army Alpha and Army Beta in 1917 due to his recently completed revision of the Binet scale. This work was especially important as "many old-line psychologists regarded the whole test movement with scorn" and its success helped to sway not only the general public but the academic community as well (Terman 1930a, p. 325). Since his arrival at Stanford in 1910, the majority of his time had been consumed by his work on Binet's scales. Terman also benefited from access to the large network of public schools that Cubberley had managed to cultivate as dean. This network provided many of the students who were used as participants in Terman's pilot version of the Binet scale (Dahlstrom, 1985). Rather than bearing Terman's name, the scales became known as the Stanford–Binet Scales, not the Terman-Binet Scales similar to the Binet-Simon Scales, reflecting the perceived central role the university played in the scales' development (Beauvais, 2016).

The 1916 publication of Terman's *The Measurement of Intelligence: An Explanation of and a Complete Guide for the Use of the Stanford Revision and Extension of The Binet-Simon Intelligence Scale* included translations and adaptions of the original French items and his technical approaches to norming the instrument (Becker, 2003), which was "favorably received … but I did not foresee the vogue it was to have and imagined that it would probably be displaced by something much better within a few years" (Terman, 1930a, p. 325). Perhaps Terman is being purposefully modest in his autobiography. At the time of the scales' publication, the large-scale use of intelligence tests during World War I had not yet occurred but would be integral to popularizing the instrument. Regardless, Terman had an unwavering confidence in intelligence tests and their applicability, utility, and efficiency in society. He would argue particularly for their use in education (Terman, 1916a, p. 5) as they would

> contribute more to a real understanding of the case than anything else that could be done. It is necessary to determine whether a given child is unsuccessful in school because of poor native ability, or because of poor instruction, lack of interest, or some other removable cause.

Terman outlined the uses for intelligence tests for students with a range of abilities. His motivations for using these measures to help identify "superior children" included "the future welfare of the country" (Terman, 1930b, p. 5) and raised similar concerns that those of high intellectual ability were those who would become leaders in various fields of endeavor and by holding children to an educational system where they all must experience education at the same rate was only doing them a disservice. Terman also realized that high intellectual ability was not enough and that intellect would not will itself out as a consequence. Teachers required better training in order to identify advanced ability and provide acceleration. Teachers also needed professional development to work in special classes created to meet the needs of children with advanced abilities (Terman, 1915, 1920). Terman's *The Intelligence of School Children* (1919) was intentionally written "for the rank and file for teachers, school supervisors, and normal-school students. Its purpose is to illustrate the large individual differences upon the everyday problems of classroom management and school administrators" in hopes of filling this professional development gap (Terman, 1919, p. xi).

There is linearity in Terman's views on the nature and measurement of intelligence to his investigation of gifted children and definition of giftedness. Terman defined intelligence as follows: "An individual is intelligent in proportion as he is able to carry on abstract thinking" (Terman, 1921a, p. 128). He envisioned that intelligence tests could be used to adjust curriculum to reflect the innate abilities measured by these tests (Terman, 1921b). In the face of his near religious zeal in regard to the science of psychology and utility of intelligence tests, he recognized their boundaries to express intelligence: "We must guard against defining intelligence solely in terms of ability to pass the test of a given intelligence scale. It should go without saying that no existing scale is capable of adequately measuring the ability to deal with all possible kinds of materials on all intelligence levels" (Terman, 1921b, p. 131). However, IQ tests—particularly the Stanford–Binet—were recognized as the best measure possible during this time period, so it remained the standard-bearer for intellectual measurement for decades and is currently in its fifth edition (Becker, 2003).

Thanks largely to the testing of Army recruits during World War I, the acceptance and importance of mental tests were secured. Terman began shifting his efforts to the study of gifted children. Upon his arrival at Stanford, Terman had been the recipient of reports regarding gifted children. He, too, was conducting his own case studies and collecting data on children with high IQs as part of his efforts to standardize and develop technical qualities for the Stanford–Binet (Cravens, 1992). Ironically, despite Terman's ongoing work with gifted children conducted at Stanford, the university wavered regarding an early entrance application for a 14-year-old girl named Betty Ford. In the early 1920s, when Terman was commencing his studies, his research findings had limited influence with university policies and attitudes which reflected broader societal views that despite intellectual abilities ready to take on the challenges of university work, 14-year-olds could be corrupted by college life. In a letter to Harry Hollingworth (Leta Hollingworth's husband), Terman bemoaned,

> She had a straight A record in high school and about 20% more credits than she needs for university entrance. It remains to be seen whether our Committee on Admissions will refuse admittance on account of her age. There is a strong prejudice here in our Admissions Committee, against taking in prodigies. They are so afraid these supposedly one-sided bright children won't have a good time socially in the University. Isn't it enough to make one furious?
> *(L. Terman, personal communication to H. Hollingworth, March 25, 1926, in Terman, 1910–1992)*

Interactions and experiences like these only convinced Terman that his next research endeavor was that much more important and required. As Terman moved into the next phase of his research agenda, his theoretical beliefs and axioms are important to consider:

> [he] defined intelligence as the ability "to carry on abstract thinking." He strongly believed that exams such as his Stanford–Binet and the National

Intelligence Tests were valid and reliable measures of ability and that intelligence remained relatively constant. Convinced of the essential correctness of Galton's theories on hereditary genius ... [and] in his work that test score differences among ethnic, national, and occupation groups could be explained in terms of inherited intelligence.

(Chapman, 1988, p. 129)

California's Gifted Children

Terman's longitudinal study of gifted children coupled with his development and application of the Stanford–Binet IQ test shaped and defined Terman's career. In 1911, Terman had embarked on a small-scale study of 31 children with IQs over 125 based on the reports of gifted children he had been receiving since his arrival at Stanford (Jolly, 2008a). Coupled with the massive boost in intelligence testing and measurement, established due to the large-scale testing that was conducted during World War I, Terman was well-positioned to begin the longitudinal study that would define and consume the majority of his remaining working years. The intimate links between Terman's work with intelligence tests and the longitudinal study of gifted children were due to Terman's definition of giftedness, which revolved solely around IQ—those students with IQ scores of 135 were categorized as moderately gifted, 150 as exceptionally gifted, and 180 as profoundly gifted (Jolly, 2008a).

In 1913, applying Stern's conversion of Binet's mental age to the Intelligent Quotient (IQ), Terman recognized validation of the Binet-Simon scale for the American context would have "great importance for the education treatment of ... talented children" (Terman, 1913, p. 104). Focusing on the most able students, he proposed research to better understand "what performance may rightly be expected of ... 125 per cent intelligence at the various age levels" (Terman, 1915, p. 537). Ultimately, Terman envisioned the intelligence test as a tool to bring superordinate classifications in terms of race, mental stability, and genius (Lagemann, 2000).

After long-awaited grant funding, an initial $20,000 award from the Commonwealth Fund was provided to Terman in 1921 to advance the study of gifted children (From Correspondent, 1921). He believed that forces machinated "the inauguration of research in this field" (Terman, 1925, p. vii). He associated these forces with

> the nature of superstitions, regarding the essential nature of the Great Man ... moved by forces which are not to be explained by (a) the natural laws of human behavior; (b) the widespread belief, hardly less superstitious in its origins, that intellectual precocity is pathological; (c) the vigorous growth of democratic sentiment in ... America ... which has necessarily tended to encourage an attitude unfavorable to a just appreciation of native individual

differences in human endowment; and (d) the tardy birth of biological sciences, particularly genetics, psychology and education.

(Terman, 1925, p. vii)

The revision of the Binet-Simon scale as the Stanford–Binet and its success with an American audience provided an instrument with which to identify children for his study. The basic purpose of his research was to determine to what degree the gifted child varied from the average child. Terman's longitudinal study of approximately 1,500 intellectually able Californian youngsters stands as a foundational milestone in the study of gifted children (Boring, 1959; Chapman, 1988; Cravens, 1992; Jolly, 2004; Minton, 1988). In Terman's initial proposal to the Commonwealth Fund, he delineated the six main goals of the study. These included (1) the administration of two intelligence measures, (2) collection of achievement data across four to five content areas, (3) domain-specific testing to a specific number of students, (4) revision of methods for collecting demographic data, and (5) collection of data from subjects over a ten-year period. In 1922 the Commonwealth Fund provided an additional $14,000 in funds to collect extra data along with $14,000 of matching funds from Stanford to support the continuation and expansion of the study (Terman, 1925). These extra monies allowed for medical examinations to be conducted and inventories of personality and character to be given to the children.

This study was not only expansive in scope but also in geographical size, spanning the length of California. This required grant staff, field assistants, and a small army of trained volunteers (Jolly, 2008a). The recruitment and hiring of staff for work on the grant also identifies some of the first interactions between Terman and Leta Hollingworth contrary to earlier reports indicating that "strangely, she and Terman seem to have had little or no contact with each other" (Stanley, 1976, p. 39). Terman's initial correspondence with Hollingworth was in regard to a graduate student who had to come work as a field assistant and study with Terman: "I want to thank you most sincerely for letting us have ... Miss Goodenough ... [she] is hard at work in Los Angeles and making progress like a steam engine. I feel she is utterly dependable, both as to intentions and judgment ... I feel that I can't thank you sufficiently for your help" (L. M. Terman, personal communication to L. S. Hollingworth, October 15, 1921; in Terman, 1910–1992). Florence Goodenough eventually became Terman's chief research psychologist during the initial phase of his longitudinal study, earning her Ph.D. under his guidance in 1924. At the University of Minnesota, she established her own career as a prominent psychologist and developed the Goodenough Draw-A-Man test as a measure of intelligence (Jolly, 2010).

The majority of field assistants and psychologists were women, as females were thought to have the best temperament to work with children. Whatever the motivation for this woman-centric work, it provided women with opportunities to pursue graduate-level educations at one of the nation's leading institutions of higher education. In 1920, the National Academy of Sciences ranked Stanford as a Leading Doctorate Producing Institution (Harmon & Soldz, 1963). In 1920, just a year before Terman's study commenced, only 62 women held Ph.D.s in psychology and membership in the American Psychological Association (APA) remained overwhelmingly male until World War II (Bryan & Boring, 1944; Hogan & Sexton, 1991). In addition to Florence Goodenough, other female graduate students who received their doctoral degrees under Terman's supervision while working on the first phase of the longitudinal study included Catherine Morris Cox, Barbara Stoddard Burks, Dorthea Williams Jensen, and Maud A. Merrill (Terman, 1930a).

Nine surveys and tests from approximately 1,500 students were collected, amassing the largest data bank on gifted students at the time. These data provided "a pathway of a process—maturation in superior persons—in selected population that was large enough to make certain generalizations about a group of humans, namely geniuses" (Cravens, 1992, p. 186) and was typical of psychologists during this era that did not consider individuals beyond their group membership (Cravens, 1992). Data included (1) two intelligence tests (one being the Stanford–Binet); (2) the Stanford Achievement Test; (3) a test of general knowledge of science history, literature, and the arts; (4) an interest survey and knowledge test regarding plays, games, and hobbies; (5) an additional survey about children's interests; (6) a reading record kept over a two-month period for each child; (7) a Home Information Blanks that canvassed parents on 25 traits over 16 pages; (8) a survey for teachers to rate students on the same 25 traits; and (9) the Whittier Scale, which provided a grade of the home environment (Terman, 1925). The Home Information Blanks, alone, provided approximately 37,500 separate points of data. Up until this point, the knowledge about gifted children was limited and that regarding their home lives even more so (Terman, 1925).

The children recruited for the study were gathered through teachers' nominations and then filtered by IQ score. Occasionally accidental or unexpected discoveries were made when the incorrect child was sent for evaluation or a nominated child was absent and another was sent in his or her place (Terman, 1924a, Terman 1924b, 1925). This method of recruitment happened to yield a very narrow participant population that was overwhelmingly White from English, German, or Scotch ancestry or predominately Jewish with grandparents determining children's "ethnic origins." Another byproduct of this type of selection included the family background of the children: Fathers were classified either in professional or semi-professional careers with few in skilled or semi-skilled trades, and both the mean and median incomes $4,705 and $3,333 respectively reported by families were well over that of the average American family ($1,236) reported for 1925 (Terman, 1925). At least one-fourth of the gifted students had a parent who had graduated from college, and on average parents in Terman's study had completed twice as much schooling as the average adult (Terman, 1925). Terman was also interested in the prevalence of eminence in children's family backgrounds. Several families could name Presidents, Vice Presidents, writers, generals, Supreme Court

Justices, and important political leaders as part of their family trees, which Terman identified as evidence of Galton's theory of heritability of genius. However, Terman recognized the limits of these data and believed more exact data would be needed to "reveal the laws by which superior mental ability is transmitted," again due to its hereditarian nature (Terman, 1925, p. 111).

Terman's initial observations of the data collection focused on the greater number of boys than girls identified by the sample. He attributed this to the widely held belief at the time that males were more variable than females, which was supported by the study's evidence that "exceptionally superior intelligence occurs with greater frequency among boys than girls" (Terman, 1925, p. 54). This may have been a result of students initially being identified by teachers who generally favored boys (Jolly, 2005). Subsequent data revealed that females did just as well as males in academic outcomes but in different content areas (Burks, Jensen & Terman, 1930).

Terman also began to amass the first data on gifted children's lives outside of school. The stereotypical view of gifted children was that they deviated tremendously from the average child and spent the majority of their free time alone and reading. The results of Terman's study revealed that gifted children were sought out as companions in school at the same rate as control group children despite being much younger than their classmates. Not surprising, gifted children from the study simply read more, a greater variety, and for longer periods of time than the control group (Terman, 1925).

Lacking representation in Terman's sample despite their presence in the general population were children from ethnic backgrounds, including African American, Italian, Portuguese, Mexican, Japanese, and Chinese children. Due to laws excluding children of Chinese descent from attending public schools at this time, these children would not have been present in recruitment schools and Terman did not recruit in the segregated "oriental schools" despite 80% of the nation's Chinese population residing in California in the 1920s, the largest concentration in the country at the time (Kuo, 1998; Terman, 1925). The lack of children from Mexican ethnicity is equally troubling but for differing reasons. In 1927, 10% of California's school population was of Mexican ancestry and attended public schools in some southern Californian districts (especially in Los Angeles county where the percentages ranged as high as 60–80%), yet the number of Mexican American children in Terman's study were negligible (Sanchez, 1993).

The outliers that did qualify for the study were intriguing to Terman and his research team. He devoted a section of *Genetic Studies of Genius, Vol. III: The Promise of Youth* to explain the perceived remarkableness of their ability and accomplishments, which challenged Terman's hereditarian views of intelligence and revealed themselves in terms of race and class (Stoskopf, 2002). Terman envisioned many uses for the Stanford–Binet, including detecting "significant racial differences in general intelligence," differences that could not be compensated for by schooling or environment (Terman, 1916b, p. 91). The initial data from the longitudinal study supported Terman's hypothesis, revealing "the racial stock most prolific of gifted children are those from northern and western Europe, and the Jewish. The least prolific are the Mediterranean races, the Mexicans, and the Negroes" (Terman, 1924a, p. 363).

The evidence does not suggest that Terman considered or reflected as to whether recruitment methods were biased for his study or if the IQ assessment itself was flawed, as the Stanford–Binet had been norm-referenced with children chiefly attending school in approximation to Stanford University. This included a considerable population of the university's faculty children, few non-Whites, and students who by and large were overwhelmingly middle-class (Beauvais, 2016; Chapman, 1988; Terman, 1916a). During the development of the technical qualities for the first edition of the Stanford–Binet, there was no contemplation afforded to the impact of environment on aptitude or achievement performance on this sample of students.

These outliers, which challenged Terman's hereditarian views, recorded in *Genetic Studies of Genius, Volume III*, included case studies of children that were characterized as handicapped by their race, home environment, or questionable moral role models (Burks et al., 1930), beginning with Family A, a Japanese American family, where four of the five children qualified for Terman's study in 1922. The father had abandoned the family, leaving them in destitute circumstances living on an isolated ranch. Despite the challenging situation, all the children excelled academically and had superior scores on the Stanford–Binet. Terman held great uneasiness for the children given the prejudice shown toward children from mixed marriages and the financial uncertainty confronting the family (Burks et al., 1930).

Another example, Harriet, "a gifted Negro girl ... striving under the handicap of prejudice against her race" (Burks et al., 1930, p. 286) scored IQ 147 on the Stanford–Binet. Her father had only achieved an eighth-grade education and her mother a sixth-grade education. She worked as a cook and maid while Harriet's two older sisters left school early to support the family after the premature death of their father. Harriet aspired to work in the social services, but her situation was described as "hopeless," given that there was little money for a university education and there was limited access to skilled jobs for African Americans (Burks et al., 1930).

Consequently, Terman also championed the idea of meritocracy and leading through the measurement of talent, the theory that ability above all should determine one's advancement through society rather than birthright, inherited wealth, nepotism, or cronyism. The IQ test would be the centerpiece when selecting these individuals. Meritocracy explained Terman's own elevation from a farm boy from Indiana to a position as one of America's early eminent psychologists and would partially explain these outliers in his longitudinal study (Jolly, 2008b; Leslie, 2000).

Even though Terman was focused almost exclusively on group membership, he did take a personal interest in a handful of the students that came to his attention, which also confounded his findings. With the royalties from the sale of the Stanford–Binet, Terman was in a unique position to help some of the study's participants by providing financial assistance to aid with university tuition and associated costs (Jolly, 2008a). He also helped secure admission to Stanford and other elite universities. He wrote numerous letters of recommendation for the young men and women in his sample. At the height of the United States federal government's forced internment of Japanese Americans during World War II, Terman interceded on behalf of a participant family who had asked for his help to avoid detention. His letter to the federal government ensuring their loyalty to the United States facilitated halting their removal to an internment camp (Leslie, 2000).

Terman's death in 1957 did not cease the collection of data from the longitudinal study and data collection continued well into participants' adulthood, with a 93% return rate being reported in the last volume, *The Gifted Group at Mid-Life: Thirty-Five Years' Follow-Up of the Superior Child* (1959), and in some cases the data collection would only cease with some participants' death in old age (Burt, 1961; Leslie, 2000). The longitudinal study data was originally planned to be collected over a ten-year period, but *Genetic Studies of Genius* instead morphed into a lifetime study for many participants and continued to follow some well into their nineties. The study is published in four volumes and covers nearly as many decades (*Genetic Studies of Genius, Vol. 1* (1925); *The Early Mental Traits of 300 Geniuses: Genetic Studies of Genius, Vol. 2* (1926; Vol. 2 does not include data from the study but is a historiographical account of 300 notable figures); *The Promise of Youth: Follow-Up Studies of a Thousand Gifted Children, Vol. 3* (1930); *The Gifted Child Grows Up: Twenty-five Years' Follow-Up of Superior Group, Vol. 4* (1947); *The Gifted Group at Mid-Life: Thirty-Five Years' Follow-Up of the Superior Child, Vol. 5* (1959).

At the outset of the longitudinal study, Terman believed that a high IQ in childhood would naturally equate to eminence in adulthood. His hypothesis did not bear out this assumption. Instead Terman's findings opened up a new set of investigative questions regarding "the disconnect between gifted performance in childhood and adult eminence" (Subotnik, Olszewski-Kubilius, & Worrell, 2011, p. 6), apart from criticisms with the selection process itself and issues in regard to bias with the Stanford–Binet. The realization that IQ was and is not enough to guarantee adult eminence ushered in a new line of inquiry, and researchers began to wrestle with the psychosocial and environmental factors that impact the intellectual, academic, and social-emotional development of gifted children (Leslie, 2000; Subotnik et al., 2011).

11
MOTHER OF GIFTED EDUCATION

Leta S. Hollingworth

If Terman is considered the father of the gifted education, Leta S. Hollingworth is most often referred to as the "mother of gifted education" (Stanley, 1976; Tannenbaum, 1983). Her work paralleled Terman's as she worked on the East Coast of the United States at Teachers College and in New York City Schools. Terman's focus on the 1,500 students in his study was considered as a collective group, while Hollingworth was very much interested in her studies' participants at both collective and individual levels (Pritchard, 1951).

Born Leta A. Stetter in Chadron, NE, on May 25, 1886, in an earthen dugout on her grandfather's property, she grew up in America's Midwest, like Terman, but did not have the nurturing environment of a large family that he had enjoyed. Her mother died while giving birth to her youngest sister when Leta was only four years old. She was raised first by her maternal grandparents and then later retrieved by her father and his new wife. Her stepmother was often emotionally abusive to Leta and her sisters. Interceding, her teachers recognized Leta's intellect and encouraged her to attend university after her high school graduation in 1902. By paying her own tuition and fees through a series of campus jobs, she attended the University of Nebraska and chose teaching as a profession, one of the few careers open to women at that time (Benjamin, 1975; Hertberg-Davis, 2014; Klein, 2002).

Upon her graduation in 1906, she would teach at several rural high schools, similar to the ones Terman had first taught at when he had left Central Normal School. While at the University of Nebraska, she met Harry Hollingworth, whom she would eventually marry in 1908. His doctoral studies in psychology with James McKeen Cattell at Columbia University would lead Harry to New York City in 1907 (Poffenberger, 1957). Leta would eventually join him in New York and they would marry in 1908. Left to her own devices, she grew bored and restless as teaching was closed to her now that she was a married woman. Ever curious and with a genuine desire to extend her own graduate studies, "Leta returned to school to study psychology, thanks to the money she and Harry had earned working for Coca-Cola (Benjamin, 2013, p. xiii). She eventually completed her dissertation, "Functional Periodicity: An Experimental Study of the Mental and Motor Abilities of Women During Menstruation" and earned her Ph.D. in 1916 under the direction of E. L. Thorndike at Teachers College where she would eventually obtain a faculty position of her own (Benjamin, 1975; Hertberg-Davis, 2014; Klein, 2002).

A First Encounter Becomes a Life's Passion

At Teachers College, Hollingworth initially taught courses in educational psychology, which included one on mental testing. Similar to Stedman, Hollingworth's interest in gifted children came after an initial encounter with an exceptionally precocious child who immediately piqued her curiosity (Jolly, 2007b). Hollingworth acknowledged her own lack of familiarity with "children who are alleged to possess extraordinary intellectual powers and abilities" which were limited to newspaper accounts of such children as William Sidis and Winifred Stoner. She noted the lack of attention given to "the intelligence of such children [which] has not been quantitatively measured" (Garrison, Burke, & Hollingworth, 1917, p. 102).

In 1916, Child E, aged eight years four months, was brought into her mental testing course, as "a child of exceptional intelligence was desired for demonstration before a class in the psychology and treatment of exceptional children in Teachers College, and this child was suggested on account of his remarkable school record" (Garrison et al., 1917, p. 103). Child E, whose real name was Edward Hardy, propelled Hollingworth's interest in gifted students. Up until this point her portfolio of research did not include gifted children; however, from this point forward her research focused almost exclusively on gifted students, procedures and instruments for identification, and the development of curriculum and pedagogical practices to best meet their educational needs (Jolly, 2007b). Child E would be included in the original cohort of her own longitudinal study and he would also appear as a case study in *Children Above 180 IQ* (1942). Her first article on gifted children in 1917 was about Child E, detailing characteristics of a child with a 187 IQ with a follow up article in 1922 detailing his progress. Still new to working with prodigious children, Hollingworth reached out to Terman for consultation and advice. In a correspondence to Terman in 1921, Hollingworth's delight with such an inquisitive child as E is evident:

> Edward spent the afternoon with me, and we had a delightful time. So many minor incidents happen, showing the quality of his mind. For instance,

> I wanted to measure his weight in pounds, but the scales stood so that the side measuring kilograms only was visible. I said, "We'll have to move the scale out, so I can see the number of pounds." At once Edward said, "No, no you can see the number of pounds it is by looking at the kilograms." He took it for granted that I could transmute kilograms into pounds as instantly as he can! I think that it is interesting that in Test 2 on Alpha he performed the mathematics involved in the solutions of the problems entirely without using the side of the page to figure on.
>
> (Hollingworth, personal correspondence to L. M. Terman, September 30, 1921, in Terman, 1910–1992)

In 1922, her follow-up article expressed that Child E had not regressed toward the mean but that he had continued to progress in his studies and achievements, and his scores on aptitude tests remained in the superior range (Hollingworth, 1922). Child E also had not succumbed to the fallacy of what some believed was "early ripe, early rot." What was obvious to Hollingworth was that children like E would not do well in regular lockstep classrooms, which were designed for children of average ability. Apart from establishing a greater understanding of gifted children, Hollingworth sought to create learning environments that matched their intellectual abilities, which distinguished her research from that which Terman was undertaking.

P. S. 165

Shortly after the follow-up study with Child E concluded, Hollingworth was provided the opportunity to open a school in the New York Public Schools in cooperation with Teachers College expressly for gifted children—P. S. 165, which would operate from 1923–1925. Teachers College's long history in collaborating with neighborhood schools began in 1887, and P. S. 165 was in keeping with this early tradition and commitment to authentic environments for students' learning and researchers' investigating. From the earliest days of Teachers College, "it thus proposed to work within the schools, not outside the schools. A school [Teachers College] of observation and practice" (Russell, 1900, p. 20).

Hollingworth seized on the opportunity to use P. S. 165 as a research laboratory, noting that little was known concerning the educational needs of gifted students. Students were selected based on an IQ score, measures of achievement, distance from the school, overall health, and parental approval (Cobb, Hollingworth, Monahan, Taylor, & Theobald, 1923). Her work at P. S. 165 was instrumental to her writings "Provisions for Intellectually Superior Children" (1924a) and *Gifted Children: Their Nature and Nurture* (1926), which is considered the first textbook on gifted children. Stedman's classroom contributions influenced Hollingworth and were cited as one of the foundations of her chapter on "Organization and Curriculum" in *Gifted Children: Their Nature and Nurture* (1926) and continued to be referenced as a foundational text by other researchers and practitioners. Much of the content included in this text was based on the research and findings from her time at P. S. 165. The student population of P. S. 165 reflected similar demographics when compared to the sample used in Terman's longitudinal study. Primarily, the overrepresentation of students from Jewish descent failed to present a sample truly representative of the larger population in Manhattan. Hollingworth commenced her longitudinal study, following this particular group of students over the next 15 years (Hollingworth, 1936a).

At P. S. 165, Hollingworth advocated for students to have access to libraries with various reference books, classrooms to be fitted with shelves to display collections, and moveable desks and chairs to accommodate the recommended group work rather than secured to the floor, which was common practice. In recognizing gifted students' asynchronous development, Hollingworth also encouraged oral reports or the use of the typewriter for students whose fine motor skills had not caught up with their advanced thinking abilities (Hollingworth, 1926).

The laboratory environment of P. S. 165 provided ample opportunity for Hollingworth to initiate some of the theories she had regarding the education offerings for gifted children. Hollingworth supported acceleration as a practice in schools but also believed that gifted students would benefit from an enriched curriculum. She recognized the qualitative differences within the upper range of IQ scores and established two distinct classes at P. S. 165. One class of students had an IQ range from 150–190, whereas the other class had an IQ range from 135–150 (Cobb et al., 1923). Each of these classes offered acceleration and enrichment opportunities to meet students' learning needs. The initial enrichment lessons focused on biography, as this was a course of study that fell outside of the normal curriculum. She conducted the first several lessons herself and observations of the two classes revealed distinctly different levels of questioning and group discussions which confirmed her hypothesis for the need of two separate classrooms. Hollingworth typically could be found at the school on most days working with students and collecting data (Hollingworth, 1924b).

Based on the observations and findings from the studies conducted at P. S. 165, Hollingworth produced *Gifted Children: Their Nature and Nurture* in 1924. This text filled a gap in the literature and provided a platform for Hollingworth to document her thoughts regarding curriculum, systemic issues about schooling, teacher selection, pedagogical issues, and asynchronous development. She also used the text to dispel the pervasive myths or misperceptions about gifted children (Jolly, 2006b).

Critics of segregated classes for the gifted children argued that they encouraged conceit and jealousy in children in addition to being undemocratic in nature. Given that there was no empirical evidence to support these claims, Hollingworth, instead, felt that the opportunity classes at P. S. 165 provided a challenging academic curriculum and peer interactions that were commensurate with their abilities and interests. She noted, "A pupil coming into special classes often meets his rival for the first time" (Hollingworth, 1926, p. 301) and also hypothesized that if feelings of jealousy existed these could be attributed to the children's parents rather than the students. These and additional findings from P. S. 165 would counter many of the myths and erroneous ideas that had been circulating about gifted children.

Another focal point was the teacher of gifted children. Hollingworth sought teachers with the right set of dispositions and attitudes to work with gifted children: "The teacher must be free from unconscious jealousy and from unconfessed bias against gifted children" (Hollingworth, 1926, p. 306). Other essential characteristics included a sense of humor, patience, and high intelligence. Teachers also needed to move away from the commonly practiced whole class recitation and instead embrace and institute small-group work and inquiry learning.

At the end of the three-year period, the opportunity classes were completed and achievement outcomes were compared with a control group of similar ages and IQ range who attended regular classes in nearby elementary schools. The results were perhaps not what Hollingworth and her colleagues had expected:

> It was found that in accomplishment in subject matter there was no appreciable difference between the segregated and non-segregated groups. In the case of intellectually superior children, accomplishment in the subject matter measured by standardized tests was very superior wherever these children were located.
>
> *(Pritchard, 1951, p. 57)*

Until greater refinement to measures of achievement and additional measures of "personal satisfaction and social adjustment" could be developed and introduced, the results would remain absent from the research literature (Gray & Hollingworth, 1931, p. 261).

Similar to Terman, Hollingworth's intent was to gather longitudinal data on the students who were included in the opportunity classes at P. S. 165. She continued collecting data regarding the educational trajectories and home lives until 1936, when she was presented with an opportunity to participate in another collaboration between Teachers College and New York Public Schools—P. S. 500, The Speyer School. Initially resistant to abandoning her longitudinal work, the pull to be back in the classroom and answer some of the unfinished questions from P. S. 165 was too great a motivator (Hollingworth, 1942; Jolly, 2007b).

P. S. 500—The Speyer School

The Speyer School, P. S. 500, had originally been established as a Teachers College laboratory school in 1901. Its location on the Lower East Side of Manhattan attracted students of "shop-keepers, teamsters, janitors, policemen, and street-car conductors" (Lagemann, 2000, p. 115). In 1936 P. S. 500 was designed to include exceptional children significantly above and below the norm (Hollingworth, 1936a, 1936b). Two classes of 25 students had IQs over 130 and these were designated the Terman classes, and seven classes of students had IQs between 75 and 90 (Pritchard, 1951). All students were between seven and nine years old and, unlike the students who participated in Hollingworth's classes at P. S. 165 who were predominantly of White and Jewish descent, the students of P. S. 500 were more representative of the greater New York City area (Hollingworth, 1990; Rudnitski, 1996).

During the operation of P. S. 165, the defining characteristics of gifted children, range of their capabilities, classroom practices to address their advanced learning needs, and fundamental knowledge of this particular population were established. P. S. 500 provided the opportunity to revisit some of the issues that P. S. 165 left unanswered, including the best age to transition to high school given accelerated programs of study and questions of social and emotional maturity. Approximately 45 studies were added to the literature on gifted education based on the work carried out at P. S. 500 during the two years the special classes operated (Hollingworth, 1938). With the baseline knowledge established, the rationale for the Speyer School differed from P. S. 165 in its intentionality. From the outset it was established that

> we know that these pupils—they know and no others—will possess as adults those mental powers on which the learned professions depend for conservation and advancement. Also, we know that they will be the literary interpreters of the world of their generation. And they will be the ones who can think deeply and clearly about abstractions like the state, the government, and economics. We know this because we have seen a group like this "grow up."
>
> (Hollingworth, 1938, pp. 297–298)

Hollingworth gauged that students with an IQ of 130 could cover the standard classroom curriculum in half the time it took a regular student and those with an IQ over 170 could do it in a quarter of the time. She queried as to the best use of this extra time, "How shall we choose the materials from the world's stock of knowledge with which to enrich the intellectual life of these gifted pupils?" (Hollingworth, 1936a, p. 87). Again, one has to remember that Hollingworth's ideas related to achievement were strongly tied to measured IQ: "The world's work is arranged in a hierarchy, with reference to degrees of intellect. 'The top one per cent' can do all that the rest can do and some things that none of the rest can do" (Hollingworth, 1936a, p. 88). Whatever the curriculum, it should be to prepare these gifted students for either professions in the "conservation of knowledge" (IQs over 130) or the "advancement of knowledge" (IQs over 160; Hollingworth, 1936a, p. 88).

Students were not accelerated through the curriculum in the traditional sense, but rather provided opportunities for advanced curriculum. So once they completed the traditional curriculum in a half or a quarter of the time, Hollingworth and her colleagues moved them on to experimental curricula that had been developed specifically for students at P. S. 500 (Pritchard, 1951). Advancing through the typical curriculum at an accelerated pace allowed time for students to study other topics or subjects. These were some of the earliest forms of what is commonly referred to today as curriculum compacting (Reis & Renzulli, 2010).

Hollingworth (1938, pp. 298–299) also believed "initiative and originality" should influence educational experiences for P. S. 500 students. To reach this eventuality, Hollingworth considered it necessary for them to have an understanding of how things came to be over time through special units of study. She named these curriculum units *The Evolution of Common Things*, developing topics that addressed clothing, transportation, communication, and natural resources (Hollingworth, 1938). Each unit included a timeline of the unit's topic, and regardless of the content, a child's responsibility to society was emphasized (Rudnitski, 1996). The lack of acceleration through the normal curriculum was predicated on Hollingworth's belief that the students at P. S. 500 should not enter high school before 13 years of age. Research on the social and emotional impact of acceleration was underdeveloped and from Hollingworth's point of view, "pushing them into the company of pupils so much older than themselves that social contact is impossible" would be detrimental to the student (Hollingworth, 1936a, p. 89). Complications also arose due to what Hollingworth described as immaturity, but would now be interpreted as asynchronous development: "To have the intelligence of an adult and the emotions of a child combined in a childish body is to encounter certain difficulties" (Hollingworth, 1942, p. 282).

One of Hollingworth's last articles before her death in 1939 spoke to the identification and education of future leaders among the gifted population: "Whatever may be his other qualities, if a person is stupid he will not be wanted as a leader" (Hollingworth, 1939, p. 575). She felt that intelligence was a strong indicator of possible leadership ability (Hollingworth, 1939). However, these abilities were to be nurtured, and Hollingworth identified five behaviors that would hinder the full development of this potential: "(1) to find enough hard and interesting work at school, (2) to suffer fools gladly, (3) to keep from becoming negativistic toward authority, (4) to keep from becoming hermits, (5) to avoid the habits of extreme chicanery" (Hollingworth, 1939, p. 586). Given that the publication was so close to her death, this particular element of giftedness was not explored in great detail and remains under researched and explored sporadically during the past 100 years (Matthews, 2004).

The Profoundly Gifted

In 1939 Hollingworth's premature death from stomach cancer, a condition that she had been living with for over ten years, left her life's work unfinished. Her death came as quite a shock to those in her professional community. Hollingworth, Goodenough, and Terman were in the midst of working on the *Thirty-Ninth Yearbook of the National Society for the Study of Education* upon Leta's death. In a letter to Lewis Terman, Florenec Goodenough wrote,

> I don't know what to say about Leta Hollingworth's death. I tried to write you about it then but I could find no words and I still have not. I can not [sic] understand why neither you nor I had not been told of her illness. I understand that she had been in the hospital for about two months.
> *(F. Goodenough, personal communication to L. Terman, December 11, 1939)*

In 1942, three years after Hollingworth's death, her husband published a collection of case studies that Leta had been collecting on children with IQs of 180 and above. She was in the midst of organizing over 20 years' worth of data. Leta first began chronicling children of above 180 IQ in *Gifted Children: Their Nature and Nurture* and in her initial articles on gifted children. *Children Above 180 IQ* would be a collective and comprehensive account of their family backgrounds, educational histories, mental measurements, physical measurements, and character and personality traits (Hollingworth, 1942; Jolly, 2007b), which reflected her interest in the individual rather than in group membership, as was the focus of Terman's research (Pritchard, 1951).

This text also presented the opportunity for Hollingworth to discuss the definition of genius, upon which—she conceded at the time of the publication—there was still disagreement as to the corresponding IQ score (Hollingworth, 1942). However, she felt that Terman's original estimation of 140 IQ provided too large a population for a phenomenon that was thought to be so rare. Hollingworth and Terman also differed in their perception of genius. Terman's five volumes were titled *Genetic Studies of Genius*, as he had from the outset labeled children with a qualifying IQ score "geniuses." Hollingworth felt that the term "genius" should only be applied once students had been acknowledged in their fields as top producers. This usually occurred after they had graduated from university. She explained,

> The term "genius" has been use by Terman—and following him by many others—to denote children testing at or above 140 IQ. In the light of the developmental data herein presented, it would appear that the term "genius" is misapplied, unless we wish to define "geniuses" persons who represent approximately the best fourth of all students being graduated from American colleges.
> *(Hollingworth, 1942, p. 247)*

Only those in the top 1% could make the contributions that would rate at the genius level and only after some type of work recognized by experts in the field as exceptional (Hollingworth, 1938). She also highlighted that once children began to near 170 IQ, difficulties were likely to occur as they often were misunderstood and had very few "likeminded" peers. Highly and profoundly gifted children had distinctive social and emotional needs that differed from the average gifted child (Beauvais, 2016; Benjamin, 1975; L. Hollingworth, 1938, Hollingworth, 1942). She also suggested that emotional education might be even more paramount than pure intellectual training.

Child E, who initiated Hollingworth's interest in gifted children in 1917, was one of the case studies included. He was in his early 30s at the time of *Children Above 180 IQ*'s publication and had received a Ph.D. at the age of 22, finding employment teaching history at a seminary (Hollingworth, 1942). A female student included from the Speyer School was also one of the 12 case studies; incidentally it was discovered that her father had been a participant in Terman's longitudinal study.

Although the 12 cases highlighted the uniqueness of each child, Hollingworth did observe several commonalities across cases. The children with above 180 IQ exhibited early abilities in speech and reading that led to further accelerated achievement in school. However, this generally led to difficulties in regular school environments without the intervention of acceleration and development of their abilities by schools and teachers. The path to eminent achievement in adulthood became far less linear or inevitable for some of these children (Hollingworth, 1942).

12
THE RESIDUE OF EUGENICS

Eugenics, a popular movement in early 20th-century America, was originally popularized by Sir Francis Galton. At the core of the movement was a set of assumptions linked to practices to improve the genetic "stock" or qualities of society. As Galton (1865, p. 318) described,

> No one, I think, can doubt, from the facts and analogies I have brought forward, that, if talented men were mated with talented women, of the same mental and physical characters as themselves, generation after generation, we might produce a highly-bred human race, with no more tendency to revert to meaner ancestral types than is shown by our long-established breeds of race-horses and fox-hounds.

The eugenics movement in the United States infiltrated many sectors of American society (Margolin, 1993) and was part of the Progressive Era agenda that investigated the implementation of scientific management to advance society, organizing as a movement during the first two decades of the 20th century (Selden, 1999, 2000). Some Progressive reformers sought out environmental improvements, while others pursued the goal through eugenic programming (Selden, 1994), which was evoked in the name of social-efficiency by administrative progressives. By 1928, universities across the United States offered nearly 400 courses that included eugenics content with approximately 20,000 students registering (Cravens, 1978; Selden, 2005). Both Lewis Terman and Leta Hollingworth ascribed to eugenic beliefs, which also bled into their research agendas and views about the role of gifted children in society. Based on Terman's "early contact with the work of Galton and his own studies on genius and stupidity he has, on the whole, held to the standpoint which stresses the great importance of heredity rather than environment in the makeup of intelligence" (Young, 1924, p. 38).

The state of California, in which Terman lived for his entire professional career, had a particularly active eugenics agenda and the most aggressive forced sterilization program in the United States during the early 20th century. Several Stanford University academics were known to be deeply involved in the movement. For example, David Starr Jordan, President of Stanford University (1891–1913), was the first Chairman of the Committee on Eugenics of the American Breeders Association (1903) and outlined the Committee's objectives:

> to investigate and report on heredity in the human race; to devise methods of recording the values of the blood of individuals, families, peoples and races; to emphasize the value of superior blood and the menace to society of inferior blood; and to suggest methods of improving the heredity of the family, the people, or the race.
>
> *(as cited in Selden, 1999, p. 1)*

Terman, too, was an active member of eugenic organizations and is listed as a charter member on The Human Betterment Foundation (HBF) (Eugenics Archive, May 8, 1934). The HBF supported the research of eugenic sterilization and the dissemination information for planned reproduction for the improvement of society throughout California (Briggs, 2013) and at the sixth Annual Eugenics Research Meeting held in 1928 Terman was a member of the subcommittee on psychometry along with E. L. Thorndike, C. C. Brigham, and Robert Yerkes (Eugenics Archive, 1928).

Hollingworth, too, openly wrote about eugenic principles and the duty that parents of gifted children had to society. They could fulfill this duty by having multiple children in order to assure that the best and brightest would be more representative in the American populace. Hollingworth (1929, p. 3) noted that "gifted children existing within the period since mental tests have been available have very few siblings, the average being about one brother or sister," and this was based on the idea that "high intelligent persons simply do not want to have many children, and are at the same time enabled by their mental powers to learn rapidly how to avoid what they do not wish" (Hollingworth, 1929, p. 4). She appealed to the perceived elevated powers of reasoning of these parents, by explaining "that society at large needs gifted children" and this might help sway their attitudes towards having more children (Hollingworth, 1929, p. 7).

The 1930s witnessed a decline in the appeal of eugenics beliefs and activities due to its increasing and aggressive use by Nazi Germany leadership and growing opposition by the American Catholic Church (Leonard, 2005). Even though the field of gifted education did not continue to expand upon these eugenic concepts, Hollingworth's and Terman's eugenic assumptions clouded the research conducted during this foundational period (Rudnitski, 1996). One of the central instruments employed during the eugenics movement—the IQ test—also was the instrument used to identify children for gifted programming.

13
CHALLENGING THE STATUS QUO

Tests of intelligence, namely the Stanford-Binet, played a large role in the identification of gifted students. These tests did have their limitations, which were acknowledged:

> (1) They measure only intelligence; (2) They give information as to the present mental status; but very little on the nature and course of future development; (3) They give no hint as to the nature or cause of retardation or nature of the treatment demanded by any given case; (4) They give small indication of specific abilities outside the relatively limited fields from which the tests are drawn; (5) They give very little indication of the emotional, environmental and physiological factors in individual development.
> (Richards-Nash, 1924, p. 213)

Closely related was the discussion of the interaction of nature and nurture and the impact of environment on intelligence. Research began to challenge the deeply held hereditarian viewpoints including those held by Florence Goodenough, Terman, Hollingworth, and many other prominent psychologists of the time, and eventually to impact the conception of giftedness. A pivotal example came from researchers at the Iowa Child Welfare Research Station (ICWRS) during the 1930s.

The research conducted at the ICWRS focused on how the conditions of schooling from preschool and elementary school impacted mental development and growth. Beth Wellman led in publishing and promoting the research station's position and findings. Wellman and the station had previous interactions with Terman and Goodenough. In 1923, Bird T. Baldwin, former director of ICWRS (who had passed away unexpectedly in 1928 on the eve of his marriage to Wellman), was invited by Terman to take the initial anthropometric measurements of the nearly 1,500 children in his longitudinal study. Wellman, a research associate and graduate student at ICWRS and another graduate student, Marguerite Drew, accompanied Baldwin to California in the summer of 1923 to assist in this endeavor. It was during this this trip that Wellman became acquainted with Terman and Florence Goodenough, who was Terman's graduate student and working as the chief research assistant on the longitudinal study (Crissey, 1990; George, 2012; Terman, 1925).

These ICWRS studies posited that children who attended preschool significantly outperformed on IQ measures those who did not attend school (Wellman, 1940). A number of children included in the study were from orphanages. Wellman and her colleagues found that those children who spent the longest time housed in the orphanage and who did not attend preschool had IQs that were generally lower than those who attended preschool (Wellman, 1940). Wellman also examined a group of superior preschool children querying whether a stimulating preschool environment had provided their gains in IQ. In a study of 57 non-preschool and preschool children correlational conclusions could only be drawn:

> The mean mark received by the preschool children was significantly higher than the mean mark received by the non-preschool children. Although it cannot be said definitely that the better school achievement of the preschool children was due to their preschool experience, the evidence points in that direction.
>
> *(Wellman, 1940, p. 388)*

Findings emphasizing the influence of environment were not limited to the *Yearbook* and had appeared in mainstream publications such as *Time* magazine and *Ladies' Home Journal* (Minton, 1984).

Hollingworth's and Terman's work paralleled each other and emerged from a hereditarian view of intelligence. As the 1920s progressed, social scientists and other psychologists began to challenge hereditarian and eugenic principles and started to consider how environment impacted intelligence and school achievement. The 1940 *National Society for the Study of Education's Thirty-Ninth Yearbook* was one such platform where these assumptions were challenged (Minton, 1984). This debate between nature and nurture unfolded in the Yearbook when Terman, Hollingworth, and Florence Goodenough (representing nature) and Stoddard and Wellman (representing nurture) engaged in a heated battle using their research as tools of war. At the core of the argument was the extent to which nurture impacted intellect (Minton, 1984).

The National Society for the Study for Education had played an intermittent role in gifted education since the field's inception, publishing several yearbooks devoted to gifted education: in 1920 *Classroom Problems in the Education of the Gifted*, followed by *The Education of the Gifted* in 1924, both edited by

Guy M. Whipple; in 1940, the *Thirty-Ninth Yearbook: Intelligence Its Nature and Nurture* (also edited by Whipple). Although not directly focused on gifted education, the yearbook did include actors from the field of gifted education and the debate included within the volume would be consequential for the field.

As Terman developed the Stanford-Binet in the 1910s, hereditarians held sway over the concept that intelligence developed from nature (Minton, 1984). Hollingworth's graduate training had been completed under E. L. Thorndike, who also supported these hereditarian views (Beauvais, 2016). As Terman and Hollingworth began their longitudinal studies in the early 1920s, they were guided by scientific ideas that social class and race differences were products of heredity. However, by 1937, Terman softened his stance and acknowledged the possibility that group differences could be attributed to the environment, but his reaction to the ICWRS findings seemed to abandon this attitude (McNutt, 2013; Minton, 1984; Terman & Merrill, 1937). Hollingworth never wavered in her beliefs. In a letter to Terman she stated, "There is no power on earth (unless in Iowa) I am convinced that can change the relative status of 130 IQ's and 160 IQ's, or any other range you want to mention" (L. Terman, personal communication, to F. Goodenough, November 4, 1939).

Terman, Hollingworth, and Goodenough's strategy was to rebuke the work of the Iowa Station calling it "dangerous" and claiming the methodology was fraught with errors and lacking in perspective. They began collecting evidence to refute the Iowa findings. These exercises were somewhat reminiscent of Terman's exchanges with Walter Lippmann in the 1920s. The dissemination of the Iowa work in mainstream publications made the situation even more alarming to the hereditarian group. In Goodenough's correspondence to Hollingworth, Florence goes so far as to question Wellman's objectivity:

> I am really quite concerned about Beth Wellman. Perhaps you do not realize how completely her whole life and energies have been bound up with this question for the past four or five years at least. Needless to say we cannot consider that side of it as far as presenting and interpreting the evidence is concerned ... Terman thinks that she has deliberately attempted to present her data in a way calculated to deceive the reader. I cannot agree with him in this. I have known Beth very intimately for a number of years, and I am personally entirely convinced of her sincerity. What has happened is, I am, confident, that she has deceived herself.
>
> *(F. Goodenough personal communication to*
> *L. Hollingworth, April 5, 1939)*

Terman's slowly evolving views perhaps had not prepared him for the confronting results emerging from the Iowa Station and certainly challenged the long-standing idea that IQ was fixed and could not be altered. As the definition of giftedness was so closely tied to that of IQ, the idea that IQ could be transformed based on environment antagonized a system, in the construction of which Terman had been instrumental (Minton, 1984; Selden, 2000).

In the end, strictly hereditarian views of intelligence were nearly out of mode and the ways in which the environment impacted an individual's role in all aspects of society would increasingly become a point of research and consideration. The ICWRS findings and "the effects of environmental enrichment anticipated the kind of research and educational programming carried out in the subsequent reform era of the War on Poverty in the 1960s" (Minton, 1984, p. 172).

Summary

Growing out of a period of great scientific and societal change, gifted education was established in an attempt to separate scientific fact from myth in regards to gifted children. Employing tools—specifically the IQ test—Terman and Hollingworth set upon a path intertwined with a set of underlying assumptions that would in some ways misguide and slow the field in terms of addressing the needs of minorities and students from poor backgrounds. Through a 21st-century lens, it is easy to cast judgment on this particular aspect of their work. However, Terman and Hollingworth were researchers of their time, documenting the initial characteristics and behaviors of gifted children, which have been upheld, discarded, and extended over the past 100 years by subsequent researchers.

The 1920s could be described as gifted education's "golden era." This period established and offered an extremely narrow definition of giftedness that revolved around a single IQ score, typically derived from the Stanford-Binet. The cut-off IQ score ranged from 120–140, depending on the parameters set by the school district or program administrators, and greatly influenced by the researchers of the era. The status quo of this definition would remain unchallenged for nearly 50 years, when factors such as creativity, home environment, and socioeconomic status influenced a growing and multi-factored understanding of intelligence. Stewart (1999, p. 56) argued, "Terman gave us a default definition for the century. Giftedness became an outcome on a test ... [and] a score becomes the great divide. It separates those who do from those don't receive special attention" and perpetuated an idea that children should be separated based on the test scores rather than having their educational needs addressed. The next era in gifted education would witness the introduction of alternate theories of learning, greater attention to curricular development, and the growing dissatisfaction with the initial definition proffered by the early pioneers in the field.

SECTION III

By Jennifer L. Jolly & Jennifer H. Robins

14
THE GROWTH OF GIFTED EDUCATION

The 1920s and 1930s witnessed the establishment and rise of gifted education as a legitimate field of study with Lewis M. Terman and Leta S. Hollingworth providing the impetus and leadership for developing a baseline of research, which would eventually influence educational practice and provide evidence for an impending advocacy movement. Toward the end of the 1930s, Hollingworth (1936a, p. 90) reflected,

> Educators are the only official guardians appointed by society for gifted children in addition to their natural guardians, the parents. Courts seldom see them (for they are not delinquent). Physicians do not deal with them as such, and incidentally do not as often as with other children (for they are healthy). Legislators do not consider them; (there are many laws dealing with mentally defective children, but none dealing with the gifted).

The momentum that gifted education gathered during these foundational decades would not be extended into the 1940s. The founding years of the field were governed by the development of tentative understandings of gifted children and dominated by the work of two main researchers, Terman and Hollingworth. The 1940s and moving forward were far more diffuse and included an expanded research trajectory, the influx of new researchers, an expansion of curriculum and pedagogy for gifted students into classrooms and schools, the search for talent in which the gifted and talented would be central figures, and the establishment of advocacy organizations. This collective course of events, however, did not occur in a linear fashion and encountered varied levels of interest and support. Paul Witty, who would establish himself as a researcher in the 1930s, lamented in regards to the turn gifted education had taken during the 1940s after its foundation as a field just two decades earlier:

> Studies show that from 1920 to 1940, scarcely a beginning was made in recognizing and providing for especially bright pupils throughout our school system. During World War II, educational facilities were curtailed sharply and opportunities for gifted pupils were affected adversely. It appears that one of greatest shortcomings of school systems today is their failure to recognize and conserve human ability and talent. We need better prepared teachers, more abundant and varied materials of instruction, and generally improved conditions for learning in order to avoid further waste of our greatest human resources—bright and gifted children and youth.
>
> *(Witty, 1949, p. 264)*

Unsurprisingly, World War II interrupted much of the research being conducted on gifted children. With the Japanese bombing of Pearl Harbor on December 7, 1939, the energies expended toward investigating matters of gifted children were to a large extent placed on hold while efforts were consolidated towards the war. Similar to those psychologists who volunteered their expertise in World War I, a new group of psychologists and educational psychologists offered their capabilities to all facets of the war machine, including those involved with the work on gifted children (Jolly & Robins, 2014).

With World War II's end, several vulnerabilities were exposed for American society and national security. Military recruits' mathematical and scientific knowledge assessed during the war revealed that their abilities and knowledge were too low to maintain the technological expertise needed as the United States emerged from World War II only to find itself embroiled in the Cold War with the Soviet Union and its communist allies. The Soviet Union and the United States did not engage in traditional armed conflict but instead carried out their struggle through surrogate wars in other nations, reconnaissance work, propaganda, political antagonism, and the economic support of friendly governments (Gaddis, 2006). America would need to build and maintain a pool of talented mathematicians and scientists, and efforts in developing this resource were to be a priority moving forward as part of the strategy to sustain its established leadership position in the global hierarchy that had emerged after the war (Jolly, 2009a; Jolly & Robins, 2016). A growing vocal criticism over the state of American high schools was also taking place, led most notably by Admiral Hyman G. Rickover. As a part of this effort to maintain the United States' new world position, the federal government also began to pass a series of legislative measures and establish agencies to support the training and development of America's talented young people—with a particular focus on technology and the sciences. This strategy was implemented with the goal of cementing America's place as *the* world leader. The country's most talented and able youth featured substantially in this plan. The American government was now in the business of talent identification and development.

Academically advanced youth would be cultivated as a resource in America's Cold War effort against the Soviet Union. Renewed interest in gifted youth and their abilities and potential contributions were initiated. By not cultivating these talents and abilities, the potential losses and contributions to society were incalculable (Rickover, 1959). One of the leading supporters of gifted youth, Rickover, a U.S. Navy Admiral, is most often remembered as the father of the nuclear submarine program. However, following the launch of the first Soviet satellite, Rickover became quite outspoken regarding the state of the American educational system, characterizing it as the cult of mediocrity.

In *Education and Freedom* (1959), Rickover outlined his philosophies and ideas for reform. He believed that schools and classroom teachers ignored the needs of its most talented students as the "slower group [set] the pace" (1959, p. 117). This caused a loss of interest in school and provided an artificial sense of superiority as students had never been properly challenged. Rickover felt that "the most effective step we can take immediately is to unshackle our talented youth from the lock step of average and below average" (1959, p. 115). He also proposed the establishment of 25 demonstration schools where children of high ability and talent would be taught by teachers of equally high intelligence and controlled by a private agency. A. Harry Passow, a professor in gifted education at Teachers College, vehemently disagreed with Rickover's proposal, countering that if gifted education was going to succeed it needed to happen within the framework of universal general education (Wolters, 2008). These proposed demonstration schools never came to fruition.

This renewed interest in gifted students brought about federal intervention along with state level education units that were established to oversee those with special needs. Unfortunately, response from federal and state entities was uneven. This echoed earlier attempts to meet the needs of gifted students through policy making. The U.S. Office of Education established the Section on Exceptional Children and Youth in 1931. However, this office had no genuine authority or fiscal license (Jolly & Robins, 2016; Zettel, 1982). The 1940s saw a limited sequence of states enacting legislation to provide special classes for gifted children. These included California, Oregon, Pennsylvania, and Wisconsin, but only two states provided funds to support these classes (Knight, 1952; Santayana, 1947). Aside from these events, any further interest in the field remained relatively dormant until after World War II.

Competing Paradigms and Perceived Inadequacies

At the same time that calls were being made to identify and cultivate the talent pool that existed in America's youth, debates regarding equity and excellence began to take hold in regards to the education of the gifted during the 1940s and

1950s. In trying to uphold the principles of a democratic society, the concept of equality became confused and synonymous with sameness and thus applied to educational institutions. Gifted education would find itself caught between these two competing ideologies. By providing students with the same types of curriculum and pedagogy regardless of academic ability, the school system disallowed children with advanced learning needs the opportunity to develop their talents (Keys, 1942).

Teachers College hosted the Conference on the Education of Youth in America between November 18 and 19, 1946, just over a year after the close of World War II, to revivify the conversation around education in the United States. Within the conference structure, Committee No. 4 (1947) promoted the notion that the United States must be proactive in the early identification and development of its young people in order to contribute to society at large. The committee even went so far as to recommend developing a roster of names from which the identification and talent development process might begin. As a systematic recommendation, the committee also suggested that schools begin talent searches each year and proposed that the top one-tenth of 1% of these students' names be made public so that "special treatment" could be rendered from relevant stakeholders including business, industry, universities and colleges, and research foundations (Thut, 1947, p. 224). This recommendation met with resistance and was likened to the many lists devised under Hitler's Nazi regime (Thut, 1947).

Notables from both within and outside the gifted education community began to speak out on behalf of gifted and talented students. At the 1948 U.S. Conference of Mayors in New York City, James B. Conant named and placed gifted and talented youth at the center of maintaining America's leadership position in the world. He noted:

> Thanks to our public schools we are today, I believe, finding and developing a larger percentage of our potential talent than in any other nation, with the possible exception of the Soviet Union. But I am convinced there is a considerable untapped reservoir in many sections of the country because of the inadequacies of the elementary and secondary schools.... To the extent we fail to discover and utilize the potentialities of the youth of each generation, we are dissipating our greatest source of wealth; the young people of the nation.
>
> *(Conant, 1948, p. 52)*

Hollingworth (1939) stressed that intellect was needed at the highest positions of power and gifted youth could be identified and developed into knowledgeable and capable leaders. Russell (1941 p. 381) stated,

> [Hollingworth] saw the problem, and rightly I think too, not only in terms of respect for the individual but in the light of the welfare of the State. ...

> [N]o government will succeed or long endure which keeps stupid people at the top. It must devise means to discover and educate the able, and for its own welfare give them positions of influence and power.

The war provided a state of emergency that galvanized "training for leaders who will fearlessly locate, relentlessly attack, and intelligently bring to desirable solution the problems with which democracies [were] faced" (Bruner, 1941, p. 397). A new type of leader was needed, and gifted and talented young people provided the optimal pool from which to source this type of leadership for service in the private and public sector (Witty, 1953). Given "the present disastrous state of the world … the best abilities of mankind to prevent our civilization from dissolving into chaos" allowed gifted education researchers and practitioners to argue for the needs of gifted children (Pitner, 1941, p. 407).

> If gifted children's leadership potential was developed, they could, make outstanding contributions to the progress and human welfare of our nation; indeed, the very survival of the democratic way of life may lie in their hands. Many of them will serve as leaders in government, industry, labor, and crafts; some will be the inventors, engineers, and scientists, the artists, composers, and writers, the leading doctors, educators and farmers or their time.
> *(Scheifele, 1953, p. vii)*

Leadership acumen and talent would guide industry and business. These leaders were also expected to offer specific skills such as reasoning, patience, consideration, and expert knowledge in their respective fields (DuPont, 1941; Worchester, 1956).

15
LEGISLATIVE INITIATIVES

The Servicemen's Readjustment Act of 1944

The first set of legislative measures that impacted talent building was the Servicemen's Readjustment Act of 1944, more widely known as the G.I. Bill (G.I. short for Government Issue), which seems an unlikely inclusion in the history of gifted education (Jolly, 2013). However, this Act would deeply transform the near entirety of America's vast social and economic strata, providing the country with a professional and academic talent pool (Hindley, 2014). The bill's fundamental canons provided home loans, unemployment pay, and education and vocational training for World War II veterans. The bill was passed in anticipation of returning war veterans; even as the bill was being signed into law by President Roosevelt on June 22, 1944, the Allied forces were fully engaged in the European Theater's Operation Overlord (the Normandy Invasion). By September of 1945, millions of veterans began accessing the benefits afforded them by the G.I. Bill (Bristol, 2006).

The G.I. Bill provided assistance to World War II veterans, something that had been severely lacking for veterans returning at the end of World War I. The American Legion played a central role in the G.I. Bill's formation. The Legion was founded as an advocacy organization in 1919, shortly after the end of World War I, for veteran services and rights. When the Legion lobbied Congress to request recompense on behalf of soldiers, Congress responded with the World War Adjustment Compensation Act in 1924. Bonuses were allocated according to length and type of posting during a soldier's service. However, if the bonuses amounted to more than $50, certificates were issued. These certificates were not redeemable until 1945 and were valued between $1,000 and $1,500. The onset of the Great Depression only five years after the passage of the Compensation Act led veterans to protest and demand immediate economic relief

(Department of Veterans Affairs, n.d.). The economic difficulties of the Great Depression and the lack of World War I veterans' benefits resulted in the loss of talent for an entire generation of young men.

The highest profile of these protests was the "Bonus March" in 1932. Twenty thousand veterans marched on Washington, D.C., in order to bring attention to their dire financial circumstances and to accelerate the payment of their certificates by 13 years. Waves of marchers joined the initial group over the summer of 1932 and soon unsanitary conditions grew in these improvised camps. President Hoover responded by sending in armed military troops under the command of Army Chief of Staff, General Douglas MacArthur. The marchers eventually dispersed and another four years elapsed before Congress authorized the early payment of the certificates (Bristol, 2006; Hindley, 2014).

In consultation with the American Legion, Roosevelt urged Congress to craft a bill that would address the needs of World War II veterans. Roosevelt (1943, p. 2) believed that veterans had been "compelled to make greater economic sacrifice than the rest of us, and are entitled to definite action to help take care of their special problems." Others like James B. Conant (1943, para. 26–27) believed that post-war America for returning veterans should be

> determined by their merit, their talents, their character, and their grit, they and their relating will feel this is a good land, and a land of freedom come what may… we shall set up machinery, state machinery of course (but Federally financed), to see to it that the returning soldier is retrained and placed in the kind of employment for which his talents are suited.

The G.I. Bill provided postsecondary educational opportunities to a generation of young men and women that would have been otherwise out of reach. The Veterans Administration oversaw the G.I. Bill and education benefits, which included tuition, fees, and books, plus a monthly stipend for a maximum of 48 months (dependent on length of military service; Bristol, 2006).

Postsecondary attendance (and home ownership) now extended beyond the privileged few, and "university [attendance] came to define and ensure the ongoing production of a White middle class, rather than solely a training ground for the moneyed elite" (Herbold, 1994–1995, p. 106). Access to universities was now available to first-generation Americans, minorities, Catholics, and Jews, and those representing large swaths of socioeconomic strata (Bound & Turner, 2002; Mettler, 2012). Not everyone perceived the G.I. Bill as a harbinger of access to educational opportunity. Although supportive of veterans' benefits, James B. Conant, President of Harvard University, cautioned that institutions of higher education could be overrun and prone to accepting unqualified applicants. This belief was unfounded (Robins, 2010).

Despite the universal democratic nature of the bill, not all veterans benefited equally. For example, Black ex-servicemen did not experience the same type of opportunity as their White counterparts, and much of this was attributable to the poor educational environments present before the war, the continued poverty upon their return, and lack of opportunity (Herbold, 1994–1995).

Of the 16 million military personnel who served during World War II, approximately half enrolled in university and/or training programs using their G.I. Bill benefits (Bristol, 2006). Although not specifically intended for gifted and talented individuals, this surge of new college and training program attendees included some of the most able and talented students, who may not have had the means or opportunity to attend college otherwise. Selected recipients included individuals that would eventually contribute to gifted education. For example, Julian Stanley, known for his work with mathematically talented youth, served in the Army's chemical warfare division, eventually earning his Ed.D. from Harvard using G.I. Bill benefits (Benbow, n.d.). Additional notables include Supreme Court Justice William Rehnquist, U.S. Senator Bob Dole, author Joseph Heller (*Catch-22*), Civil Rights activist Medgar Evers, and actor Paul Newman (Mettler, 2012).

Ted Sherman represented a more typical example of how the G.I. Bill intervened in the development of talent. While a young boy, he was identified as gifted and skipped second grade. He then boarded at a school for fatherless boys. Sherman eventually joined the Navy. Using the benefits from his G.I. Bill, he earned a B.F.A. from Philadelphia University of the Arts and found a successful career in advertising (Sherman, 2007). Sherman's narrative is reiterated by servicemen and women, with the first wave of G.I. Bill graduates earning 432,058 bachelor's degrees in 1950. This was more than double the 186,500 conferred in 1940, illustrating the near-immediate impact of the G.I. Bill (National Center for Education Statistics, 1993).

Successive versions of the G.I. Bill have been available to U.S. servicemen, including the present-day Montgomery G.I. Bill. This large-scale intervention by the federal government is an example of opportunity intersecting with talent, providing considerable possibilities for both individual and societal growth (Jolly, 2013).

National Science Foundation

In 1942, not long after America's entry into World War II, weighty conversations began to occur in relation to the scientific community, government collaboration, and research support. In 1945, President Roosevelt requested Vanneaver Bush, head of the Office of Scientific Research and Development during the war, to develop a proposal for the federal government's support of science at the war's conclusion. The result, *Science—The Endless Frontier,* became the framework for what would ultimately become the National Science Foundation (NSF; Mazuzan, 1994).

The National Science Foundation Act of 1950 was passed with support from President Truman in direct response to the focus on science research and training. As a federal agency its aims were "to promote the progress of science, to advance the national health, prosperity, and welfare, to secure national defense"

(National Science Foundation, n.d., para. 1). This act concentrated its efforts on strengthening and refocusing math and science curricula while promoting these fields in high school while also providing resources for research and development in the sciences (Jolly & Robins, 2016). When signing the bill Truman (1950, para. 3–4, 8) shared,

> The establishment of the National Science Foundation (NSF) is a major landmark in the history of science in the United States. Its establishment climaxes 5 years of effort on the part of the executive branch, the Congress, and leading private citizens. Three months after I assumed the Presidency in 1945, I received a report ... [that] recommended the creation of an agency, such as the National Science Foundation, to promote the development of new scientific knowledge and new scientific talent. It was assumed at that time that the world was close to an enduring peace. The Foundation was to be an instrument in promoting reconstruction, and in maintaining our wartime momentum in scientific progress.
>
> The fact that the world has not found postwar security in no way lessens the need for the National Science Foundation. On the contrary, it underscores this need.
>
> The Nation's strength is being tested today on many fronts. The National Science Foundation faces a great challenge to advance basic scientific research policy. Its work should have the complete support of the American people.

The NSF received funding, albeit never at the amount requested or thought necessary to fully fulfill its mission. The foundation began by supporting individual research projects, scientific conferences and symposia, as well as the travel of scientists to international meetings (Mazuzan, 1994).

The National Science Foundation's six main objectives included:

> (a) to initiate and support scientific research and programs across all levels, (b) to award scholarships to students in the sciences, (c) to cultivate the exchange of ideas among scientists in the United States and their colleagues around the world, (d) to promote the development of various scientific methods and technologies for both research and education, (e) to identify the needs in the various branches of science, and (f) to establish a national clearinghouse of scientists.
>
> *(Zettel, 1982, p. 52)*

As the scope of NSF's work enlarged funding was provided to create resources for expanding science curriculum in schools. These projects included Biological Science Curriculum Study (BSCS) biology courses, School Mathematics Study Group (SMSG), Jerome Bruner's somewhat controversial Man: A Course of

Study (MACOS), and the Physics Science Study Committee's (PSSC) Physics. The majority of these curricula were introduced just before or shortly after the launch of Sputnik I (Urban, 2010). The resources offered by the NSF provided funds and resources for talented scientists and dissemination of their findings. The newly developed science curriculum also provided additional rigor and challenge for students who were ready for the advanced academic content.

National Defense Education Act

The next piece of major legislation borne from the Cold War was the National Defense Education Act (NDEA; P.L. 85–684) in 1958, which directly named and impacted gifted education and talented youth and individuals. In a 1998 interview, A. Harry Passow was asked to recall the Act and its resulting impact on gifted students with advanced academic needs:

> The National Defense Education Act (NDEA) was passed in 1958 and it provided the impetus for curriculum reform in science, math, and foreign languages, later expanded to other subjects, that lasted into the '60s. The NDEA (1958) was originally designed to improve the math and science curriculum for bright students, as well as the teaching of math and science in general. The programs that emerged were available to all levels of students, but were most appropriate for the brighter students. It was acknowledged that bright students needed a differentiated curriculum in the content areas in order to maximize their educational development. Consequently, there was more recognition of the specific curricular needs of the gifted and talented than there is today [at the end of the 20th century].
> *(Kirschenbaum, 1998, pp. 194–195)*

The NDEA aligned with initial ideas proposed by Rickover and Conant as gifted individuals were tapped to provide a pipeline of future scientists and mathematicians, thus linking them to national security and the country's survival (Passow, 1960). Prior to this, preservice courses for future teachers and graduate courses in gifted education were meagre. Disjointed and uncoordinated calls were made "for more perceptive, intensive, and sustained consideration" regarding the gifted (Newland, 1955, p. 292). However, rekindled attention toward gifted and talented youth and their education materialized and crescendoed with the Soviet launch of Sputnik I on October 4, 1957, which introduced a brief but intense interest in this student population. Simultaneously, the American educational system as a whole was also scrutinized, with calls for greater rigor and reform (Jolly, 2009).

The end of World War II brought to bear the beginnings of a new war that would witness the United States and Soviet Union, once former allies, carve up a geopolitical map according to political and economic ideology that would continue through the last half of the 20th century and, with the successful introduction of nuclear weaponry at the end of World War II, brought the possibility of aggression to an intensified level. The Soviet Union's launch of Sputnik I momentarily tipped the scales of Cold War aggression in their favor and elevated the fears of the American public to new heights. If the Soviets could launch a satellite into orbit, they now possessed the means to propel nuclear warheads on intercontinental ballistic missiles (Mazuzan, 1994). Sputnik also stimulated the efforts of the United States government to reevaluate the pursuit of excellence and development of talent (Jolly, 2009a), "forc[ing] a national self-appraisal that questioned American education, scientific, technical and industrial strength. ... They saw ... its toughest competition, particularly in the areas of science and technology and in science education" (Mazuzan, 1994, para. 39).

In U.S. Commissioner of Education Lawrence G. Derthick's (1959) report, he questioned, "Will we Americans work and sacrifice to extend to all our youth the best in American schools?" (1959, p. 1). NDEA ensured that some of the work and sacrifice could occur in American public schools and universities. As a part of this strategy, the advancement and promotion of the country's most able and brightest would aid in the ongoing Cold War with the Soviet Union, providing manpower fueled by talent and knowledge (Passow, 1960).

A shift in the nation's educational priority focused on:

> [motivating] the discovery of intelligent and talented young men and women stimulat[ing] them to devote themselves to the sciences, foreign languages, technology, and in general to those intellectual pursuits that will enrich personal life, strengthen resistance to totalitarianism, and enhance the quality of American leadership on the international scene.
>
> *(Fleming, 1960, p. 132)*

The Soviets' launch of Sputnik provided an inadvertent interest in gifted education that advocates for this group of students only hoped to inspire. The legislation instantaneously put the needs of gifted and talented youth at the forefront of educators and advanced the status and recognition of gifted children and educational needs not observed since the foundational years of the field during the 1920s and 1930s (Jolly, 2009a).

The Act

A series of bills had been introduced in Congress to address the educational needs signaled by the launch of Sputnik, beginning in the spring of 1958. Apart from providing focused assistance for gifted children, the NDEA was also a significant moment in the federal government's involvement in public education (Butz et al., 2004). The NDEA provided the first comprehensive federal education legislation, with unparalleled levels of funding to support this ambitious plan (Flattau et al., 2006). Despite the level of funding, the Act's focus did not address elementary school education in any substantial or meaningful way (Urban, 2010). Instead, the focus concentrated on high school and university education reforms and assistance, illustrating the urgency with which it was thought that talented young people could help in service during the Cold War. Aiding talented elementary school children was thought too far away to contribute to the immediate problem at hand.

Carl Elliott, Representative from the Seventh Congressional District of Alabama and Chairman of the Subcommittee on Special Education of the House of Representatives, and Senator Joseph Lister Hill, also of Alabama, co-authored the bill that eventually became the NDEA. Rep. Elliott's speech at the National Education Association Conference on the Academically Talented Student in early February of 1958 addressed how gifted students would "fit into this legislation" (Elliott, 1958, p. 143). His speech highlighted the predicament of academically able boys and girls who were stymied by current educational practices and systems. The elements of the act sought to bring relief to these circumstances and develop a resource that would benefit American society as a whole. Elliott (1958, p. 143) noted, "Improv[ing] the quality of education for all children will greatly aid the gifted, or academically talented."

The National Defense Education Act was a curious title for the legislation, yet an inspired choice. Given the climate of the nation, congressional representatives could sell this type of spending on defending the nation—even if the defense would be achieved in the form of educational outlets and initiatives (Davis, 2011). As Terizan (2008, p. 312) noted, "in linking science education programs for American youth to military preparedness and economic strength," these expenditures would be on America's "critical resources." The NDEA provided $1 billion over four years, providing approximately 40,000 scholarships, 40,000 school loans for postsecondary education, and 1,500 graduate fellowships. These funds targeted academically capable students who would otherwise not have the financial means or direction to pursue undergraduate or graduate education (Fleming, 1960). The NDEA also offered states matching funds to improve elementary and secondary mathematics, science, and foreign curriculum and instruction, which also included better equipment and materials, along with professional development for teachers (Anderson, 2007). The additional funding allowed for resources to be devoted to strengthening and expanding the types of science and mathematics courses offered to gifted and talented students in American schools, particularly at the high school level. Title V of NDEA also allocated funds for targeted guidance counselling and testing and identification of gifted students (Fleming, 1960),

Researchers and educators in gifted education recognized the opportunity that Sputnik's launch presented and took advantage of the renewed interest and targeted goals included in NDEA for academically talented youth (Barbe, 1958). The identification and implementation of programming for academically gifted and talented students was an aggressive agenda pursued predominantly at the secondary level. A summary of the act concluded,

The National Defense Education Act [was] and unparalleled move by the federal government to assume leadership in providing for loans to students, program development, fellowships, guidance, counselling, and testing, institutes, and research studies. In the main, it [was] directed toward improving educational services for the able student and supplying creative manpower.
(Fliegler & Bish, 1959, p. 413)

Gifted children had long experienced a capricious existence in the public's estimation and in schools (Barbe, 1958; Jolly & Bruno, 2010). Researchers and practitioners within the field prudently took the opportunity that NDEA presented: "Once a forgotten element in our schools, the gifted student has become the center of controversy. The great debate in education is now focused on how to teach gifted students for their role as technological and political leaders" (French, 1959, p. v). The gifted education community approached with a cautionary sense of optimism as their memory was moderated by the previous decade, where the needs of gifted students were all but forgotten.

Shifting Constructs

Title V of NDEA provided for the identification of academically talented students, presenting both theoretical and practical challenges for researchers, practitioners, administrators, and students. Prior to the passage of NDEA, traditional constructs and views of intelligence and giftedness had begun to shift. Forces outside gifted education, particularly those in psychology, contested the long-held conceptions of giftedness, and the evolution of a "comprehensive theory of giftedness which could explain why and how individual talent matured" (Passow, 1960, p. 143) continued throughout this period. John Stalnaker had discussed these issues surrounding identification at the Academically Talented Student National Education Association (NEA) Conference.

From the establishment of the field, Hollingworth and Terman tied giftedness to intelligence (synonymous with IQ) and resulting achievement (Jolly, 2009a). Hollingworth's definition of giftedness provided a cut-off score of 130 IQ, or the top 1% of children (Hollingworth, 1926), while Terman held his definition to an even higher standard equating giftedness and genius with a 140 IQ (Terman, 1930b). These definitions proved to be limiting, and even Terman and Hollingworth acknowledged other traits might be applicable to the conception of giftedness but held steadfast to intelligence as the sole marker due to the certainty with which they felt it could be measured (Jolly, 2004). Hollingworth (1939), shortly before her death, submitted that giftedness was multifaceted and a reconsideration of the definition to include creativity and leadership would be fruitful in pushing the field forward. NDEA provided the opportunity to explore how the concept of giftedness and its identification could be expanded.

Despite the theoretical shifts and recommendations for a more sensitive means for identification, IQ scores and achievement measures were still extensively used to identify students for gifted and talented programs under NDEA's Title V (Martinson, 1960). Even so, there were competing agendas as to what percentage of the population should be identified. The widely accepted definition of giftedness suggested that 2–10% of the school population were comprised of gifted students (Fliegler & Bish, 1959). James Conant, now President Emeritus of Harvard and Chairperson of the Educational Policies Commission, suggested more generously that 15–20% of American high schoolers should be identified as academically talented students (Conant, 1958b). Conant also held influential positions and key roles on the National Defense Research Committee, National Science Foundation, and Atomic Energy Commission. These positions allowed him exceptional influence in the movement to identify America's best and brightest students.

Fleming (1960, p. 132) summarized the immediate impact and realized goals of the NDEA:

> The National Defense Education Act recognized that education is a national unifying force, and it regards an educated citizenry as the country's most precious resource. Its ten Titles are designed to motivate the discovery of intelligent and talented young men and women and stimulate them to devote themselves to the sciences, foreign languages, technology, and in general to those intellectual pursuits that will enrich personal life, strengthen resistance to totalitarianism, and enhance the quality of American leadership on the international scene.

The White House Conference

The NDEA strengthened interest in gifted education, and this was evidenced at the 1960 White House Conference, which focused on "opportunities for children and youth to realize their full potential for a creative life of freedom and dignity" (U.S. Department of Health, Education, and Welfare, 1967, p. 22). The White House conferences, established during William Taft's presidency in 1910, focused on "problem typical of the decade" (U. S. Department of Health, Education, and Welfare, 1967, p. 1). Conference attendees represented an array of governmental and nongovernmental agencies and voluntary organizations that focused on the welfare of children.

The National Association for Gifted Children (NAGC), established only seven years earlier, was represented by its President, Ann Isaacs. Specific recommendations were made on behalf of gifted children that included (1) all schools be required to make special provisions for the education of gifted, talented, and creative students, using high-order thinking skills; (2) state departments of education assume greater responsibility for their education; (3) teachers acquire better understanding of the nature and needs of gifted students; and (4) more sensitive means of identification be developed, especially to find those students from diverse and underserved populations (NAGC, 1960). Conference recommendations were evidenced in the research agendas of gifted researchers and the implementation of programming for gifted children during the post-Sputnik era. Additional recommendations would surface a decade later with the release of the Marland Report in 1972 (Jolly & Matthews, 2014).

16

TECHNOLOGY AND SCIENCE DRIVEN REFORM

Searching for Talent

Interest in science education emerged during the 1940s as part of the Progressive education reform agenda. Even though high school enrollment increased, the number of students selecting science courses was not reflected in this growth (Terizan, 2008). Science education would be informed by two distinct factions—those who thought science underwrote democratic citizenship and those who considered science education as a guide to everyday life decisions. Those favoring democratic citizenship believed that "science education for expert leadership in a meritocracy required rigorous, discipline-based courses with the brightest students who had been carefully selected on the basis of their academic achievements and intellectual promise" (Terizan, 2008, p. 311).

One of the main motivators behind America's need to build its scientific talent pool was the perceived lack of technological and scientific talent during World War II and the ongoing talent deficiency moving forward into the Cold War. Talented youth and gifted young people of the United States figured prominently in this capacity-building scheme. America's lack of eminent and leading scientists highlighted its unpreparedness and exposed its vulnerability requiring scientific training as an instrument of national defense (Jolly, 2009a).

Precursors to private mobilization efforts of scientific talent by the federal government included competitions like the Westinghouse Science Talent Search (STS; now known as the Intel Science Talent Search), which originated in 1942 soon after the United States entered World War II (Davis, 1951; Edgerton & Britt, 1946; Terizan, 2008). An outgrowth of the Science Service (known today as the Society for Science and the Public), founded in 1921 by Edward W. Scripps and William Emerson Ritter, the organization sought to keep the general public apprised of scientific breakthroughs. These programs and organizations were implemented to improve science teaching in the United States and encourage high school students' interest in science through the development of original research projects (Kaye, 2001). The objectives of the STS were:

1. to discover and foster the education of boys and girls whose scientific skill, talent, and ability indicate enough potential creative originality to warrant the granting of scholarships;
2. to focus the attention of large numbers of scientifically gifted youths on the need for developing their scientific and research skill and knowledge in order that they can contribute to the rehabilitation of an insecure world and, with the aid of science, help the world to achieve peace; and
3. to aid in making American adults grow aware of the varied and vital roles played by science in world affairs and in the general welfare of our people. (Davis, 1951, p. 236)

The enduring popularity and importance of these organizations and competitions are reflected in their longevity and relevance in advancing scientific talent in young people.

In 1951, the Ford Foundation established The Fund for the Advancement of Education as a philanthropy to support the advancement of the field of education in American schools and colleges (The Fund for the Advancement of Education, 1957). The Fund focused on five programs that allowed for early college entrance:

1. joint effort by three preparatory schools and three colleges (Harvard, Yale, and Princeton) in which grades 11–14 were treated as one continuous path;
2. the Atlanta Experiment in Articulation and Enrichment in School and College, which focused on enrichment;
3. the collaboration between the Portland, OR, public schools system and Reed College to identify exceptional students early and enrich their educational opportunities;
4. the School and College Study of Admission with Advanced Standing, which enriched and accelerated education in grades 11–14 by giving students college-level work in high school in 1955 (this program became the Advanced Placement program when the College Entrance Examination Board took over); and
5. the Program for Early Admission to College(The Fund for the Advancement of Education, 1957, pp. 2–5).

In an effort to develop diverse abilities of advanced students, the Program for the Early Admission to College was formed through The Fund. In the fall of 1951, 420 early entrance freshmen students took their place in the network of universities and colleges set up to accelerate their educational path (The Fund for the Advancement of Education, 1957). Initial program outcomes appeared promising: All participating colleges considered the program to be effective; program participants outperformed their classmates (and control group); when identified, difficulties adjusting to campus life were negligible and quickly surmounted; and among the total graduating classes, more program participants planned on attending graduate school (The Fund for the Advancement of Education, 1957). Even though funding for the program concluded at the end of the decade, all but one participating university continued on with the program, realizing the benefits for both the university and the students. The positive findings from the program also helped to change the attitudes of even some of its most vocal critics.

The National Association of Secondary School Principals (NASSP) reacted quite negatively to the Early Admission to College program when it was first announced (Meister, 1956) and issued a statement to its members opposing the program, stating that they would not support a program that curtailed students' secondary education, echoing similar statements about the strategy of acceleration. NASSP would:

> Present ... the implications of the unsound practice of curtailing secondary education and the subsequent admission of students to college before graduation [and] point out as effectively and as forcibly as possible these dangers, even with the alluring inducement of funds provided by the Ford Foundation. [They] must make citizens generally aware of the sinister implications of such a program especially if a scholarship award is offered to their sons.
>
> *(Meister, 1956, p. 221)*

However, results from the program evaluation swayed this influential organization and altered its position upon the realization that the students had excelled and "no serious educational tragedies have resulted. On the contrary, these early-admitted students have fared better than expected, in every way" (Meister, 1956, p. 221).

Tangential to accelerated studies, the Advanced Placement (AP) program began in 1953–1954 as part of the School and College Study of Admission with Advanced Standing and supported financially by The Fund for the Advancement of Education and taken over in 1955 by the College Board (Douglas, 1959). In June 1954, the first conference on the Advanced Placement program, including professional learning for high school and college history teachers, was offered.

During the first school year, 18 schools offered AP courses. Over the next two years, the numbers increased to 38, then 104, and by 1956–1957, the number rose to 212 schools. During the 1957–1958 school year, 356 schools offered AP courses to students (Keller, 1958). The subsequent growth remained steady and the advantages for gifted and high-ability students soon became clear to principals and teachers who worked with these students and witnessed the AP program's benefits firsthand.

During this period, the AP program created a great deal of anticipation as a new educational contribution. The program "has been called, and rightly so I believe 'one of the most encouraging recent innovations in education'" (Keller, 1958, p. 11). Dudley (1958, p. 1), director of the AP program, noted:

> The more mature level of study and discussion and examination demanded in the Advanced Placement classes provided the stimulus which our superior students need if they are to receive the education best suited to their high potential—for the very fast student, like the very slow student, needs a pace different from the average.

Students also recognized the advantages and benefits of participation in the program:

> Not only did Advance Placement work permit me to begin my college studies without having to fumble with the fundamentals in the two advanced courses I have, but it also oriented me both to a system of study and to an appreciation of what my immediate goals in studying should be .... It is disturbing to see other students who are willing and able to absorb concentrated advanced knowledge held back because they must spend half a year learning fundamentals that are rightly learned in high school.
> (Keller, 1958, pp. 7–8)

The gains for students were not lost on principals or teachers. F. Hamilton Whipple, principal of Memorial High School in New York, explained the two objectives for the implementation of the program at his school, which began in the spring of 1956. In the process, the school began identifying rising seventh-, ninth-, and tenth-graders for participation in Advanced Placement courses (Whipple, 1958). Whipple (1958, p. 24) explained,

> An Advanced Placement Program has as its first objective the stimulation of superior students in order to induce them to use their talents to the utmost. A second objective is advanced placement in college on the basis of Advanced Placement examinations prepared by the College Board and given in May of the senior year.

Teachers also were impressed with the AP program and understood the curricular challenges it offered students who were most in need:

> America's security and future rests, to a great extent, upon the best development of the potentials of scholarship creativity and leadership in our young people. At present, when much attention is focused upon re-evaluating and redirecting education in terms of the maximum development of the able student, the Advanced Placement Program is one of the provocative and realistic approaches to the problem. By providing challenging experiences

to meet the needs and abilities of these students the program is effectively serving the welfare of the nation.

(Engelstein & Miller, 1958, p. 32)

Some high schools went so far as to align their gifted programs with the AP courses. Midwood High School in New York offered a vertical AP program that began in the tenth grade and followed students through graduation (Bernstein, 1958). Gifted students were divided into two groups: those who showed an interest in math and science and those with an interest in the humanities. All gifted students undertook the AP courses and corresponding exams in order to avoid repeating the material when they enrolled in college (Bernstein, 1958).

Another important program established during the 1950s and still in existence today is the National Merit Scholarship Corporation. Begun in 1955, its objectives included the following:

(a) identify and honor academically talented U.S. high school students; (b) stimulate increased support for their education; and (c) provide efficient and effective scholarship program management for organizations that wish to sponsor college undergraduate scholarships.

(National Merit Scholarship Corporation, 2008, para. 2)

The National Merit Scholarship Program was an independent nonprofit entity whose entire focus was to identify high school seniors who would most profit from a college education (Stalnaker, 1957). In 1956, the National Merit Scholarship Corporation granted its first four-year college scholarship to 556 students designated as Merit Scholars using a nationwide screening program. The committee looked at students who were "the most promising students for college work" (Holland & Stalnaker, 1958, p. 10). The National Merit Program played an important role in meeting the needs of the exceptionally gifted by providing "qualified students an opportunity to go to college" by offering an environment that extended and fulfilled their abilities and talents (Brickman, 1958, p. 124).

These targeted scholarships and national talent search programs were not only to benefit gifted and talented students but society would also benefit from their future contributions. As Stalnaker (1957, p. 266) summarized:

If national scholarship and talent-searching programs can stimulate the interest of the country in our able youth, encourage high school students to do better work, and increase the number of scholarships offered, they will serve the schools and the nation.

Prior to these programs' establishment, America's brightest students had limited, if any, systematic and nationally available options to develop their strengths and talents. The Advanced Placement and National Merit programs remain in existence six decades after their establishment.

The Academically Talented Student National Education Association (NEA) Conference of 1958

The NEA and co-sponsor the Carnegie Corporation invited interested individuals to New York City in order to discuss the educational future of academically talented high school students. Also included in the conference schedule were particular initiatives and programs. On February 6, 1958, this two-day conference convened less than six months after the launch of Sputnik I and just a week after the successful launch of the American satellite, the Explorer. Many individuals who were actively contributing to the research base on gifted children were on hand to present their findings. These included Walter Barbe, Gertrude Hildreth, Mariam Goldberg, John Gowan, Ruth Martinson, Harry Passow, Sidney Pressey, Ruth Strang, Virgil Ward, and Paul Witty. Ann Isaacs, President of the National Association for Gifted Children, served as an advocate for gifted children and George Roeper as an educator who had founded the Roeper School, which was designated a school for gifted children in 1956. Stakeholder institutions also participated in the proceedings, including the Educational Testing Services (ETS), Harvard University, the National Merit Scholarship Corporation, and administrators from state departments of education, superintendents, principals, and practitioners representing a cross section of American high schools (Conant, 1958a).

ETS's participation at the conference was not accidental. Its president, Henry Chauncey, James Conant's former assistant for many years, spoke at the conference. Conant had been ETS's first Chairman of the Board and both had been instrumental in identifying the Scholastic Achievement Test (SAT) as an instrument for university admission. In 1933, as President of Harvard, Conant began providing scholarships to gifted boys at Harvard University who would not otherwise be able to afford the cost of an Ivy League institution. He felt that opportunity should be offered to those who merited the benefit, not just those who had attended elite boarding schools and privileged backgrounds. However, he needed a way to evaluate applicants based on merit. Chauncey brought him the SAT. The SAT was adapted from the Army Alpha as a college admissions test by Carl Brigham, who had also helped Yerkes during World War I on the Army Alpha and Beta (Lemann, 2000). In 1957, the SAT was administered to approximately half a million high school students and the number of colleges and universities requiring it for admission steadily grew (PBS, 1999).

Coincidentally, the conference was already in the planning stages when the Soviets launched their satellite into orbit as the identification of talented youth was an ongoing priority after World War II. Sputnik only galvanized the purpose of the conference, focusing on the issues of academically talented students. The conference program scheduled participants for 12-hour days, not leaving a minute wasted, with the identification of educational options at the forefront of the agenda items (Conant, 1958a).

The conference was conceptualized by James Bryant Conant. For more than a decade, Conant extolled the abilities, particularly in the areas of leadership, of gifted and talented students. Simultaneously he had undertaken a study of the American "comprehensive" high school and believed these students were vital to the United States' long term prosperity and ability to compete with the Soviet Union. Perhaps Conant's own high school experiences at Roxbury Latin School in Boston, MA, influenced his own concepts about the potential impact rigorous high school environments could have on American youth. His science teacher, Newton Henry Black, was instrumental in Conant's development and interest in chemistry. What Conant failed to realize was how exceptional this type of interaction and intercession was on his behalf by a teacher (Bartlett, 1983). Black provided the type of mentoring and enrichment that is commonly recognized as best practice for gifted youth (Tannenbaum, 1983). Black went so far as to secure credit for Conant's freshman chemistry course at Harvard through extra work undertaken at Roxbury. Black also mapped out a course of university study for Conant that included graduate work with Harvard's Nobel Prize-winning chemist, T. W. Richards (Conant would even go on to marry Richard's daughter) (Bartlett, 1983).

Armed with his own advanced talents and abilities, Conant followed this plan and rose to become one of the most influential American scientists, diplomats, and eventually educationalists (Bartlett, 1983; Smurro, 2011). His influence on talented youth was particularly striking during the 1950s and 1960s. First an organic chemist in private industry and then a prominent Harvard chemistry professor, he eventually rose to become President of Harvard (a position he held for two decades). Following his presidency at Harvard, U.S. President Truman appointed him Ambassador to the newly formed West German Republic after World War II. After completing his tenure in Germany, Conant—with assistance from the Carnegie Corporation—turned his attention to the American high school system, which he surmised was in desperate need of reform. The conference served as a vehicle for reform and to highlight the needs of a group of students whose needs had been consistently neglected (Jolly, 2014a).

Identification as a Focus

John Stalnaker, President of the National Merit Scholarship Corporation, began the identification discussion with a rather dismal view of the United States educational system, characterizing American society as one of anti-intellectualism, where universities had shifted their goals away from rigorous academics to social activities, athletics, and fraternity activities. College degrees increasingly represented social status rather than the attainment of scholarship and no respect was given to the "disciplined mind" as noted by the salaries of K–6 teachers (Stalnaker, 1958).

Stalnaker observed that the universal system of education offered in America was both a strength and a challenge to the country. He felt "mass education must not come to mean reducing the best to the level of the average" (Stalnaker, 1958, p. 22); instead it should be viewed as the foundation to be able to identify students with academic promise. He supported the practice of early identification coupled with continuous entry points so those students who did not evidence early academic promise would be captured at some later point. Stalnaker also recognized the limits of a single IQ score, which was not an accurate reflection of the complex mental ability students possessed. He recommended the development of multiple measurements and assessments to depict the array of abilities and aptitudes exhibited by talented youth, which foreshadowed contemporary identification practices (Conant, 1958a).

Henry Chauncey, President of the ETS, confidant, and former assistant to Conant, furthered the discussion turning to the merits of testing and assessment. Achievement and aptitude tests provided an approach for comparable observations. These assessments, however, were too limited in the types of abilities they captured. Missing were those abilities associated with creativity and problem solving (Conant, 1958a). Chauncey also stressed the concept of potential and the importance that schools and communities at large had in developing their emerging gifts and talents: "If it hasn't been developed, it won't do them much good" (Chauncey, 1958, p. 29). In other words, putting in place identification efforts with appropriate programming and services to support talent would be squandering of human resources and capital (Jolly, 2014a).

The next speaker, Samuel Stouffer, Director of the Social Relations Lab at Harvard University, addressed the concept of encouraging those with the ability to go on to pursue post-secondary education in his speech "Problems Related to the Use of Academic Ability." Although the G.I. Bill diversified university populations to some degree, university attendance for graduating high school seniors during the 1950s was still largely dominated by White males and the exponentially growing middle class who sought university educations for their children. However, Stouffer argued that perhaps not all children from white-collar families were suited for university education, even if postsecondary attendance was part of the family culture (Spencer, 1958).

Educational Deliberations

Educational considerations for the academically talented populated the remaining sessions of the conference. Topics included special classes, acceleration, grouping, recommendations for subject-specific content, and motivation. Ruth Strang of Teachers College identified motivation of gifted children as a significant issue for both schools and parents. She maintained that "most gifted children are underachievers," given that school expectations and performance were often significantly lower than their actual abilities (Strang, cited in Conant, 1958a, p. 59). In order to counter these motivational quandaries, Strang suggested implementation of independent study programs, a different approach to grading, and additional opportunities to interact and work with peers of similar ability and interests (Conant, 1958a).

Paul Witty and A. Harry Passow next spoke about guiding gifted students. Guidance needed to be holistic and continuous, and gifted children needed to be supported in their goal setting. This was particularly difficult in some instances, as Witty stressed the inconsistency of programming, services, and resources for students in all settings—rural, suburban, and urban. To reduce these inconsistencies, Witty called for additional research and the establishment of a clearinghouse so that evidence-based practices could be collected and better disseminated (Conant, 1958a).

While enrichment opportunities such as Saturday classes or afterschool programming were options used to meet the needs of gifted learners, acceleration remained the centerpiece of academic options for gifted children. Sidney Pressey and Gertrude Hildreth emphasized that acceleration had been in place for gifted learners for many years. They suggested that the years students could shear off from their formal education instead be put toward creative endeavors or the start of career trajectories. Research evidence underscored that social adjustment had not proven to be an issue for accelerated students and even those students who were rapidly accelerated (two years or more) still flourished with the appropriate supports (Conant, 1958a).

The NDEA would be enacted just shortly after the close of the conference and echoed many of the conference's concerns in its legislative language. Although the conference addressed a host of issues, attendees failed to recognize the unique challenges faced by females, minorities, and those from lower socioeconomic circumstances. These issues would not be addressed until several decades later.

17
IDENTIFICATION, EDUCATIONAL PRACTICES, AND CONSIDERATIONS

Identification

The 1950s ushered in a reconsideration of the definition of giftedness. The exacting observance to intelligence and IQ scores loosened and

> No longer [were] people content to accept an IQ score alone as a measure of giftedness. ... The concept began to develop that the gifted child might be one who is superior not only in one activity but in many activities, and even beyond this.
>
> *(Barbe, 1959, p. 72)*

As a consensus began to build in certain circles regarding the development of talented youth, identification of these young people for specialized programming would be the first step in this process. These identification procedures included standardized tests and observational protocols, which could lead to placement in a gifted and talented program (DeHaan, 1959; DeHaan & Havinghurst, 1957). As these processes were to be fanned out in schools across the United States, procedures needed to be developed.

> [One] would not be able, by causal observation only, to distinguish the gifted pupils from the others. The gifted are not staggering under a towering load of books. Neither are they blundering along the fringes of the group trying unsuccessfully to "get in" with other children, as is sometimes supposed to be true of them. On the contrary, they are quite as carefree and as well adjusted as any children in the hallway; hence the need for inaugurating methods of identifying them.
>
> *(DeHaan, 1959, p. 75)*

In addition it was suggested that schools collect a variety of data points to help determine if a child was gifted and perhaps universal data collection of all children might be necessary (Munson, 1944). In his foundational work, Terman hoped to establish that high IQ equated to giftedness and in the process promulgated his own IQ measure, the Stanford–Binet IQ test. During the 1940s and 1950s IQ tests remained in use and were regularly supplemented or exchanged for achievement tests, which were on the rise in use and popularity. Several of the more popular achievement tests included the Stanford Achievement Test (developed with the assistance of Terman), the Otis Lennon School Ability Test, and the Woodcock-Johnson Test of Achievement (Kaestle, n.d.). Teachers were also encouraged to observe the physical, emotional, and social characteristics of children. These records would be kept as notes, photographs, or evaluations and checklists. IQ cut-off scores remained in debate (Bristow, Craig, Hallock, & Laycock, 1951).

Terman and Hollingworth also took records from parents and teachers as part of their studies of gifted children, with many school districts also adopting this process. These measures now became part of systematized identification procedures. Parents provided a first-hand level of their child's abilities and interests that proved useful to teachers, school psychologists, and counselors (Sumpton & Luecking, 1960). Still, some applied caution to these measures as it was thought that parents either over- or underestimated their child's abilities and failed to understand how his or her performance benchmarked with the overall population (Bristow et al., 1951). Teacher reports also began to be used in a more systematized basis. However, concerns were raised around the suitability of these recommendations, especially when teachers possessed no background in gifted education or understanding of the gifted child:

> Teachers ... tend to underestimate the ability of gifted children because they overlook the factor of chronological age. They factor that the gifted child may be one or two years younger than his classmates. Reactions to the personality of different children may influence the teacher's evaluation of ability. Thus, a poorly adjusted teacher may be annoyed by the brilliance of the gifted child and be jealous of him. Such a teacher may be unwilling to acknowledge the child's ability. Still other teachers do not have adequate standards of child development by which to judge the gifted child's status and hence to estimate his ability.
> (Bristow et al., 1951, p. 16)

Despite obvious limitations, these shifts in conceptions of giftedness and identification procedures provided opportunities to capture a more varied representation of gifted students.

Acceleration

Stedman and Hollingworth provided the initial foundations on educational practices for gifted students. Acceleration remained an option for gifted students, along with enrichment and special classes (Hildebrand, 1981; Jolly, 2004). The Educational Policies Commission (1950) suggested that the most effective approach to educating gifted students was a combination of the options. A national survey conducted in 1948 suggested that implementation of these best practices was limited. Of more than 3,000 cities with populations of 2,500 or more, only 15 cities reported having special schools or classes for gifted children, with largest enrollments found in New York, Cleveland, Worcester, and Los Angeles (Heck, 1953). Acceleration was one of the first strategies offered to gifted students in the 1800s (Sumpton & Luecking, 1960), and throughout the early 1900s, remained the most common programming model used with gifted children well into the first half of the 20th century (Educational Policies Commission, 1950). Witty (1954) noted that, if acceleration was warranted, it caused more harm if gifted students were not allowed to accelerate (Wilson, 1951). DeHaan and Havighurst (1957) found that two to three years of acceleration did no harm to gifted students and one to two years appeared optimal, especially for students who were prepared mentally and socially. "Acceleration offers opportunity for a gifted pupil to move at a pace appropriate to his ability and maturity and to complete an educational program in less than the ordinary amount of time" (DeHaan & Havighurst, 1957, p. 122). Acceleration provided educational experiences on par with gifted students' intellectual abilities (Educational Policies Commission, 1950).

During this period three types of acceleration dominated: grade skipping; rapid- or special-progress classes, in which the material for each grade was covered in a faster period of time; and early entrance to kindergarten or college (due to a prior grade skip) (DeHaan & Havighurst, 1957; Sumpton & Luecking, 1960). There were several apparent advantages to early entrance, including students' option to enter a career path one to two years earlier, and complete school without skipping a grade (Sumpton & Luecking, 1960). Rapid progress was an option most often used at the junior high level and allowed groups of students to finish more years of study in a truncated period of time (Sumpton & Luecking, 1960).

The advantages of acceleration really spoke to the rate at which gifted students were capable of learning. Acceleration aided gifted students in developing at their individual tempo instead of hindering their learning needs. The practice alleviated boredom and the lack of challenge often experienced in the students' age-based grade level classrooms; allowed students to become creative, productive adults who finished school early to begin their careers; and provided students with opportunities to work with peers with similar interests and advanced abilities. Abraham (1957) also suggested that acceleration was one of the most cost-effective ways to provide for gifted students, as no extra resources were needed. Drawbacks of the strategy included lingering misconceptions regarding the practice that students might omit learning concepts or content, encounter social or emotional complications as they transitioned to their new grade level, and be ostracized for being the accelerated student (Keys, 1942; Sumpton & Luecking, 1960).

Enrichment

Enrichment at its very core was thought of as an antidote for deficient curriculum. Cutts and Mosely (1957, p. 37) defined enrichment as "the substitution of beneficial learning for needless repetition or harmful idleness" and stated that it embodies the following criteria: (1) challenge students' full abilities; (2) broaden the knowledge base; (3) deepen understanding; (4) increase skill level; (5) develop students' love of learning; (6) offer new methods of learning, thinking, and sharing; (7) encourage initiative; and (8) provide a creative outlet for students (Cutts & Mosely, 1957). They cautioned that enrichment should not be an "excuse [for] haphazard planning or lack of planning, or impulsive, superficial following of will-o'-the-wisps" (Sumpton & Luecking, 1960, p. 39), that both teacher and student should understand the purpose and goals of the enrichment program (Sumpton & Luecking, 1960). DeHaan and Havighurst additionally described enrichment as providing additional opportunities dependent on context and resources for gifted students to "go deeper and to range more widely than the average child in his intellectual, social, and artistic experience" (1957, p. 97) and "is not the same thing everywhere. It is not a static activity. It is relative to the child's ability, achievement, and experience, and to the ideas and skills that the teacher brings to the situation" (1957, p. 102).

Offered in the regular classroom, enrichment was also seen as a cost-efficient option and proved to be a popular programming option for gifted students. However, some controversy surrounded the practice with Abraham (1958, p. 82) arguing that, "while its heart is in the right place, it remains unproven and unsatisfying." Some teachers also misunderstood the concept of enrichment and believed that extra homework or more of the same work satisfied the criteria for enrichment.

Based on the nature of the practice, its implementation was diffuse and exemplars were varied. Regardless of how the practice was operationalized,

> Possibilities for "enriching" a given subject with respect to the intellectually gifted within regular classes are restricted only by the ingenuity, resourcefulness, and especially the energy of the teacher and his colleagues. Causing students to think rather than merely to memorize is the key concept. While departing from rote learning would enliven most classes it is doubly important for the brightest pupils.
>
> *(Stanley, 1959, p. 170)*

Special Classes

Special classes were also a popular option during this era and were based on the earlier work conducted by Stedman and Hollingworth. Witty, Conant, and Strang (1959, p. 6) who noted the increased interest in this type of programming: "During the past ten years a strong interest in special classes for the gifted has emerged, and many programs are being initiated in which gifted pupils are placed in such classes." In comparison to acceleration and enrichment, special classes were considered to have specific advantages: "Because standards of achievement are higher, each pupil is challenged to use his intellectual powers to a fuller extent than in the typical heterogeneous class" (Educational Policies Commission, 1950, p. 70). Based on ability rather than chronological age, gifted students were grouped together and introduced to a greater variety of challenging learning experiences than could have been offered in a heterogeneous, age-based classroom and taught by teachers specifically trained to meet their needs (Educational Policies Commission, 1950).

However, French (1959, p. 210) noted several potential disadvantages of grouping students by ability:

> [People] are afraid that a differentiated instructional program will prevent some children from receiving their fair share of instruction, will create an elite class, will keep the gifted from learning to understand others, will not speed up the emergence of talent, or will not significantly help because teachers do not know enough about the new provisions.

Concerns voiced during Hollingworth's experience with special classes resurfaced, including the belief that special classes were undemocratic, the fear that gifted students would become arrogant or conceited and feel superior to other students not selected for the special class (Heck, 1953), the cost of having smaller classes and additional teachers needed to provide special classes, and the question of who "want to teach the ones left? Most teachers will resent remaining with the [nongifted students]" (Abraham, 1958, pp. 71–72).

The Cleveland Major Works Program, established in the 1920s, was still in operation in the 1950s and 1960s and was one of the most successful examples of special classes for gifted students. The program's continuous direction under Dorothy Norris helped to secure the participation of children that varied greatly in ethnicity and socioeconomic status. The majority of students in Cleveland schools came from working-class families who immigrated from Russia, Germany, Hungary, Ukraine, and Poland rather than the nearly entirely White and middle- and upper-middle-class students involved in the foundational work of Terman and of Hollingworth's sample from P.S. 165 (Gold, 1984). In preparation for students' future roles in society, the Major Works Program focused on core subjects such as English, math, and the social sciences, while also being imbued with humanities curriculum so that one day "he or she were to eventually assume a leadership role in a democratic society" (Gold, 1984, p. 498).

Regardless of programming choice, Heck (1953, pp. 386–387) highlighted central principles to maintain when planning programming for gifted children:

> (a) it should provide the gifted with the same opportunity to develop their talents that is provided for the average child and for the child of low IQ;

(b) it should guard against the development of conceited individuals among the gifted; (c) it should provide for social and physical placement, as well as for proper mental placement; (d) it should develop a real enrichment program; (e) it should prevent the development of wasteful and bad social habits; (f) it should seek for each gifted child a sane, all-round development educationally, socially, physically, and morally; and (g) it should be based, on the last analysis upon the most careful study of each child.

A project that included a number of recommended practices for gifted children included the Talented Youth Project in both elementary and secondary populations across the United States, investigating a range of topics. These included the effects of ability grouping, acceleration, special courses, and counseling programs. Researchers also studied attitudes toward gifted students by teachers and peers, the impact of underachievement, and the development of an instrument to evaluate gifted programming (Passow, 1957). The findings from this study would help to inform researchers and practitioners about a new generation of gifted and talented students.

In an attempt to construct a current holistic understanding of gifted education after World War II, Harry Passow at Teachers College embarked on the Talented Youth Project. This project would "assist school administrators and their staff in different parts of the country to develop, implement, and evaluate their own programs for the gifted" (Tannenbaum, 2000, p. 34) in order provide the most effective educational opportunities for the discovery of talent (Passow & Goldberg, 1962). Two essential suppositions guided the project's work: (1) public schools should present educational experiences that matched students' individual differences, and (2) instruction and school practices should be informed by field-based research (Passow & Goldberg, 1962). The Talented Youth Project extended over 12 years and had three goals:

- to initiate and conduct studies of the nature of talent and its role in modern American life,
- to experiment with program modifications by which schools can improve their programs for the talented, and
- to summarize and interpret past and current research for schools (Passow, 1957, p. 199).

In 1954, Passow and Tannenbaum (p. 150) argued for "a well-developed framework to guide experimentation and program development efforts." They did recognize certain positive aspects available to gifted and talented youth in the educational system:

> First, our secondary schools are recognizing the need for making special provisions for talented youth and are not willing to leave these either to

chance or to the ingenuity of the youngsters. "Don't worry about the talented, they'll take care of themselves," is an approach which is neither acceptable nor accepted.

(Passow & Tannenbaum, 1954, pp. 153–154)

Passow and Tannenbaum (1954, pp. 154–155) also had particular expectations for educators, which included:

- begin to probe more deeply into the nature of talent;
- try to understand what the general objectives of their schools mean when tailored to fit children with special abilities and potentials;
- analyze existing traditions and administrative procedures to test their validity in practice;
- attempt total school planning for talented youth rather than indulge in isolated effort;
- try to increase their sensitivity to the impact of peers, parents, teachers and community on talented youth and *vice versa*; and
- recognize the enormity of planning for every conceivable talent.

18
RECOGNIZING THE NEED AND ESTABLISHING ADVOCACY ORGANIZATIONS

As gifted education evolved, so too did the needs of its stakeholders. The pervasiveness of advocacy groups and organizations across the United States grew out of the idea that public schools could be doing more to locate and educate talented youth and the belief that when schools failed to discover and nurture these students, it was a disservice to not only the child but to society at large. However, in a time where print-only journals, newsletters, postal mail, and annual meetings were the main conduits of information, two national organizations emerged as leading advocates for gifted children: the American Association for Gifted Children (AAGC) and the National Association for Gifted Children (NAGC). Both organizations had similar missions and objectives and many members overlapped in their affiliations.

The 1940s and 1950s witnessed the rise of advocacy organizations focused on coordinating efforts on behalf of gifted children. Apart from national organizations, state, regional, and local groups were also appearing across the United States. These included the Metropolitan Association for the Study of the Gifted (New York), the Ohio Association for Gifted Children, and the Pennsylvania Association for the Study of Mentally Gifted Children and Youth (Davis, 1954; Sumpton & Luecking, 1960; Wilson, 1953). However, the formation of two new national organizations marked a turning point for gifted education. National organizations created an interconnectedness among stakeholders that had previously not existed and provided a central voice for the field to disseminate information to parents, teachers, and researchers.

American Association for Gifted Children (AAGC)

Established on September 6, 1946, in New York City, the AAGC's purpose was for "recognizing, appreciating, and stimulating creative work among gifted children" (Williamson, 1948, p. 53). By forming the organization, its leaders sought to help teachers and others understand and help one group of children who seemed not to be getting the consideration they need—the gifted children. The founders of this new association felt that in a real sense here was a minority group that should be identified, understood, and worked with in such a way as to enable them to contribute most effectively to themselves and to our society.

("Editorial: Understanding the Gifted Child," 1948, p. 33)

The organization was founded by Ruth Strang and Pauline Williamson, friends and colleagues, who after much observation surmised that "the gifted were the most neglected children in our democracy" (AAGC, 1999, para. 1). Initially based at the University of the State of New York, this association was the first in the United States to solely serve the needs of gifted children. Strang served as its first treasurer and Williamson as secretary. Both women were advocates for gifted children, Strang in her capacity as a professor at Teachers College, and Williamson as a school health educator and administrator. Teachers College education economics professor Harold Clark became the organization's first president (AAGC, n.d.). Lewis M. Terman was appointed to the position of Honorary Vice President (Williamson, 1948).

The first board meeting was held on November 21, 1946, and applications for memberships to the organization had to be approved by the board members. Membership was open to a wide range of persons who were interested in gifted children, including book publishers, schools, and other institutions that focused on children (Williamson, 1948, 1953). At this first meeting, Williamson (1948) noted that the group discussed future plans it had mind, including the development of a yearbook (for scholarship funds and to help fund the organization), writing articles, and organizing a Department for Gifted Children within the National Education Association.

Just under a year later, the AAGC held its first annual meeting on November 14, 1947. At this meeting, one of the paramount points of discussion centered around outlets in which articles on gifted children could be published to disseminate information. In addition, other deliberations included identifying gifted children; ways of helping teachers and parents to understand issues surrounding the gifted; the relationship of the association to industries and professional organizations seeking personnel with special talents, to organizations offering scholarships and awards, and to motion pictures and radio; and proposals for publications (Williamson, 1948).

The AAGC had many supporters, among them Paul Witty, who realized the influence that such an organization and other organizations like it could have. He noted (p. 79), "It is hoped that the work of the American Association for Gifted Children and other organizations will lead to more widespread efforts to care for the gifted." The AAGC's goals in advancing the needs of gifted children lay in activities focused on gifted children. These included (1) developing a widespread understanding of the nature and needs of gifted children, (2) training more effective teachers to work with this population, (3) improving relationships between the school staff and parents, (4) developing more stimulating curricula, and (5) conducting more research on gifted children (Clark & Williamson, 1951, p. v).

The leaders of the organization sought to extend what was known about gifted children into mainstream education. Pauline Williamson worked with the editors of the *Journal of Teacher Education* to secure a special issue of the journal dedicated to gifted children. The issue noted the important role teachers played and an understanding of gifted children was paramount (Strang, 1954).

Perhaps the organization's most important and lasting contribution was the publication of *The Gifted Child* in 1951 (Witty, 1951). Edited by Paul Witty, the book provided an overview of important issues and research in the field of gifted education. In the introduction, Clark (Clark & Williamson, 1951, p. v), then-president of the AAGC, expressed the organization's need to "enlarge[e] our concept of ability and ... the discovery of better ways to identify the gifted in many different fields. And it is particularly interested in furthering educational opportunities for gifted children and youth."

The Gifted Child played a pivotal role in the organization's growth and was representative of the type of materials that the AAGC member strived to produce in advancing the needs of gifted children. Williamson (1953, p. 123) described the work of the members:

> Members of AAGC are responsible for its growth through: Preparation and distribution of literature including bulletins, articles, and the book, *The Gifted Child*; conferences with local, national and international groups; speeches; informal discussions; seminars; workshops; courses for teachers; administration of special schools; research; cooperation with other professional groups on joint programs; and correspondence with parents, professional, business and government leaders, as well as with administrators, teachers, and students in universities, colleges, high schools, and elementary schools.

The AAGC remained in New York City until 1986 when it moved to Wright State University in Ohio, where its mission focused on "minority gifted and health care professionals" (AAGC, 1999, para. 10). Currently, AAGC is housed at Duke University. Although it does not have a standing membership, the organization continues to offer scholarships and resources to the gifted education community (AAGC, 1999).

National Association for Gifted Children

The National Association for Gifted Children (NAGC) grew out of the determined efforts of Ann Fabe Isaacs, a concerned parent advocate rather than a researcher. After the birth of her first child, Ann earned a master's degree in counseling and guidance in 1950. Ann envisioned a different path for herself when compared to most married women in post-World War II America. She established a preschool in her own home which included many of the children from the family's Cincinnati neighborhood. Drawing on her background in counseling, Isaacs administered the Stanford–Binet IQ test to her preschool attendees. In following their progress into school, she observed how those students with the highest IQs did not fare well when they eventually enrolled in formal schooling. This phenomenon puzzled Isaacs and upon further inquiry came to realize this was not an isolated incident. This discovery provided the focus and almost obsession-like quality to her life's work over the next several decades of her life (Rogers, 2014). She would lead the organization for its first two decades until her singular point of view was challenged by a changing membership and "Ann was summarily 'discharged' by John Gowan on November 1, 1973" (Rogers, 2014, p. 268), which altered the tenor and trajectory of the organization, allowing researchers in the field to take a greater role in its direction.

Founded nearly a decade after AAGC in 1954, NAGC was a non-profit organization with three main objectives:

> (a) the formation of an association, (b) the publication of a journal, and (c) the establishment of a fund for [the] gifted with which to sponsor research and aid school systems who wished to embark on programs for their gifted.
> *(Isaacs, 1957, p. 2)*

One of the main distinguishing factors between the two organizations was Isaacs' determination to establish a journal. AAGC had failed to do so, instead concentrating on disseminating research and information through alternative outlets. By February of 1955, Isaacs had identified a tentative editorial board consisting of 30 gifted education researchers, including Lewis M. Terman, Paul Witty, Robert Havighurst, Walter Barbe, Nicholas Mosely, Norma Cutts, and A. Harry Passow. Terman deemed the list of board members "excellent" and suggested that the publication be titled *The Gifted Child* or *Gifted Child* (personal communication, February 21, 1955, in Terman, 1910–1992). Isaacs pressed for a monthly publication, but Terman interceded as he felt that there was not enough material to fit a monthly publication, and more practically the printing budget would be too costly:

> I agree with you that it would be desirable if possible to have a journal devoted entirely to articles on gifted children. However, printing costs have soared terribly in recent years and one would have to be pretty sure that the subscriptions would pay the costs. I would suggest that some group be persuaded to explore the financial situation and to make plans for the journal if it decided to launch one.
> *(personal communication, May 10, 1954, in Terman, 1910–1992)*

Even though Terman agreed to the idea of a new publication, he was perplexed as to why Isaacs thought another organization was required, even noting that he "was under the impression that the National Association for Gifted Children was the American Assn. for Gifted Children" (personal communication, December 29, 1955, in Terman, 1910–1992). He queried Isaacs:

> Now I am wondering why there should be a national association in addition to American Association. Certainly many people would be confused and will probably prefer to support the American Assn which was organized some years ago and which was responsible for the splendid book edited by Witty, entitled, THE GIFTED CHILD.
> *(personal communication, December 29, 1955, in Terman, 1910–1992)*

Isaacs replied to Terman, justifying her position:

> I am a life member of the American Association for Gifted Children and know of the Fine [sic] A.A.G.C. public which Dr. Witty edited THE GIFTED CHILD. He is also a member of our Board. Our N.A.G.C. was formed with a number of purposes in mind. You may recall our discussing them briefly when I had the pleasure of talking to you on the phone last summer, and you had agreed to be on our board. We hope to unify and establish new local study groups, create a fund for graduate research on gifted and to work with parent groups.
> *(personal communication to L. M. Terman, January 12, 1956, in Terman, 1910–1992)*

Isaacs's moxy and determination played a key role in making NAGC the leading advocacy organization in gifted education more than a half a century later, with AAGC exerting little influence or relevancy (Rogers, 2014).

The first issue of the *Gifted Child Newsletter* was published in January 1957; it later became *Gifted Child Quarterly*—the research journal that Isaacs envisioned. NAGC planned to publish the newsletter for one year and then transition to a quarterly journal once funding was confirmed. Isaacs remained its editor for 18 years (Isaacs, 1974), until researchers within the membership challenged her editorialship. Isaacs, originally a preschool teacher, was well versed in the literature, but was not a standard journal editor of peer-reviewed publications and her editorship perhaps obstructed the growth of the journal in many ways as her focus remained on advocacy rather than pushing the research trajectory of the field (Rogers, 2014).

Like the AAGC, the NAGC encouraged membership among those interested in advancing the needs of gifted children and held annual meetings. In the early years of the organization, NAGC often held their annual meeting in conjunction with organizations who had similar interests. For example, in 1956 the meeting was held with the American Association for the Advancement of Science (Isaacs, 1968). Robert Havinghurst, a professor at the University of Chicago and author of the influential *Educating Gifted Children* (with Robert DeHaan, 1957) suggested that NAGC's primary role should be one of leadership, and this was the direction the organization appropriated. *Gifted Child Quarterly* is now recognized as the premiere journal for published research in gifted education and has been advancing in special education and educational psychology journal rankings.

A third organization would emerge in 1958 as a Special Interest Division of the Council for Exceptional Children. The Council originated in 1922 as the International Council for the Education of Exceptional Children at Teachers College in New York City (Kode, 2002). In 1953, Special Interest Divisions were organized and in 1958 The Association for the Gifted (CEC-TAG) was established. In 1978, CEC-TAG would establish its own research journal, *The Journal for the Education of the Gifted* (CEC-TAG, n.d.).

The emergence of these gifted organizations was also supported by the renewed interest in gifted education beginning not long after the close of World War II. In 1948, James B. Conant (p. 52) had shared his own "wish [that] some organization identified in the public mind with concern for all American youth would take some dramatic action to demonstrate a vigorous interest in the gifted boy or girl." AAGC, CEC-TAG, and NAGC helped to fill this void and assumed their advocacy role for gifted children (Witty, 1954).

Researcher/Advocate

With the establishment of organizations like the AAGC, NAGC, and CEC-TAG the researcher/advocate emerged as a new role in the field in the second half of the 20th century. Several notable examples include Paul Witty and Ruth Strang.

Paul Witty

The establishment of these advocacy groups provided a new role for researchers—one of advocate—whereby researchers would actively use their research findings to press for appropriate school provisions alongside teachers and parents. Among the most active and stalwart of this group was Paul Witty. A native of Indiana born just before the turn of the 20th century, Paul Witty initially attended Indiana State Teachers College, where he was introduced to the ideas and theories of Sir Francis Galton, William James, G. Stanley Hall, and Charles Darwin (D. C. Heath, 1946).

In 1920, he eventually found his way to Teachers College, Columbia University, to study in the Department of Psychology, where he received his M.A. (1923) and Ph.D. (1931). At the time, E. L. Thorndike, John Dewey, and Leta Hollingworth occupied the faculty at Teachers College, providing a fertile environment for the study of psychology. In 1924, he took a position at the University of Kansas as the director of the Psycho-Educational Clinic, where Witty began his study of gifted children. Witty's "A Study of One Hundred Gifted Children" examined children who had a reported IQ of 140 or above. Witty concluded that his results did not diverge much from Terman's and Hollingworth's studies (Jolly & Robbins, 2014).

Witty differed from conventional thinking by suggesting that real genius included not only aptitude but also must be accompanied by drive (or motivation) and opportunity (Witty, 1930). Witty and Lehman (1927, p. 366) felt that "the importance of capacity is over-emphasized and the significance of drive neglected or under-estimated." IQ measures such as the Stanford–Binet did not measure such constructs as drive and Witty's research focused on determining the factors that caused some children to achieve while others, equally capable, failed to thrive (Witty & Lehman, 1927).

In 1930, Witty accepted a position of Professor of Education and Director of the Psycho-Educational Clinic at Northwestern University and would remain until his retirement in 1966. Witty would also be one of the first researchers in the field to accept a Black doctoral student, Martin Jenkins. Jenkins's research drew attention to the achievement and potential of African American gifted students (Jolly & Robins, 2014). In the 1930s, African American students were "invariably described as being inferior to the average white child" (Witty & Jenkins, 1934, p. 585). Nearly a decade later, Witty and Theman's case studies extended Witty and Jenkins's initial work and provided examples that were contrary to this deficient view and long-held biased views of gifted African American students (Theman & Witty, 1943). Theman, who was Witty's graduate student, would later go on to be director of Northwestern University's Children's School.

Another influential student of Witty's, Walter Barbe was the long-time editor of *Highlights Magazine*, and past president of the NAGC and CEC–TAG. Witty described how he came to be Witty's student and the enduring influence he had in Barbe's life:

> I chose Dr. Witty to be my major professor and advisor at Northwestern. I was in my last quarter of my junior year … was a math major who commuted 4 hours a day and had to have a course on Wednesday evening. The math class was cancelled so I took the only other possible Wednesday night class [Psycho-Educational Clinic], for which I had none of the prerequisites, but no one seemed to care. I had been working the night shift in the Pullman factory and wondered what I had gotten myself in to. (Dr. Witty was elegant looking, dressed and groomed impeccably, a complete gentleman, while I was poorly dressed and as a result of the factory work, not always completely clean).
>
> *(Barbe, personal communication to Jennifer L. Jolly, December 14, 2012)*

Under Witty's direction, Barbe would conduct a follow-up study on gifted children who participated in Cleveland's Major Works Program. And "to

Dr. Witty I can only say, 'Thank you for an exciting and great life'" (Barbe, personal communication, December 14, 2012).

Witty also used popular media to provide opportunities for gifted children to showcase their abilities. *Quiz Kids*, a popular quiz format radio program during the 1940s and 1950s, featured children with advanced aptitude who competed for prizes of savings bonds. Witty was instrumental in recruiting children from the greater Chicago area and served as the show's advisor—providing the show a sense of legitimacy—and administering individual intelligence tests to many of the children who participated (Barbe, personal communication, December 14, 2012).

Martin Jenkins

The early work by conducted by Terman and Hollingworth treated minority students in gifted populations as outliers and rather unexpected occurrences. The deeply held hereditarian beliefs tied race to IQ, leading many researchers and school personnel to disregard certain races of school children with high intellect. Paul Witty was one the first researchers to seriously begin researching minority gifted students, and he also mentored graduate students of color. Together, Witty and his various students would begin to challenge these beliefs (Jolly & Robins, 2014).

This view began to change with the work of Martin Jenkins, a former student of Paul Witty's. A line of research initiated in 1935 with Jenkins's dissertation and would continue until Jenkins began his tenure as administrator in higher education (Davis, 2014). After an initial career in engineering, Jenkins decided to study psychology and caught the notice of Witty. "[Witty] was an early supporter of the belief that Blacks were also gifted—he was not prejudiced toward any group of people" (Barbe, personal communication, December 14, 2012). Similarly, Witty and Jenkins both hailed from Terre Haute, IN, and had attended Indiana Normal School. Jenkins then began his studies with Witty at Northwestern, which had an established history of educating African American students (Davis, 2014).

Jenkins's work was particularly innovative. For the first time, the research made a purposeful attempt to distinguish Black children who did not have any White ancestry in their families (Davis, 2014; Kearney & LeBlanc, 1993; Witty & Jenkins, 1935). This case study provided great detail regarding a high-achieving African American student with an IQ of 200 (Witty & Jenkins, 1935). The evidence from the case was intended for use with the identification of racially diverse students.

In 1943, Jenkins published an article featuring the case studies of 14 Negro children with IQs 160 and above. The study sought "(1) to ascertain the origin and characteristics of the children in diverse populations; (2) to examine the origin and characteristics of the children; and (3) to follow the development of the subject over a period of years" (Jenkins, 1943, p. 159). In finding the children for the sample, Jenkins used mental test performance, achievement test results, school performance and progress, parents' occupation and education, family background, and racial composition. He countered the idea that African Americans with high IQs could not be found and instead proffered that individual differences should be the focus, not racial differences. Jenkins came to understand that teachers and other educators limited opportunities for African American students based on beliefs and misperceptions regarding IQ and race rather than the student's actual individual ability (Jenkins, 1943). In examining the upper limits of IQ, Jenkins found that if environments were controlled for, "there should be found a 'normal' proportion of very superior cases, and the upper limit of ability should coincide with the white population" (Jenkins, 1948, p. 399).

In 1943, Witty and Theman published research that followed up Theman's dissertation study on the educational attainment of gifted Black students. Theman's dissertation, "A Study of Negro Youth of Superior Intelligence," written in 1942, was actually the follow-up to Jenkins's dissertation, written in 1935. Witty and Theman's findings included (1) educational attainment on the Myer-Ruch High School Progress test was above average, but not up to the level expected of these children based on mental tests in 1934; (2) mean percentile rank on the Iowa Every-Pupil Test in Understanding of Contemporary Affairs was slightly above average; (3) GPAs for all but two students were above average; (4) a stronger interest in school was evidenced than for gifted White students; (5) English was the students' favorite subject, followed by science, chemistry, French, and history, in that order; and (6) all but one set of parents indicated their child had an interest in college (Witty & Theman, 1943).

These studies clearly illustrated that students of color were found in gifted populations and successfully challenged some of the long-held beliefs concerning race and IQ. However, systematic investigations faltered over time and were only reengaged in the later part of the 20th century.

Ruth Strang

Another example of researcher/advocate is Ruth Strang. Strang's involvement in gifted education emanated from the strong foundation established at Teachers College by Leta Hollingworth. Strang also benefitted from the early female professoriate that was supported at Teachers College. Her path to higher education was an unlikely one, as her academic aspirations were not supported by her father but by her older brother (Kronborg, 2014). First earning a B.S. in home economics in 1920, she followed this up in 1926 with a Ph.D. and finally became a member of the faculty in 1929. Gifted children were just one of several areas of Strang's research, which also included health education, guidance education, and reading development. Her scholarship in gifted education reflected the changing views about giftedness. She proffered a definition that represented inclusivity and supported the use of multiple measures to identify gifted students. In addition, Strang recognized that the interactions between environment and native ability influenced the development or trajectory of a gifted child over time (Melnik, 1960).

Strang also combined her research in reading and counseling with the study of gifted children. She suggested that autobiographies could meet the social and emotional needs of gifted children, where they may find public and historical figures who held similar interests (Burgess, 1971). As a founding member of the American Association for Gifted Children, she played an integral role in the advocacy movement afoot during the 1950s.

19
CREATIVITY AS AN EMPIRICAL INVESTIGATION

Each year the President of the American Psychological Association addresses the members of the association. 1950 was no exception. J. P. Guilford's Presidential APA address was a clarion call for research into the nature of creativity (Bycroft, 2012; Rhodes, 1961; Runco, 2000–2001). J. P. Guilford's presidential address and later his Structure of the Intellect (SOI) did much to influence the concept of intelligence, creativity, and the field of gifted education. Guilford, a professor at the University of Southern California, was one of the first researchers to propose to both psychologists and educators a move away from a unitary view of intelligence to a multidimensional interpretation. The SOI submitted that individuals could possess up to 120 different intellectual abilities (Guilford, 1959). Guilford's work prompted the systematic inquiry into the multifaceted nature of giftedness (Goldberg, 1958).

Researchers answered this appeal, engaging in a surge of research around creative constructs and processes (Bycroft, 2012). Studies of highly creative of children also provided a new line of inquiry within gifted education. While attempting to differentiate the highly intelligent from the highly creative, Torrance (1959, p. 312) found that

> Members of the highly creative group rated in the upper 20 per cent in their classes on the creativity measure but not in the upper per cent on traditional measures on IQ. Members of the highly intelligent group ranked in the upper 20 per cent on measures of IQ but not creativity. ... Although there was a mean difference of 25.6 IQ points between the highly intelligent and the highly creative groups, there was no statistically significant difference on any of the achievement measures.

School did not provide an encouraging outlook for highly creative children and their long-term outcomes. Studies of highly creative children in schools found they suffered from isolation. These children also did not suffer fools gladly, sought to have their reputations as being highly creative noticed immediately, developed a reputation for being disruptive, and had no inclination to acclimate to the majority group (Torrance, 1959). These studies and others helped to reveal what schools could do differently to meet the needs of creative children. This work would continue to be developed into the following decades, concentrating on instrument development for identification of creative behavior and programs and strategies for creativity development (Sternberg & Lubart, 1999).

One indicator of the resoluteness with which researchers responded to Guilford's call was in the number of centers devoted to studying the different aspects of creativity. Many of the centers also housed the top creativity researchers of the era. Guilford established his own center at the University of Southern California to develop instruments to measure creative thinking. Calvin Taylor at the University of Utah focused on education and organizational factors. At the University of California Berkeley, Donald MacKinnon and Frank Barron studied how creativity was required in certain fields to attain eminence. At Pennsylvania State University, Viktor Lowenfield investigated creativity and its relationship to art education. J. W. Getzels and Phillip Jackson at the University of Chicago sought to better understand the link between school achievement and creative thinking in high school students. Meanwhile, at the University of Buffalo, Alex Osborn and subsequently Sidney Parnes studied the process of brainstorming by groups and individuals (Bycroft, 2012). E. Paul Torrance, initially at the University of Minnesota and then at the University of Georgia, focused on instrument development and classroom factors influencing creative thinking (Torrance, 1959). The collective efforts of these centers, researchers, and other scholars in the field would double the output in empirical studies in creativity between 1950 and 1956 and influence the field of gifted education in forthcoming decades (Guilford, 1967).

Summary

With America's entrance into World War II, the country's main energies were directed toward achieving victory in the Pacific and European theaters of war. As the nation emerged victorious from this worldwide conflict, it found itself in a much different situation than most of its allies. Not having been occupied during the war, its infrastructure was wholly intact, which left the United States in a position of power in terms of both its physical and human resources. Although the war did elevate America to its status as the new world leader, it also revealed some major faults in human resource weaknesses, especially in the areas of science and technology. These areas of weakness presented gifted and talented students and young people the opportunity to have their needs reexamined.

The field of gifted education began to establish the structural criteria needed for growth, based on the foundations established by the early pioneers such as Lewis Terman and Leta Hollingworth. This included academic recognition by other fields, continued generation of new knowledge, research journals, professional and advocacy associations, and research conferences (Fensham, 2004). Additional activities helping to sustain field building included a diffusion of recognized practices aimed at gifted students in schools and legislation to support talented youth and their educational needs. At the close of the 1950s, as the NDEA had recently been passed by Congress, the future of gifted education appeared encouraging. However, as patterns repeat, another window of neglect was just on the horizon with the beginning of the new decade and an alternative set of educational priorities.

SECTION IV

20
BUILDING AND SUSTAINING CAPACITY

After the passage of the National Defense Education Act (NDEA) in 1958, primacies in the 1960s shifted to long overdue priorities of social justice, equity, and the civil rights of America's most marginalized and disadvantaged student populations (Corn, 1999; Cross, 1999; Gallagher, 1994). Federal legislation codifying these issues was contained in Title VI of the Civil Rights Act of 1964 (P.L. 88–352), which captured education programs and activities in states receiving federal assistance for these activities:

> No person in the United States shall, on the ground of race, color, or national origin, be excluded from participation in, be denied the benefits of, or be subjected to discrimination under any program or activity receiving Federal financial assistance.

P.L. 88-352 provided the mechanism to improve the education for children of color and push forward the desegregation of schools, which had been systematically dismissed by a large majority of state and federal educational institutions up until this point in America's history (Corn, 1999; Ford, 2011).

By the opening of the 1960s, signs were clear that NDEA would fail to provide sustainable long-term infrastructure for gifted education. Several years since its passage, the initial excitement and interest shown for gifted children and talented youth, spurred on by the launch of Sputnik I in 1957, had all but fallen off the radar of many educationalists and policy makers. Additionally, research in gifted education slowed tremendously, leaving the field unable to maintain the sizeable research output that it had begun to initiate under the NDEA legislation. These changing priorities also witnessed some school districts deprioritizing gifted programming, with the most vulnerable programs disappearing altogether. Well-established programs like those in Cleveland, OH, and San Diego, CA, did continue to offer programs and services.

After nearly a decade of educational attentions being drawn elsewhere, the close of the 1960s would present opportunities for the field of gifted education to reassert itself. The banner of gifted education was once again raised and another period of interest occurred. Although this period, too, would be short lived, the field would be in a better position to take measures to secure its future and somewhat insulate itself from the erratic and volatile educational landscape through capacity building undertaken throughout the 1970s and early 1980s, allowing for sustainment over time even when state and federal forces contracted and expanded in terms of funding and interest. This would include the cultivation of a cadre of researchers, practitioners, and advocates across the United States. These combined efforts would serve the field well over time.

Federal Interposition

The NDEA heralded a significant shift in the federal government's involvement in state education and federal funding at the close of the 1950s. Although the 1960s witnessed a declining interest in gifted education, federal interest and participation in the public education of American school children signaled the beginning of a dramatic increase and extension. With the passage of the Elementary and Secondary Education Act of 1965, the federal government invested $1 billion dollars into public education to support the education of poor and underserved children (Thomas & Brady, 2005). Federal government spending would only continue to expand with subsequent decades, even including gifted education at some minor level.

Prior to the 1960s, federal involvement and spending in America's schools was negligible. The Democratic candidate for President of the United States, John F. Kennedy, introduced his domestic program's agenda, New Frontiers, at the Democratic National Convention in July of 1960. One of the *frontiers* identified was that of education. After winning the presidential election, in his Special Message to Congress on Education in February of 1961, now-President Kennedy further outlined his education plans. Here he recognized that the federal government's obligation to educational matters had evolved in response to the Cold War (like those included in NDEA) and now included domestic issues:

> We do not undertake to meet our growing educational problems merely to compare our achievements with those of our adversaries. These measures are justified on their own merits—in times of peace as well as peril, to educate better citizens as well as better scientists and soldiers. The Federal Government's responsibility in this area has been established since the

earliest days of the Republic—it is time now to act decisively to fulfil that responsibility for the sixties.

(Kennedy, 1961, para. 33)

In addition to the ongoing Cold War threat, the United States was facing significant domestic educational challenges, which included the fact that one-quarter of the American K–20 schools were in a state of disrepair or suffering from unsustainable infrastructure. Kennedy acknowledged that, in order for the United States to attain a standard of excellence, efforts would need to cater to the population born during the previous 15 years and to assist elementary and secondary schools and colleges and universities. An increase in teacher credentialing standards and raises in teacher salaries were also necessary, in addition to the needs of special education students.

Kennedy's older sister, Rosemary, had been born with an intellectual disability. Through his family's interest in those individuals with special needs, he witnessed first-hand the benefits special education could have and its potential impact on a larger scale (Kennedy, 1961). Unfortunately, many of Kennedy's overarching educational initiatives were halted with his assassination and stalled with Congress.

After Lyndon B. Johnson assumed the presidency, his public policy agenda, the Great Society, provided Johnson his own policy identity, which was cast as a set of initiatives to tackle the challenges of poverty (Kantor, 1991). Johnson (1964, pp. 230–231) noted:

> The Great Society is a place where every child can find knowledge to enrich his mind and enlarge his talents. It is a place where leisure is a welcome chance to build and reflect, not feared cause of boredom and restlessness. It is a place where the city of man serves not only the needs of the body and the demands of commerce, but the desire for beauty and the hunger for community. ... Our society will not be great until every young mind is set free to scan the farthest reaches of thought and imagination. ... We must seek an educational system which grows in excellence as it grows in size.

From Johnson's description, it would seem that all students, including the country's gifted and talented youth, would be included in the Great Society's educational vision. However, the initial work on education legislation would instead focus on the assumptions made about education attainment and its link to eradicating poverty, which was a core tenet of the Great Society. The resulting legislation, the Elementary and Secondary Education Act of 1965 (ESEA), permanently altered the federal government's role in the educational lives of American students: "The result was to give the federal government a distinct new role in defining the nation's educational priorities and to make federal policy a central focus of the struggles over access to schooling and control of educational policy" (Kantor, 1991, p. 49). ESEA became a defining policy initiative of the Johnson administration and his presidency, creating the mechanism to long-term federal intervention into state educational matters (Rury, 2015).

21

CONTINUED GROWTH, CREATIVITY RESEARCH, AND IMPLEMENTATION

The momentum in gifted education did slow after the initial impetus from NDEA subsided. However, the research in the field of creativity did not reflect this trend. Following Guildford's APA address in 1950, which is often cited as the origin for the experimental research on creativity, research efforts grew exponentially (Rhodes, 1961; Runco, 2000–2001). Nearly a decade and a half after his speech, Guilford recognized the mainstream appeal that creativity had also gained (Bycroft, 2012) while some researchers lamented that "the words creative and creativity [were] ... loosely used and overused" (Rhodes, 1961, p. 306). Under NDEA, the identification of talented youth revealed that schools still relied heavily on IQ testing for identifying giftedness, prescribing classroom grouping, and assigning school-based programs (Jolly, 2009). Moving into the 1970s, the work done in creativity and by creativity researchers helped to expand the concept of giftedness, as well as develop instruments for the measurement of creativity and consideration of how creativity might be cultivated in children. For example, Calvin Taylor and E. Paul Torrance represented a group of researchers who impacted both the fields of gifted education and creativity.

A native of Georgia, E. Paul Torrance began as a high school teacher and served for a short time as principal. During his tenure as principal he dealt with two young male students who were troublesome yet very creative and would go on to achieve high levels of success in their adult lives. The experience with these two young men would stay with Torrance as he advanced through his career and further research (Hébert, Cramond, Speirs Neumeister, Millar, & Silvian, 2002). After working for the military as a psychologist, Torrance eventually completed his doctoral studies at the University of Michigan in 1951.

In 1958, Torrance's creativity research began in earnest at the University of Minnesota. Inspired by Guilford's work, Torrance began devising an assessment to measure creativity, specifically divergent thinking and problem solving using figural and verbal tasks. This included the figural portion of the test, which assessed the abilities of fluency, elaboration, originality, resistance to premature closure, and abstractness of titles, while the verbal section focused on fluency, flexibility, and originality (Torrance, 1972). This assessment came to be known as the Torrance Tests of Creative Thinking (TTCT) and part of "the psychometric revolution of measuring creativity" (Sternberg & Lubart, 1999, p. 7). His work in creativity continued with his appointment as Professor and Chair of the Department of Educational Psychology, Research and Measurement at the University of Georgia (Hébert, 2014; Hébert et al., 2002).

Calvin Taylor, unlike many of his contemporaries who worked in gifted education, did not come from a background teaching in public schools. Instead he earned his Ph.D. in psychology under L. L. Thurstone at the University of Chicago in 1946 and it was here that he became interested in creativity (Anonymous, 2001). Intellectually precocious, he had skipped several grades as a child and finished high school at 15 years old. Taylor took a faculty position at the University of Utah upon completing his doctoral studies and remained at the institution for the entirety of his career (Cohen, Austin, & Odoardi, 2014). Taylor organized and hosted ten conferences on Scientific Creativity funded by the National Science Foundation from 1955 to 1970. These critical conferences provided a common gathering point for creativity researchers to share their research and findings as the field grew and matured (Cohen et al., 2014).

Creativity researchers like Torrance and Taylor recognized the impact that creativity research could have on gifted education, especially the limitations of IQ-centric indicators of giftedness. Taylor (1960, p. 8) stated, "Results to date indicate that creative talent is not measured well by the use of IQ tests. The nature of traditional intelligence tests does not directly involve the ability to create new ideas or new things."

The work done in the area of creativity and its assessment resulted in the evolving definition of giftedness. Getzels and Jackson (1958, p. 75) argued that "the term 'gifted child' has become synonymous with the expression 'child with a high IQ,' thus blinding us to other forms of excellence." Over time it became apparent that IQ tests were not "within the universe of intellectual functions themselves ... an adequate sampling of *all* these functions" (Getzels & Jackson, 1958, p. 75).

Creativity and its intersection with the educational needs of gifted children developed as a dimension of creativity research and an area of concern and discussion. Torrance (1971, p. 220) lamented,

> By the time a child enters school for the first time he is on his way to learning the skills of finding out by asking questions. When he enters

school, however, the teacher begins asking all the questions and the child has little chance to ask questions. Further the teacher's questions are rarely asked to gain information. The teacher almost always knows the answer. ... Questions in the classroom are usually to find out whether the child knows something that the teachers know.

Taylor (1960, p. 12) also supported shifting the emphasis on what should be taught: "Education may teach people to recite the past and repeat past performances more often than to prepare them to develop new things or even be ready for new developments by others." These types of classroom environments did little to support the needs of students who were highly able and/or creative in their thinking. Models to develop creativity in the classroom and address teacher dispositions became a part of the discourse to integrate greater creativity into the classroom. Taylor's Multiple Talent Model provided students opportunities to display talents in a range of areas including academics, creativity, decision-making, planning, forecasting, communication, implementing, human relations, and discerning opportunities. These talents could then be incorporated into the development of the curriculum for the gifted (Taylor, 1986). This underscored Guilford's research findings, where he had found that some children scoring in the high IQ range were at the same time scoring low on divergent production, classifying this group as "creative underachievers" and suggesting that "development of creative skills in the gifted group promises the greatest payoff for individuals and for society" (Guilford, 1972, p. 240).

By the 1960s, much progress had also been made in designing measures of creativity, which would be important as the definition of giftedness became multifaceted and called for multiple measures when identifying gifted children. One of the standouts in this group was the Minnesota Tests of Creativity, later to be known as the TTCT. Constructed by E. Paul Torrance and his colleagues, this test of divergent thinking is still used today (Hébert et al., 2002). Torrance's longitudinal studies, using the TTCT to establish predictive validity, began in the 1950s with successive data collections over the next 50 years. Results revealed that particular creative manifestations and school achievement are impacted by divergent thinking (Hébert, 2014).

The gradual acceptance of creativity as a construct in gifted education prompted the proposition of the creative gifted as a new category in Special Education or Exceptional Children at the annual meeting of NAGC in 1967 (Torrance, 1979). The underlying rationale for this additional category flowed from the evidence that "there are many creative children whose problem behavior stems from differences between them and other children and between them and their teachers" (Torrance, 1979, p. 354), which caused handicapping conditions for them at school. When creatively gifted children are offered an array of strategies, supports, and resources, "they are motivated to learn in creative ways, to solve problems in creative ways, and to live in creative ways" (Torrance, 1979, p. 371).

Governor's Schools

After the fervor from the NDEA had subsided, in-school services for gifted and talented students remained limited, and alternative educational options were explored to address the academic and affective needs of gifted students. Governor's Schools were one response in these efforts. In Rickover's *Education and Freedom* (1959), a series of 25 demonstration schools had been suggested as an alternative method to educate the country's most able students. This was generally not supported and characterized as anti-democratic. However, in the 1963, the first Governor's School was established. These were not demonstration schools, as Rickover had envisioned, but instead initially dedicated to educating predominately gifted children, teach a wide range of accelerated and enriched content, address the affective needs of children during the summer months, and supplement traditional schooling. These schools became increasingly popular and diverse in their foci and offerings during the 1970s and 1980s (Winkler, Stephenson, & Jolly, 2012).

The very first Governor's School, founded in North Carolina, was initially designed as a summer program to augment the education that gifted students received during the regular school year and keep this population interested in their educational pursuits (Bray, 1991). Virgil Ward, a researcher in gifted education at the University of Virginia, spearheaded the movement to offer gifted students a differentiated curriculum based on his axiomatic focusing on the whole child, these types of curricular offerings came to fruition at the North Carolina Governor's School (Henshon, 2014; Ward, 1961).

With support from the Carnegie Foundation and other stakeholders from across the state of North Carolina, the school operated as an arm of public education. Through a series of competitive auditions in the fine and performing arts, 400 high school students were recruited to participate in a seven-week tuition-free program. Teachers were selected from high schools and colleges from around the state. The school was to be an exemplar "in differential education for the gifted, the first such institution" (Ward, 1979, p. 209). In 1964 the second Governor's School in the United States opened at McNeese University in Lake Charles, LA, with funding provided by the state (GPGC, n.d.). Underachieving and/or students with behavior problems were the original focus of the school. Dr. George Middleton led the efforts to offer a Summer Enrichment Program (SEP) in hopes of alleviating underachievement and misbehavior in the school's students. During the intake process, he realized after the administration of an IQ test that many of the students were actually highly gifted and were in need of more stimulating and challenging curriculum and activities that could be provided at McNeese's Governor's School (Winkler et al., 2012).

Governor's Schools continue to offer accelerated and enrichment options for gifted students in locations across the United States. Between 15 and 20 schools operate and are largely dependent on state budgets, as most schools remain either tuition-free or with very low fee structures (National Conference of Governor's Schools, n.d.). These schools represented one of the early networks created during this period, by providing innovative educational opportunities to meet the needs of gifted students. Although this intervention addressed an educational need, summer opportunities were not going to address the long-term necessities of America's most able students in public schools.

Studies of Mathematically Precocious Youth

In addition to Governor's Schools, talent searches and academic summer programs were instituted to shore up insufficient age-grade instruction offered in schools (Stanley, 1996). One of the earliest and best examples of these types of offerings was initiated in 1971 by Julian Stanley at Johns Hopkins University. This study set out to understand how to identify potential and develop the talent of mathematically talented youth. The study—inspired by Stanley's meeting in 1968 with a precocious 12-year-old, Joseph Bates, whose parents had arranged for Joseph to take a computer science course at Johns Hopkins—forged what has now evolved into a nearly 50-year study, with additional cohorts over the decades (Clynes, 2016; Stanley, 1996). Stanley recognized the limitations of IQ measures and sought other assessments to identify special abilities that provided information as to "type and pace of instruction" in content specific areas (Stanley, 1980, p. 8). After its initiation, the study was transferred to Camilla P. Benbow in 1986 and conducted from Iowa State, until it was moved to Vanderbilt University in 1998, where data is still being collected (Lubinski & Benbow, 2006). The data collected, and results of these studies emphasize the importance of providing appropriate academic, social, and emotional support to those with exceptional precocity in mathematics, using individualized instruction based on diagnostic testing (Stanley, 1980, 1996).

22
THE MARLAND REPORT

With the passage of ESEA in 1965, the federal government's role in public education significantly and irrevocably changed. This amplified federal role provided a pathway for a renewed interest in gifted education from the federal government (Thomas & Brady, 2005). Nearly a decade had passed since the NDEA, and the needs of gifted students began to surface once again. Sponsored by Representative John Erlenborn (R-IL) and Senator Jacob Javits (D-NY), the Gifted and Talented Children's Educational Assistance Act (1969) (P.L. 91-320, Section 806) offered the opportunity to review and evaluate the current state of gifted education. The amendment charged the U.S. Commissioner of Education

> (a) to discover the extent to which special education provisions were necessary to meet the needs of gifted and talented children, (b) to discover whether any existing federal programs were currently meeting some of those needs, (c) to evaluate how programs of federal educational assistance could become more effective in meeting these needs, and (d) to recommend what new programs were needed to meet them.
> *(Jackson, 1979, p. 46)*

Javits and Erlenborn both recognized that while the educational needs of disadvantaged children required addressing, this left the needs of gifted children woefully lacking, especially as gifted students were not a group directly addressed in ESEA. The lack of acknowledgment during this testimony that students could be both disadvantaged and gifted also illustrates the limited understanding of gifted and talented children and their diversity. In Erlenborn and Javits's testimony on behalf of the proposed legislation, they highlighted the responsibility of the federal government to act. On January 28, 1969, Javits testified in the Senate, noting:

> Today, a decade since the passage of NDEA, the Federal effort toward meeting the needs of the gifted and talented has diminished to the point that there is not one single Federal law or program devoting significant resources toward the education of gifted and talented youth, nor does the U.S. Office of Education employ anyone with responsibility in this area.
> *(Gifted and Talented Children's Educational Assistance Act, 1969a).*

Javits hoped P.L. 91-320 would mark the beginning of a long-term investment in the education of highly able children. During his testimony in the House, Representative Erlenborn voiced his belief that equal concern should be given to gifted children as it was given to

> educationally and culturally disadvantaged children .... [W]e are forgetting this other group of gifted and talented. I think that we are really going to do, if we continue down this road, is more toward mediocrity. We will be raising those from the lower level and bypassing those on the upper level and come out with mediocrity. I don't think this should be our goal. I think we should have a goal of giving the greatest opportunity to all. Let us raise those who have the greatest disadvantage and the greatest learning disabilities but let us also reach the greatest potential for the gifted and talented at the same time.
> *(Gifted and Talented Children's Educational Assistance Act, 1969b)*

Members of Congress were persuaded to act and the ESEA Amendments of 1969 (P.L. 91-320), Section 806, "Provisions Related to the Gifted and Talented Children," was passed. However, the bill did not provide for the inclusion of additional or future funding. Rather, Titles III and V of ESEA now reflected the gifted and talented within the funding parameters of respective student populations. Title III, "Supplementary Educational Centers and Service," supported local education agencies' (LEA) decision-making power, as they could best determine which types of services would support their own student bodies. Title III funds could be used to assist in identifying best practices or exemplar school programs (Zettel, 1982). Monies could now be used to support gifted students if LEAs deemed necessary, but the language was not written as a requirement. The lack of required funding decreased the likelihood of directing these program and services toward gifted students.

Title V provided grants for state departments of education, as the federal government recognized that education was primarily a local issue, and Javits stressed this point during his testimony: "Congress has long realized that education is a state responsibility" (Gifted and Talented Children's Educational Assistance Act, 1969a).

State-level personnel and administration for gifted education could be supported with grant funds, as it was noted that "9 out of 10 gifted and talented children" were from states with full-time personnel and integral to the subsequent successful administration of gifted and talented identification and programming (Zettel, 1982, p. 57).

Congress conceived these amendments as precursors to additional and expansive programming, funding, and support. In 1969, the Educational Professions Development Act (EPDA) of 1967 was extended, and Title V, Part C, Section 521 of the Higher Education Act of 1965 expanded to include the gifted and talented. These later pieces of legislation focused on the needs of teachers. The EPDA would strengthen professional development, so that educators would be better prepared to work with gifted learners, and would feature significantly in the capacity-building strategies undertaken by various entities in the field. Section 521 sought to increase the number of universities and course offerings that prepared pre-service teachers to work with advanced learners (Marland, 1972a).

These new legislative authorizations put the needs of gifted children on par with the requisites of other special learners, but without the benefits of funding. However, with no mandate or additional funding to support identification, administrative programming, or curricular provisions, the needs of gifted children fell to those school personnel and administrators who understood these students' educational needs as a priority or at least as important as other identified student needs. Members of Congress recognized the dubious nature of the unfunded legislative language and questioned whether school systems and districts would diverge or divest from current projects to support gifted children. Representative John Ashbrook (R-OH) questioned the practicality of the entire situation:

> In my State there is not going to be money available and if there is the money squeeze they claim, I can't see very much coming to pass as a result of this. ... Where there is not money involved, we both know as a practical matter, that there is not going to be a whole lot done.
> *(Gifted and Talented Children's Educational Assistance Act, 1969b)*

The Commissioner of Education, under Section 806 of ESEA, was also required to determine the current condition of education throughout the states for gifted children as members of Congress wished to better understand which states and LEAs were providing services and to what extent (Marland, 1972a). U.S. Commissioner of Education James E. Allen initially began the study, but was soon removed from his position by President Nixon, who was frustrated by Allen's stance toward school integration (Finn, 2008). Allen had been increasingly critical of the Nixon administration for "moving too slowly on school desegregation" (Herbers, 1970, para. 3).

President Nixon nominated Sidney Marland Jr. in the fall of 1970 as Allen's replacement. Marland not a stranger to public service or the Washington corridor, having just finished an appointment with the Office of Economic Opportunity (OEO). His work in public schools and as a life-long educator drew the attention of policy makers and Washington insiders (Jolly & Matthews, 2014).

Marland's career in education began in 1938 as a high school English teacher in West Hartford, CT, which was interrupted by World War II and his service in the South Pacific (S. P. Marland III, personal communication to Jennifer L. Jolly, June 4, 2009). After being discharged from the Army in 1948, Marland became superintendent of schools at age 34 in Darien, CT, a bedroom community of New York City catering to corporate executives who commuted back and forth to the city. His eight years in Darien proved highly successful and launched him to his next posting in Winnetka, IL. Less than a 30-minute commute from Chicago, Winnetka typified the moneyed suburbs of the time that lay just outside major metropolitan hubs.

Carleton Washburne, Winnetka's previous superintendent, had been an early supporter of gifted education during the Progressive Era. Marland struck up a friendship with Washburne and the two collaborated on *Winnetka: The History and Significance of an Educational Experiment* in 1963 (Jolly & Matthews, 2014). Washburne had introduced the Winnetka Plan in 1922, a Progressive Era plan that supported self-paced individualized instruction and had been cited as an early model of programming for gifted students (Washburne, 1924; Witty, 1951). Marland also recognized the needs of advanced and gifted learners, offering acceleration, enrichment, and ability grouping in Winnetka schools. He advocated "high attention to the balance between creative activities and formal learning [with an] emphasis on differentiation of content consistent with individual ability" (Washburne & Marland, 1963, p. 201). Marland also systematized students' cumulative folders so that successive teachers would be aware of students' learning needs (Jolly, 2009b; Washburne & Marland, 1963).

Marland's subsequent position as superintendent of schools was markedly different from his previous two positions, but it was this position that would bring him to the attention of Washington, DC policy makers. Superintendent of Pittsburgh, PA, schools seemed an unlikely position, after the leafy suburban outposts of Darien and Winnetka. Pittsburgh presented an entirely antithetical set of challenges, unseen in his previous, solidly upper-middle-class suburban school districts. Many schools in Pittsburgh had large African American student populations, who consistently underperformed academically when compared to White students in the district. In response, Marland and his staff established a number of novel programs and policies (Jolly & Matthews, 2014). These included hiring experienced African American teachers, attracting better qualified teachers overall, building new schools, adjusting attendance zones, changing curriculum to better reflect Pittsburgh's overall school population, introducing college preparatory programs, and establishing preschool and early childhood programs (Board of Education, 1965).

The work done with preschoolers was particularly progressive for the time period and "likely did call attention to Pittsburgh and therefore to me" (Marland, 1972b). Not the first school district to try to disrupt the "the very low achievement of the child in the deprived neighborhood" (Board of Education, 1965, p. 33), Pittsburgh was part of the first wave of districts to implement early childhood education as a way to improve school readiness, while also focusing on childhood health and nutrition. These pilot programs became the model for the Office of Economic Opportunity's Operation Head Start under the direction of Sargent Shriver (Jolly & Matthews, 2014; Marland, 1972b).

Marland inherited the task of assembling the Section 806 report upon Allen's dismissal. The Marland Report could have easily been the Allen Report. For a report that is such an important part of the gifted education narrative, Sidney Marland was a relative outsider to gifted education. Still, his prior experience as a high school teacher and later superintendent provided him with experiences to signal that this student population required educational reprioritizing. He harnessed the full resources and expertise of the Office of the Commissioner to assemble the report (Jolly & Matthews, 2014).

Assembling the Assets

When the Marland Report was commissioned in 1968, the U.S. Office of Education (USOE) offered no financial assistance to states or LEAs to support gifted and talented students, nor were any staff allocated at the federal level to oversee the needs of this student population (Marland, 1972a). This lack of priority and concern for gifted students was part of an ongoing trend, which had witnessed peaks and valleys of interest. Overall, the 1960s could be characterized as a low point of interest and educational priority for the gifted. After the spotlight from NDEA faded, it was difficult to isolate one sole cause for this disinterest in gifted children. Perhaps it was an amalgam of forces pushing priorities of disadvantaged children toward the forefront, combined with another round of apathy toward high-ability students, thus preventing Congress from maintaining the type of interest realized with NDEA. Marland (1972a, p. 1) noted, "For many years, interested educators, responsible legislators, and concerned parents have puzzled over the problem of educating the most gifted of our students in a public education program geared primarily to a philosophy of egalitarianism," yet harnessing any real change had been difficult to institute and sustain.

The development of the Marland Report necessitated not only commandeering the vast resources of the USOE, but also consulting experts in the field of gifted education from across the United States. Panel experts included Catherine Burch, Louis Fliegler, Joseph French, Marvin Gold, David Jackson, Ruth Martinson, Paul Plowman, Joseph Renzulli, Irving Sato, William Vassar, and Virgil Ward (Marland, 1972a). A sample of school staff and state department personnel, along with identified gifted advocates were also surveyed.

Data gathered from Project TALENT, a longitudinal study of approximately 450,000 secondary students, also informed the report. Other informants included A. Harry Passow and Abe Tannenbaum of Teachers College, Jacob Getzels of the University of Chicago (based on his work in the area of creativity), and James Gallagher.

Gallagher, now at the Frank Graham Porter Center at the University of North Carolina, had only just left his former role as Deputy Assistant Secretary for Planning, Research, and Evaluation in the Department of Health, Education, and Welfare (HEW). In his position at HEW he had testified in support of funding the Marland Report (Jolly & Robinson, 2014). During his testimony to Congress on whether students learned at different rates, Representative Quie (R-MN) inquired as to whether "one could speed up a learner"; Gallagher agreed and also added,

> I think the answer is yes and I think conversely is you can slow them down. ... If the teacher presents one program, she almost has to focus it at the medium level where the majority of the youngsters are. That means that material being presented is too easy for the youngster who is very bright. You have to develop a series of activities, which will allow each youngster ... to progress at their own rate of speed.
> *(Needs of Elementary, 1969)*

In additional testimony, he went on to speak again in support for gifted students who did not come to the immediate attention of school officials and policy makers:

> So while they do not cause great or immediate concern, or create a crisis, the way that a delinquent youngster or a youngster who is emotionally disturbed causes to the school system, we can say that particular attention paid to them has long-term benefits, not only for the individual, but also for the society.
> *(Gifted and Talented Children's Educational Assistance Act, 1969b)*

Organizations such as The Association for the Gifted (TAG) of the Council for Exceptional Children, the American Association for the Gifted, the Council of State Directors of Programs for the Gifted, and the Frank Porter Graham Child Development Center at the University of North Carolina were also asked to inform the report (Marland, 1972a). Based on these data sources, the Marland Report provided: (1) the extent to which existing special education programs were addressing the needs of gifted and talented students, (2) the identification of federal programs already employed to meet their needs, (3) the evaluation of how current programming could be more effective, and (4) the recommendation of new programming (Marland, 1972a).

Volumes 1 and 2

The results were reported out in two volumes. The report to Congress, Volume 1, described the population of gifted and talented students, provided the argument for special programming, highlighted model programming, reported the results from the survey of states, and defined the USOE's role and response. Volume 2 consisted of appendices that included background papers and the supporting documents that were used to produce the first volume. The appendices included a review of the existing research literature on gifted education, an analysis of the Advocate Survey sent to experts in the field, an analysis of the hearings held by regional commissioners of education, state laws for the gifted, selected results from Project TALENT, four case studies with exemplar programs for the gifted (California, Connecticut, Georgia, and Illinois), and a current assessment of the USOE's endeavors on behalf of gifted children.

The report's establishment of a federal definition of gifted and talented remains as its central and enduring impact on the field. The definition reflected the multidimensionality of giftedness that had been under deliberation in the prior decades, which reflected recommendations to move away from the unitary view of giftedness and strict adherence to IQ. The multifaceted definition remains largely intact today, more than 40 years later (with the exception of psychomotor ability, which was removed in 1978; Jolly & Robins, 2016). The advisory panel incorporated best practices and findings from the research literature into the recommended definition and underscored the need for multiple measures to inform identification:

> Gifted and talented children are those identified by professionally qualified persons who by virtue of outstanding abilities, are capable of high performance. These are children who require differentiated educational programs and/or services beyond those normally provided by the regular school program to realize their contribution to self and society.
>
> Children capable of high performance include those with demonstrated achievement and/or potential ability in any of the following areas, singly or in combination:
>
> 1. general intellectual ability
> 2. specific academic aptitude
> 3. creative or productive thinking
> 4. leadership ability
> 5. visual and performing arts
> 6. psychomotor ability.
>
> *(Marland, 1972a, p. 10)*

The report continued its definition by indicating:

> It can be assumed that utilization of these criteria for identification of the gifted and talented will encompass a minimum of 3 to 5 percent of the

> school population. Evidence of gifted and talented abilities maybe determined by a multiplicity of ways. These procedures should include objectives measures and professional evaluation measures, which are essential components of identification.
>
> *(Marland, 1972a, p. 11)*

The current federal definition reflects some of the qualities offered in the 1972 definition including high ability in multiple domains and the need for services outside of the normal school curricula to develop these domains fully:

> The term 'gifted and talented,' when used with respect to students, children, or youth, means students, children, or youth who give evidence of high achievement capability in areas such as intellectual, creative, artistic, or leadership capacity, or in specific academic fields, and who need services or activities not ordinarily provided by the school in order to fully develop those capabilities.
>
> *(ESEA Title IX General Provisions, SEC. 9101, 22)*

The Marland Report also exposed a lack of existing services for gifted children and the majority of prevailing services extended to a very restricted segment of the gifted population that routinely excluded underserved populations. Despite half of all states indicating some type of legislation regarding the education of gifted children, this legislation provided intent only, with no fiduciary responsibility between states and LEAs to meet the needs of gifted children. States suggested their legislative initiatives and funding mirrored those of federal interest and governmental support. If the USDOE did not recognize the needs of gifted students, why should states? The report also conceded that the lack of federal, state, and local support for gifted students' development was a massive loss to the nation, but also to the students themselves (Marland, 1972a).

The concerns raised by members of Congress regarding the feasibility of the inclusion of language concerning the gifted and talented in ESEA under Titles III and V were not unfounded. The suggestion that available funds could be used for gifted programming and services was not enough. Unless stipulated for a specific purpose or program, monies typically were disbursed at the discretion of the state or LEA administrator (Marland, 1972a) with approximately only one-quarter of states indicating that they used ESEA funds for gifted and talented students.

The report also recommended that a more nuanced approach to identifying gifted students was required. In addition, the misperceptions and mythology surrounding gifted children needed to be eradicated, particularly the attitudes of policy makers and the general public, principally the false concept that gifted students did not require special educational interventions—that they would get by on their own. The federal government's failure to acknowledge the needs of gifted and talented learners in policy provided de facto permission for states to also ignore the needs of these learners (Marland, 1972a).

The survey conducted as a result of the report also highlighted the correlation between full-time state personnel and a greater rate of identified gifted students within the state. It was noted that an assigned person at the federal level within the USOE could significantly increase the number of identified gifted and talented students nationwide. Marland extrapolated this evidence to ultimately argue for the Gifted and Talented Program Group to be assigned to the Deputy Commissioner for School Systems, which would eventually morph into the Office of Gifted and Talented Education (Marland, 1972a).

An Inventory of Services

The Marland Report catalogued the first analysis of services offered for gifted and talented students by state. The level of service was considered as an indicator of priority given to gifted children. Included in this survey were questions pertaining to state-level staff for the gifted, legislation, professional development, and the implementation of federal funding for gifted education (Marland, 1972a). If states did have personnel, it was one individual at the state department of education. This individual typically had no support staff or additional resources.

Curiously, states did provide in-service and pre-service training to teachers at high rates of implementation with more than 60% of states indicating one or a combination of both types of preparation for teachers (Marland, 1972a). The survey specifically queried as to what were the specific barriers to more inclusive and complete services. There were many perceived barriers, including insufficient funding (the most frequently cited), competing priorities, poorly trained and inadequate numbers of personnel, deficient referral and identification procedures, an absence of public interest, a dearth of legislation, and actual classroom space (Marland, 1972a). The state survey unequivocally revealed the low status of gifted students and the choices school personnel were forced to make among student populations, with gifted students often sacrificed when choices were made for programming and services: Exposed by the Marland Report, as a result of the state survey, was the overall failure by the majority of states to address the needs of gifted and talented learners.

> Most of the states have recognized that the education of the gifted is an area of substantial educational need and have tried, in a variety of way, to put some available resources to work in this area. It is also clear that these efforts have been overwhelmed by the more crisis-oriented issues of the deprived child, the disruptive child, the child who cannot learn, etc. The limited resources available are absorbed by these problem areas before such long range educational issues as the gifted are considered.
>
> *(Marland, 1972a, p. 168)*

The Marland Report also provided concrete steps from which the USOE could proceed toward serving gifted and talented children. These included:

1. Gifted and talented children were attended to as a specific educational need. Thus a crippling assumption, that these children could somehow "make it on their own," was officially undercut. Previous efforts benefitting gifted and talented children had entered the schoolhouse via the back door, through programs under the National Defense Education Act, the National Science Foundation, and others. Now gifted and talented children were seen as worthy of assistance in their own right—a significant step forward.
2. A definition of "gifted and talented" was attempted for purposes of identifying this population. Significantly, the definition was a broad one and not circumscribed by a view of giftedness that focused on cognitive superstars. The new definition sought to encompass not only generalized intellectual ability, but also specific academic aptitude, original and creative abilities, leadership abilities, talent in visual and performing arts, and psychomotor abilities.
3. Staff attention within USOE was to be directed toward improving the educational lot of gifted and talented children.
4. Elements of a national strategy for the education of the gifted and talented began to take shape.

(Jackson, 1979, p. 47)

For the first time in the history of gifted education, the field had a succinct, if imperfect, way forward with *support* from the federal government.

23
CAPACITY BUILDING

The Office of Gifted and Talented

The establishment of the Gifted and Talented Program Group within the USOE came almost immediately after the issuance of the Marland Report and assigned the Deputy Commissioner for the School System to supervise the Group, which would use the survey results from the report as a blueprint for its agenda (Harrington, Harrington, & Karns, 1991). The Group became the Office of Gifted and Talented (OGT) in February 1972. Despite the call for greater support that the Marland Report generated and the idea that unfunded mandates held little sway, the OGT was not provided any programmatic funds. This was highly problematic as the office attempted to operationalize its agenda and advocate for a national policy. The most salient points of the survey on which the OGT decided to focus its efforts included:

1. Raising the profile and priority of provisions and funding for gifted and talented students.
2. Identifying and bringing greater awareness to minority and underserved gifted and talented students.
3. Addressing the discrepancy and uneven responsiveness at the state level in terms of legislative provisions and state level personnel.
4. Changing the unfounded beliefs that gifted students could realize their potential without any specialized intervention and/or programming.
5. Bringing greater consistency to the identification process which ranged from testing procedures, funding for instrumentation, and changing attitudes of educational leaders and teachers.

6. Evidencing that differential programming for the gifted and talented did produce measurable positive outcomes.
7. Providing the leadership and guidance at the federal level that LEAs, parents, and other stakeholders expected.

(Jackson, 1979)

As the OGT had no programmatic funding to support its efforts, Marland and the OGT accessed the Educational Professions Development Act to secure funding to train leaders and expand programming at the state level in gifted education. This would eventually be known as the National/State Leadership Training Institute on the Gifted and Talented (N/S-LTI-G/T). Again the focus was on state-level training, as those states with stronger programming and state-level support tended to have greater numbers of gifted students, as detailed in the Marland Report (Jackson, 1979; Jolly, 2014b; Marland, 1972b).

The OGT pursued other stakeholders such as private foundations, companies, businesses, and community groups. These stakeholders were asked to invest in and support gifted programs and services. A concerted effort toward raising the media profile of gifted children was made with a number of TV and radio appearances, and through op-ed pieces and popular magazine and journal articles (Jackson, 1979).

Gifted and talented organizations, in conjunction with the OGT, also provided opportunities to raise awareness of gifted children through programs such as Exploration Scholarships. The authority to administer The Presidential Scholars program was moved to the OGT. The OGT encouraged states to take advantage of the funding available through ESEA and its various provisions. Additional funding applications through the National Endowment for the Arts and Humanities and the National Science Foundation were identified as potential sources for gifted and talented students with domain-specific talents (Jackson, 1979).

The OGT finally received specific funding in 1974 and was eventually funded as a separate entity in 1976, with the passage of the Special Projects Act of P.L. 93–830, Section 404, which provided categorical funding for gifted and talented students for the first time in the history of the federal government (Harrington et al., 1991; Jolly & Robins, 2016, Zettel, 1982). Its first director, Dorothy Sisk, was one of five directors in the Bureau of the Handicapped in Health, Education and Welfare (HEW). The Commissioner of Education during this time, Dr. Ernest Boyer, recognized the importance of gifted education and ranked it among the top seven programs within the HEW. "Commissioner Boyer viewed the role of the Office and Gifted and Talented as integrative, working closely with all programs …. [H]e reinforced the idea … as an office where new ideas were to be initiated through stimulus grants, and disseminated to impact education for all students" (Dorothy Sisk, interview; in Seevers & Shaughnessy, 2003, p. 30).

Despite the findings from the Marland Report and apart from those few policy makers who were already sympathetic to the needs of gifted and talented children, few others were convinced that the gifted required any additional programmatic support in school, as their advanced abilities already put them ahead of their peers.

Yet when, in 1977, Commissioner Boyer surveyed his staff for topics of national interest, gifted education was selected as one of the six topics, with Sisk named as Task Force Chair. From the fall of 1977 through May of 1978, twice-monthly task force meetings were held focusing the following topic: "minority and disadvantaged gifted, leadership training, and visual and performing arts" (Fox, 1978, p. 284). An additional focus of these meetings comprised gifted females and the lack of the awareness toward their needs (Fox, 1978).

The task force results also revealed that in the five years since the Marland Report, an increase from 4% to 12% of gifted and talented children were now receiving educational programming and services that matched their needs. Three additional states had passed legislation providing educational assistance to gifted and talented students, moving from 21 to 24 states (Harrington et al., 1991). A similar study conducted in 1978 by the Council for Exceptional Children reported that despite modest progress, gifted and talented students remained educationally depressed (Harrington et al., 1991). However, these findings did little to persuade Congress to act.

The OGT was disbanded in 1982 as part of a larger strategy to dismantle the Department of Education. When Congress rejected the request to eliminate the Department of Education as part of President Reagan's policy of returning power to states, gifted education became the collateral damage of a philosophical struggle of wills, as offices within the department were defunded or disbanded (Harrington et al., 1991).

National/State Leadership Training Institute on the Gifted and Talented (N/S-LTI-G/T)

Despite its somewhat cumbersome acronym, the N/S-LTI-G/T provided gifted education an effective mechanism to build capacity throughout the United States, something unachievable until this point. Capacity development at the state level would provide a framework to support ongoing gifted programming and cushion the blows resulting from cyclical cutbacks or lack of interest at the federal level.

The Marland Report had revealed a patchwork of state programs and services for gifted children suggesting that only a small fraction of the two million gifted students were having their academic needs addressed (Jolly, 2014b; Marland, 1972a). The Marland Report included a State Survey indicating that 21 states had legislation specifying certain incentives to local education agencies (LEAs) that provided special programming for gifted students. Upon further investigation, the actuality of these legislative measures "merely present[ed] intent," not actual practice (Marland, 1972a, p. 3). Ten additional states had proposed or were planning legislation, but no actual legislation existed. This left 19 remaining states with no provision or services for this population of students (Marland, 1972a).

The N/S-LTI-G/T was a strategy to stabilize existing programming and proliferate the spread of programming for gifted students.

> The basic rationale for the LTI has always been that in order for gifted and talented students to achieve the instructional benefits that would best develop their abilities and talents, and in order for gifted child education to achieve the level of presence and recognition called for at the federal level, decision makers had to be involved at both state and local levels at the crucial points where educational policy is made.
> *(Jackson, 1979, p. 55)*

The formation of the institute came less than six months after the release of the Marland Report in August of 1972. The lack of funding for the OGT necessitated an alternative approach to capacity building at the state level. Funded through grant monies made available by the Educational Professions Development Act and administered by Ventura County Superintendent of Schools, the N/S-LTI-G/T focused on building gifted education leadership through state networks. The following five goals guided their work:

> (a) to establish and maintain a working communication network among Central Office of Education, Regional Office of Education, State, and local educational agencies; (b) to formulate and initiate regional team activities involving unique planning and program development for the gifted and talented; (c) to train selected individuals both nationally and regionally at regular training institutes or workshops (of sufficient duration); (d) to develop, reproduce, and disseminate some appropriate documents, publications, and media products on the gifted and talented through N/S-LTI-G/T-sponsored workshops and institutes; and (e) to increase public consciousness, awareness, and knowledge about the gifted and talented.
> *(Plantec & Hospodar, 1973, p. 18)*

The first institute, held in Squaw Valley, CA, in July 1973, was "designed to develop in each participating state, a team which would be trained to administer programs for gifted and talented children and youth in their respective states" (Plantec & Hospodar, 1973, p. 6). This significant meeting included 17 states and United States territories participating in sessions conducted by leaders in the field of gifted education, including James Gallagher, Ruth Martinson, Irving Sato, and Bill Vassar. Participants' outcomes included developing state plans and becoming familiar with existing resources for gifted students. State plans were comprehensive in nature and set realistic objectives and timelines. Also included were persons responsible for carrying out the work, populations impacted, and stakeholders who could be accessed to advocate and promote on behalf of gifted students and gifted education (Plantec & Hospodar, 1973).

From 1973 to 1976, N/S-LTI-G/T prepared more than 1,000 participants who developed programmatic proposals and reinforced existing programs for gifted children in a series of three national conferences and nine regional conferences (Jackson, 1979; Johnson, 1977). These conferences presented opportunities to recruit members for additional training at N/S-LTI-G/T national institutes. Five-member teams were purposeful in their composition, including parents, teachers, administrators, and community members with the proviso that one non-educator be included on the team (Jackson, 1979).

A groundswell of education programming for the gifted emerged as a result of the successive N/S-LTI-G/T institutes. Forty-eight state teams participated and authored state plans, accounting for nearly every state in the nation and territories. Many of these plans were put into practice almost immediately. For example, several programs in Maryland's Prince George's County established a range of options for high school students incorporating Advanced Placement courses, early college admission, opportunities to study topics of interest in depth, and mentorships. At the elementary school level, cluster grouping in regular classrooms, interclass grouping for specific subjects, and pull-out programs for gifted students were indicated (Johnson, 1977).

Georgia used N/S-LTI-G/T planning to further bolster its network of gifted programs. Before participating in the institute, Georgia had undertaken a state survey in 1971. In this survey, Okefenokee, GA, noted the lack of any provisions for gifted students in its nine school systems. The project made provisions for improved parent involvement, enhanced curriculum design, and strengthened identifications practices for underserved children. The LEA in Okefenokee considered that specific services for gifted students could be a measure to help reverse the high rates of poverty in the region:

> Low education levels within much of this area inhibit its ability to increase its wealth from within. ... Adequate educational opportunity for potential leaders would reverse this trend. Within this area, in which one-half of the rural families are termed poverty cases according to annual family income, there is critical need for specialized personnel services ... if potentially gifted students are to be helped.
>
> *(Johnson, 1977, p. 39)*

These are only two examples of hundreds that were implemented as a result of the work completed at the institutes. The work of participant teams provided much-needed goal setting and curriculum development that had not existed in any of these areas previously.

Another objective of the N/S-LTI-G/T was the construction of a network of gifted and talented professionals that was greatly achieved through ongoing support from N/S-LTI-G/T staff members who provided follow-up visits, the creation of ties across all levels of educational strata, the dissemination of a monthly newsletter, technical assistance, the organization of smaller regional conferences targeted at local issues and those strategies for underserved gifted children, and an early version of the trainer of trainers model, where those already trained would return to their local schools and communities and be available to help those seeking training and professional development in gifted education (Jackson, 1979).

N/S-LTI-G/T also published and circulated more than ten books and smaller publications to help support its original goals and objectives. A diverse range of titles aimed at administrators and practitioners included *Developing a Written Plan for the Education of the Gifted and Talented* (Sato, Birnbaum, & LoCicero, 1974), *The Identification of the Gifted and Talented* (Martinson, 1974), *Parentspeak* (Coffey et al., 1976), *Providing Programs for the Gifted and Talented: A Handbook* (Kaplan, 1975), and *Promising Practices: Teaching the Disadvantaged Gifted* (Miley, 1975). For example, Sandra Kaplan's *Providing Programs for the Gifted and Talented: A Handbook* (1975, p. 8) provided a framework for gifted programs across the United States. The imprint of her work remains evident in contemporary programming as she explained her rationale for a holistic program:

> A program for the gifted and talented provides multidimensional and appropriate learning experiences and environments which incorporate the academic, psychological, and social needs of these students. The implementation of administrative procedures and instructional strategies which afford intellectual acquisition, thinking practice, and self-understanding characterize a program for the gifted and talented. A program assures each student of alternatives which teach, challenge, and expand his knowledge while simultaneously stressing the development of an independent learner who can continuously question, apply, and generate information.

These collective activities impacted state policy and planning. In an evaluation of the N/S-LTI-G/T, it was found that "of the top twenty-five states with which the LTI has had the greatest amount of interaction since 1972, sixteen (64 percent) ranked among the states having the highest percentage of policy changes" linked with LTI pursuits (Jackson, 1979, p. 57). Additional positive outcomes included an increased public profile for gifted students and programs, growth in the number of students being identified for gifted programs, and a surge in professional development in gifted education (Jackson, 1979).

Leadership Capabilities

In addition to the infrastructure and networking of the OGT and the N/S-LTI-G/T, building leadership capacity within the field was identified as a priority—a direct recommendation of the Marland Report (Marland, 1972b). An early program to build such capacity included the Teaching the Talented (TTT) program housed at the University of Connecticut, also funded through the Educational Professions Development Act and other grant monies from the U.S. Office of Education. Beginning in 1969, the program targeted teachers and school personnel to

> prepare persons who could assume positions as teachers and leadership personnel concerned with talent development of youngsters from

disadvantaged backgrounds. ... [I]t was further anticipated that all persons completing the program would develop a vigorous commitment and sincere sensitivity toward working with educationally deprived youngsters.

(Gear, 1974, p. 10)

From 1969 to 1974, 46 fellows participated in the program, completing 72 internships in a range of roles within schools and educational agencies. These participants also earned 22 Ph.D.s, 13 master's degrees, and three sixth-year diplomas, and a further eight dissertations were in progress when the evaluation report was published in 1974. The ultimate goal for TTT fellows was to serve as change agents upon completion of the program (Gear, 1974).

Another leadership program established in 1977, the Graduate Leadership Education Program (GLEP), drew participants from across the United States and was characterized as

a turning point in the field on two counts. First, it occurred at a time when leadership development in the school setting was formally recognized as part of gifted education; and second, it was the first collaborative attempt by recognized leaders of the field to identify and develop the leadership potential of a talented group in order to maintain strong leadership and forge new directions for gifted education.

(Rudnitski, 1994, p. 265)

With funding from the U.S. Office of Education, Teachers College administered the grant in collaboration with the University of Kansas, the University of Georgia, the University for Connecticut, Purdue University, the University of Virginia, and the University of Florida. In total, 54 fellows participated in five cohorts. Fellows undertook their respective university's graduate program curricula and also participated in GLEP activities including Summer Institutes and field experiences, and were encouraged to write and present on gifted education to a range of audiences. A 15-year follow-up study of 38 GLEP fellows indicated mixed results:

[I]t is difficult in the current climate to discern whether or not the "generation of leaders" for gifted education did end the cycles of interest. Their commitment and contributions to the field, though still in progress, confirm that in many respects the Graduate Leadership Education Project on the Gifted/Talented fulfilled its mission for awhile.

(Rudnitski, 1994, p. 270)

Forty years since the establishment of the program, its the impact is still difficult to gauge. Several of the GLEP fellows are counted amongst the current leaders in the field of gifted education, while others have made contributions at the state and local level and others have left the field altogether.

24
ACKNOWLEDGED NEGLECT AND COMPETING PRIORITIES

The OGT and N/S-LTI-G/T offered much-needed structure and support for gifted education to the states at the federal level. Moving forward from the issuance of the Marland Report, sporadic financial aid came forth from the federal level. Unlike special education students, gifted students did not possess students' education rights and funding that were protected by federal law. Beginning with ESEA of 1966 under Title VI, the Education of Handicapped Children Act established $3.5 million in formula grants over a two-year period for children with special needs ages 3 to 21. This was replaced with the Handicapped Act of 1969 and raised the commitment for funding to $630 million, which was available for special education grants to states. In 1975 the Education for All Handicapped Children Act passed and for the first time identified and defined free appropriate public education (FAPE) for all children with disabilities (McCann, 2014). The likelihood that gifted children would have been included in the federal handicapped designation is unknown. NAGC and the CEC-TAG were at an impasse as to whether gifted children should be labeled handicapped. In testimony to the U.S. Office of Education, Ann Isaacs, President of NAGC, stated:

> Educators who would play politics and call the gifted by any name merely to get money for their programs are a disgrace to the profession, or are not themselves gifted, or feel they aren't, so sympathize not with a loathing for this labeling. ... The willingness of educators to link giftedness with the handicapped is living evidence of inadequate understanding of the gifted concept.
>
> *(as cited in Rogers, 2014, p. 264)*

This testimony certainly rendered gifted children absent from any further consideration within the special education legislation. In 1977, funding was offered at $250 million (U.S. Department of Education, 2006), and in 1999, under the Individuals with Disabilities Education Act (IDEA), funding had reached $5.3 billion—and by 2013 risen to $12.6 billion (McCann, 2014). The level of federal funding for gifted education in 2016 was $12 million. The comparison in funding dollars is stark when simply considering the number of students identified for gifted and special education services. In 2013–2014, 6.5 million students in public schools received special education services (NCES, 2016), while approximately 3.1 million gifted students were identified and enrolled in services (OCR, 2012). Although there are twice as many identified special education students, the funding available represents an amount ten times as large. A reduction in special education funding is certainly not suggested, but rather greater funding for gifted education. Regardless of the impetus, the lack of guaranteed funding can in part be traced to the absence of gifted students and gifted education in the original federal special education legislation.

In the absence of legislation and consistent funding sources, gifted students required legislative advocates to advance their case at the federal level. Senator Jacob Javits (R–NY), a supporter of gifted education since the Marland Report, emerged as a major defender of gifted education. By the early 1970s, Javits had been a long-serving member of Congress with a reputation as a liberal Republican (U.S. House of Representatives 1947–1954 and U.S. Senate 1957–1981) (Winker & Jolly, 2011). He was the son of an Orthodox Jewish immigrant family, who was raised on the Lower East side of New York City and considered progressive in his legislative record, supporting such legislative measures as the National Endowment for the Arts and the Civil Rights Act (Javits, 1981; Winkler & Jolly, 2011).

For fiscal years (FY) 1976 to 1978 Javits and Representative Dominick Daniels (D–NJ) proposed what would eventually become P.L. 93–830, which included a provision for "Special Projects," including gifted and talented education. Initially allocated $12.25 million, the Ford administration decreased funding to $2.56 million annually (Harrington et al., 1991; Jolly & Robins, 2016; Zettel, 1982). In 1978, Javits and Representative Carl Pursell (R–MI) sought out Congress for increased funding, each proposing what would eventually become P.L. 95–561, Gifted and Talented Children's Education Act. This legislation provided state education agencies access to grant monies to improve the education for gifted and talented students, which was interpreted quite widely and could include research, demonstration grants, statewide planning, and professional development for teachers. Funding was approved at $6.2 million per year between 1978 and 1981 (Harrington et al., 1991; Jolly & Robins, 2016; Zettel, 1982).

Ronald Reagan's presidency, beginning in 1980, curtailed the progress that Javits and his colleagues were making at the federal level for gifted education. In 1981, Congress authorized the Elementary and Secondary Education

Consolidation Act and categorical programs were eliminated and replaced by block grants, returning greater decision-making and funding responsibility back to individual states. Congress had disrupted Reagan's ultimate goal of eliminating the Department of Education altogether, so Reagan lingered in appointing his last cabinet member—the Secretary of Education (Jolly, 2015). Terrell H. Bell, Reagan's choice for Secretary of Education, recalled,

> I knew [Reagan's] quest for this last member of his cabinet had been delayed because of lack of conviction concerning its importance.... He emphasized his interest in schools and colleges and his firm conviction that education should be primarily a state rather than a federal responsibility.
>
> *(Gardner, 2005, p. 106)*

Under Reagan's leadership, this "new federalism" allowed states to distribute funds to LEAs (Caraley & Schlussel, 1986; Jolly & Robins, 2016). Reagan's larger agenda was to reduce the role of the federal government in American education (New York State Department of Education, n.d.). During Reagan's tenure in office, federal aid to schools was reduced by 15%, or $1 billion. What occurred next was inevitable with education budgets reduced and no specific funding earmarked for gifted education, and as experience had borne out before, states were apt to spend monies on student populations perceived to have challenges of greater and/or more immediate priority. This negligence toward gifted children would soon impact an already stressed education system.

A Nation at Risk

Near the end of Reagan's presidency, gifted children once again became the centerpiece of interest. Just over a decade after the release of the Marland Report in 1983, *A Nation at Risk* was released and "define[d] the problems afflicting American education" (U.S. Department of Education, 1983, p. 1), including significant gaps in the education of gifted children (Gallagher, 1994).

Almost immediately after accepting the position, Terrell Bell found himself in the midst of a groundswell of mounting anxiety regarding the nation's student performance on national and international assessments and the role the federal government should play in interceding and addressing these deficiencies. Much of the criticism originated from within Reagan's own political party toward American public education (Fiske, 1986; Jolly, 2015). With supposition and conjecture in ample supply from members of Congress and the mainstream public, Secretary of Education Bell reasoned that a Commission should be impaneled to fully understand the gravity of the situation in order to make evidence-driven recommendations to address those challenges facing America's educational system (Gardner, 2005; Jolly 2015). It's fair to suppose that the White House was not overly interested in investigating a situation it had partly created, so Bell created a cabinet-level commission to help unravel the questions regarding American student performance.

Bell appointed commission members representing educational stakeholders that were as diverse as the children in American schools and the Commission's work would be completed over 18 months. Bell insisted that the findings be published and circulated broadly, regardless of the President's opinion of the report (Jolly, 2015). The 18-member panel set forth a rigorous eight-point plan, which included:

1. To review and synthesize the data and scholarly literature on the quality of learning and teaching in the nation's schools, colleges, and universities, both public and private, with special concern for the educational experience of teenage youth;
2. To examine and to compare and contrast the curricula, standards, and expectations of educational systems of several advanced countries with those of the United States;
3. To study a representative sample of university and college admission standards and lower division course requirements with particular reference to the impact that the enhancement of quality and the promotion of excellence standards may have on high school curricula and on expected levels of high school academic achievement;
4. To review and to describe the educational programs that are recognized as preparing students who consistently attain higher than average scores in college entrance examinations and who meet with uncommon success the demands placed on them by the nation's colleges and universities;
5. To review the major changes that have occurred in American education as well as events in society during the past quarter century that have significantly affected educational achievement;
6. To hold hearings and to receive testimony and expert advice on efforts that could and should be taken to foster high levels of quality and academic excellence in the nation's schools, colleges, and universities;
7. To do all other things needed to define the barriers to attaining greater levels of excellence in American education; and
8. To report and make practical recommendations for action to be taken by educators, public officials, governing boards, parents, and others having vital interest in American education and a capacity to influence it for the better.

(U.S. Department of Education, 1983, appendix A)

Gifted education scholars and experts were given an opportunity to weigh in on these topics and were called together at Harvard University to testify. A sample of those who provided testimony included Alexinia Baldwin of the State University of New York; June Cox, executive director of the Gifted Students Institute in Fort Worth, TX; John Feldhusen of Purdue University; James Gallagher of the

University of North Carolina; Joseph Renzulli of the University of Connecticut, Albany; Julian Stanley of Johns Hopkins University; and Abraham Tannenbaum of Teachers College (U.S. Department of Education, 1983).

The final report was written and presented in consumable and accessible language for all Americans, not just the policy wonks who roamed the halls in Washington, DC. One of the report's most memorable passages is an indictment of the American educational statement which reveals the changes that occurred over the 20 years since the passage of the NDEA in 1958 and the reform measures insisted upon by Rickover and Conant:

> If an unfriendly foreign power had attempted to impose on America the mediocre educational performance that exists today, we might well have viewed it as an act of war. As it stands, we have allowed this to happen to ourselves. We have even squandered the gains in student achievement made in the wake of the Sputnik challenge. Moreover, we have dismantled essential support systems which helped make those gains possible. We have, in effect, been committing an act of unthinking, unilateral educational disarmament.
>
> *(U.S. Department of Education, 1983, para. 2)*

The report's final version was no longer than 40 pages and presented the commission's recommendations, which revolved around five central topics—the curriculum and content, standards and expectations, time in school, teaching, and leadership and fiscal support.

A sequence of support for gifted students appears throughout the recommendations. From the introduction, individual differences in learning are addressed and advanced students are used with an example of "a curriculum enriched and accelerated beyond even the needs of other students of high ability" (U.S. Department of Education, 1983, para. 3). Within the standards and expectations section, a recommendation was made for textbook support to address the needs of gifted and talented students. Within the recommendation of time, the commission put forth that ability or chronological age should not limit a child's progression through school. Leadership and fiscal support recommendations encouraged the collaboration among federal, state, and local entities to meet the range of gifted students' needs. One major indicator of risk reported for gifted students included that "over ½ of the population of gifted students do match their tested ability with comparable achievement in school" (U.S. Department of Education, 1983, para. 10). Despite gifted students' appearance throughout the document, the direct influence that *A Nation at Risk* had on gifted education is difficult to evaluate. Gifted education advocates did use the document to gain services and resources for gifted children based on the language pertaining to their educational needs, but the major paradigm shift that was expected following the NDEA never materialized despite the evidence presented (Jolly, 2015).

The report also proposed a nationwide system of standardized tests, providing an annual benchmark of student progress (Jolly, 2015) or measure of achievement: "call[ing] for a nationwide system of tests marked a new era of federal educational policy, an era in which equal educational opportunities would be measured ... in terms of standardized test" (New York State Department of Education, n.d., para. 2). This recommendation could not envisage the accountability movement that would soon overshadow the work of classroom teachers and schools across the nation and inadvertently further deprioritize the needs of gifted students (Jolly, 2015; Jolly & Makel, 2010).

Jacob K. Javits Gifted Children and Youth Education Act

A Nation at Risk exposed some glaring chasms in the education of gifted children and after considerable and continued efforts, particularly by Senator William Bradley (D–NJ) and Representative Mario Biaggi (D–NY), Congress finally passed legislation to help rectify this problematic condition (Harrington et al., 1991). In 1987, the Jacob K. Javits Gifted and Talented Children and Youth Act (P.L. 100–297, or The Javits Act, as it came to be known) was ratified by Congress. Named after Jacob Javits, who had passed away the previous year in 1986, the Act was funded at $7.9 million per year from FY 1988 to 1993 (Harrington et al., 1991; Jolly & Robins, 2016) and "focused resources on identifying and serving students historically underrepresented in programs for learners who are gifted and talented 'including economically disadvantaged individuals, individuals of limited English proficiency, and individuals with handicaps'" (Renzulli, Callahan, & Gubbins, 2014, p. 340). The National Research Center on the Gifted and Talented was also conceived out of the Act's funding, creating the first national research center devoted to gifted and talented education (Renzulli et al., 2014). The Javits Act has sustained intermittent levels of funding over the subsequent three decades. Unlike the laws that have protected special education funding and programming, gifted education has been fiscally vulnerable during periods of budget crises or disinterest toward the educational needs of gifted students.

The Every Student Succeeds Act (ESSA) of 2015, which reauthorized No Child Left Behind of 2002 (and the original ESEA of 1965), funds the Javits Gifted and Talented Students Education Program, including the National Research Center and grants focused on identifying underserved gifted populations and to improve the K–12 schools' ability to meet the needs of gifted and talented students. ESSA provides two new requirements in relation to gifted and talented students. One addresses student performance. Previously, states only had to report on students' performance for those at proficiency and below. An advanced performance level is now included in state report cards. Title II professional development funds must be devoted to strengthening teachers' and other school personnel's abilities to meet the needs of gifted and talented students. Title I funds earmarked for students from low-income families can now be used for identification and service of gifted students (National Association for Gifted Children, n.d). The passage of this group of provisions was the most comprehensive response to the needs of gifted learners in over three decades.

National Excellence: A Case for Developing America's Talent

A decade after *A Nation at Risk* was released, the U.S. Department of Education released *National Excellence: A Case for Developing America's Talent* (1993), which examined the state of gifted education as the last decade of the 20th century closed. The report (1993, p. 3) highlighted a "quiet crisis," accusing America of "squandering one of its most precious resources—the gifts, talents, and high interests of many of its students." The collective evidence rendered a bleak picture for the country's most able students. Gifted students already knew much of the curriculum before the school year started, and teachers were making few adjustments to the curriculum despite students' prior knowledge. The sum total of these conditions was the underachievement of many gifted students (U.S. Department of Education, 1993). The report recommended seven steps to improve the educational landscape for America's educationally most able:

> (a) set challenging curriculum standards; (b) provide more challenging opportunities to learn; (c) increase access to early childhood education; (d) increase learning opportunities for disadvantaged and minority children with outstanding talents; (e) broaden the definition of gifted; (f) encourage appropriate teacher training and technical assistance; and (g) match world performance.
>
> *(U.S. Department of Education, 1993, p. 10)*

Despite the ability for the field to grow in terms of leadership, research, and infrastructure, sustained and coordinated systematic impact in schools remained an issue for the field. A lack of coordinated efforts between federal recommendations and state and local commitments have often led to inaction for gifted students or other priorities being identified by LEAs. When recommendations are made with few to no resources to support their implementation—little of consequence happens, and history has illustrated that gifted students and their educational needs are not chosen as a priority (Jolly & Kettler, 2008; Landrum, Katsiyannis, & DeWaard, 1998).

25
GIFTED EDUCATION'S FAILINGS
Underserved Populations

Henry Morehouse originally proposed the concept of the Talented Tenth in 1893 arguing, "In the discussion concerning Negro education we should not forget the talented tenth man. An ordinary education may answer for the nine men of mediocrity; but if this is all we offer the talented tenth man, we make a prodigious mistake"; and, "The tenth man, with superior natural endowments, symmetrically trained and highly developed, may become a mightier influence, a greater inspiration to others than all the other nine, or nine times nine like them" (Morehouse, 1896, p. 183). DuBois popularized Morehouse's concept of the Talented Tenth in 1903, explicating on educational pathways and emphasizing the role of exceptional talent for Black society: "The Negro Race, like all races, is going to be saved by its exceptional men. ... From the very first it has been the educated and intelligent of the Negro people that have led and elevated the mass, and the sole obstacles that nullified and retarded their efforts were slavery and race prejudice" (DuBois, 1903, p. 33–34). Although the Talented Tenth was part of a larger conversation in regard to educational curriculum for African Americans at the turn of 20th century, with Booker T. Washington advocating for vocational training and DuBois speaking out for greater liberal arts training, DuBois recognized the concept of potential and high ability and the need to nurture this ability by creating opportunities for African Americans to excel (Worrell, 2014).

Apart from the recognition DuBois provides for the identification and support for intellectual possibilities, the field of gifted education that began to take root over the next several decades after DuBois's introduction of the Talented Tenth failed to embrace his ideas and in fact rejected the idea that the most talented minds could be found amongst minority populations—a view perpetuated at the establishment of the field of gifted education and largely tied to the hereditarian views of intelligence held by Terman and Hollingworth, "which often erected road blocks to opportunity for certain groups, notably blacks" (Chapman, 1988, p. 175).

The critical work completed by Jenkins in the 1930s and 1940s sought to change the discourse around gifted African American students. Jenkins's studies found that even though African American students might achieve high scores on an IQ test, "limitations [are placed] on the development of the highly gifted Negro. These superior deviates are nurtured in a culture in which racial inferiority of the Negro is a basic assumption" (Jenkins, 1948, p. 401). Jenkins underscored the concept that IQ alone was not enough to ensure school performance or later success in life.

The 1960s observed underrepresented students emerge as a greater focus of education research; however, rarely were gifted populations included. Still, as Gallagher (1966, p. 51) indicated, "the nature of the problem of talent loss makes most of the research relevant, since neither the existing identification procedures nor typical school programs satisfactorily identify or develop potential talent." The limited research that did exist on culturally diverse students indicated that the differences between races were principally attributed to environment and the importance of early intervention and development of ability and talent (Gallagher, 1966), again supporting the earlier work of Beth Wellman and Martin Jenkins.

At the close of the 1960s, just as preparations for the Marland Report were underway, John Gowan (1969, p. 251) submitted the following recommendations and conclusions based on the emerging research literature base at the time regarding disadvantaged children:

- While much is known about the gifted child, and about the disadvantaged child, comparatively little is known about the disadvantaged gifted youth; much more research is necessary.
- Research in these areas and in their interface may be expected to benefit general education, as well as special education, by uncovering new and salient aspects of both curriculum and guidance.
- As Guilford says, we are moving toward education defined as the goal of stimulating whatever factors of intellect the student possesses. This implies choice of curriculum and invention of specific teaching methods for practice in improving specific abilities.
- Administrative procedures (such as grouping) are less important than breakthroughs in the quality of curriculum and guidance which will interest and predispose the child to learn.
- For these objectives to be successful there must be a program of (1) curriculum innovation, (2) individual guidance to improve self-concept, (3) group guidance with model figures to maintain morale, (4) remedial skills taught by a sympathetic teacher.

- We know little about the effects of massive amounts of guidance on bright children but some early probes are promising. Residential schools seem useful as experiments because they provide this.
- The identification, stimulation and exploitation of exotic factors of intellect in the case of disadvantaged gifted; particularly in the behavioral and figural areas, appear to have real promise; here is another example where curriculum and test modification needs to take place.
- The use of modeling and model figures from the community is particularly helpful in group guidance activities with disadvantaged children.
- Unusual kinds of guidance, such as have been illustrated earlier, may be especially relevant in upgrading and preserving the creativity of disadvantaged gifted youth.
- In general, the remedy for the problems presented by disadvantaged gifted children is to start in early and involve them in as many types of guidance and curriculum, and with as many diverse adult models as possible, enlisting the cooperation of the home background whenever feasible.

Despite indications from Gowan and Gallagher, the research trajectory remained uneven and irregular and there existed a "dearth of research and writing on the gifted of the black population" leading into the 1980s (Cooke & Baldwin, 1979, p. 388).

Intermittent approaches did exist to support talent development, particularly of African American students. The National Achievement Scholarship Program (NASP) for Negroes and the National Scholarship and Service Fund for Negro Students were developed to help prepare Black scholars. For example, NASP was established in 1964 "to call attention to the most able Negro youth and to help financially as many to attend college as funds permit," since many Black students did not qualify for the National Merit Program at the time (Roberts & Nichols, 1967, p. 1). Unlike National Merit Program students, NASP students were nominated by teachers and administrators, rather than qualifying through their PSAT scores.

Data from the inaugural group of NASP finalists found they scored above college freshman on vocabulary tests, and NASP finalists on average possessed higher goals than National Merit Finalists and significantly above average students. Finalists' median family income was higher than all other non-White families, parents of nominated students also had higher levels of education in comparison to other non-White families, and on average nominated students and finalists came more commonly from two-parent households when compared to other non-White students, underscoring the importance of home environment (Roberts & Nichols, 1967). In 2015, the NMSC administered its last cohort of students. The United Negro College Fund has rebranded the program has the Achievement Capstone Program and helps students financially once they graduate from a historically Black college or university (*The Journal of Blacks in Higher Education*, 2015).

The 1970s began to witness greater efforts to unravel the issues around under-identification and focus research attention to these issues. Hillard (1976) and his colleagues undertook an investigation into cross-cultural assessments through observations based on the work of E. Paul Torrance in creativity and African American cultural commonalities. Primarily based on students in the San Francisco Unified School district, and moving away from traditional IQ tests to identify gifted children, these researchers developed inventories of characteristics to be completed by teachers and parents (Hilliard, 1976). Researchers representing a number of different fields concluded that "the gifted child is poly-dimensional, can integrate the opposing polarities of style within himself, and can perform appropriately in terms of a variety of educational and social situations" (Hilliard, 1976, p. 102).

Torrance (1977) also developed his own set of behaviors for his Checklist of Creative Positives to aid in identifying culturally different students, referring to them as "creative positives." The Baldwin Identification Matrix collected subjective and objective data in order to provide a more holistic process to identify African American students, including creativity, psychomotor ability, and leadership skills, in addition to achievement and aptitude (Conceptual Foundations Network, 2011). Baldwin described some children of color as those "who fly in the face of traditional indicators" and needed to be honed and polished until they shone and created this matrix as an alternative to traditional measures (Conceptual Foundations Network, 2011). The field began to systematically address the issues of the under-identification of students who did not come from the majority culture for gifted programming. This included "minority students, economically disadvantaged students, underachievers, and other nontraditional students" (Ford, 1995, p. 52).

Following the Civil Rights movement, there was a growing consensus that talent potential was being lost with unidentified minority students (Renzulli, 1973). In a study to increase the identification of minority middle school students, Davis (1978) asked community members to complete a questionnaire recommending Black children in the community who they considered gifted across a number of factors including cognitive, psychosocial, and talent-specific. Of the 15 students nominated, 13 were classified as having advanced cognitive ability, 13 were found to have superior psychosocial abilities, and 13 were identified as having a domain-specific ability. There were also a number of students who were identified across categories.

Still, programs like these were insufficient to provide long-term identification, support, cultivation of talent, or research:

> Subsequent research and social pressure have brought to the fore the need to examine unique paradigms for discovering and developing this talent, because behaviors often considered aberrant in the dominant culture belie

the rough diamond of intellect and talent waiting to be polished to the brilliance it is capable of exhibiting.

(Cooke & Baldwin, 1979, p. 393)

Schools were not particularly effective at identifying and serving gifted students who were economically, ethnically or racially diverse, as teachers and educators did not recognize these characteristics together in one student. Criteria for the Javits Gifted and Talented Students Act of 1988 changed in order to help address these issues. The grant funds were provided to

> schools in the identification of, and provision of services to, gifted and talented students (including economically disadvantaged individuals, individuals with limited English proficiency, and individuals with disabilities) who may not be identified and served through traditional assessment methods.
>
> *(Sec. 5465 Program Priorities)*

26
COMPETING CONCEPTIONS AND DEFINITIONS OF GIFTEDNESS

The long-held belief that giftedness was defined solely by IQ was gradually being replaced and even greater acceptance regarding the idea that "There is nothing inevitable about the use of the I.Q. in defining giftedness" (Getzels & Jackson, 1958, p. 75). The late 1970s and early 1980s observed the introduction of a number of models of giftedness from scholars in the field. Building on the momentum from the Marland Report and borrowing from other fields of study, scholars began to offer alternative theories as to the nature of giftedness.

When Spearman proposed his *general factor* (g) of intelligence in 1904 in the seminal paper "General Intelligence Objectively Determined and Measured" using his pioneering statistical method of factor analysis, it was thought that intelligence was a single feature of the mind. Raymond B. Cattell (a student of Charles Spearman, Cyril Burt, and R. A. Fisher at King's College) graduated with a Ph.D. in 1929 and spent the rest of his career investigating factors of personality and intelligence (Revelle, 2015). Building on Spearman and Thurstone's work on the factor structure of intelligence, Cattell, in collaboration with his student John Horn, extended Spearman's single g-factor theory to "the theory of 'fluid and crystallized general abilities,' which states that with more refined analytical methods the general ability factor now measured by intelligence tests will be found to be not one factor but two" (Cattell, 1963, p. 1). These two factors are fluid (gf) and crystallized (gc) intelligence. Fluid intelligence or abilities are used in novel problem solving and driven by physiological influences, while crystallized intelligence is contingent on educational opportunities, context, and culture (Kaufman et al., 2013; Kaufman & Sternberg, 2008; Worrell, 2013). These ideas have been influential in the IQ test development and identification of gifted students (Kaufman et al., 2013; Worrell, 2013).

In 1978, Joseph Renzulli's Three-Ring Definition provided an alternative to the U.S. Office of Education definition of giftedness, which he found lacking in several key areas. These included the absence of psychosocial factors, the inclusion of nonparallel categories, and the misapplication of the definition by schools and practitioners (Renzulli, 1978).

Even though there was a recognition of the broadening conception of giftedness, Renzulli's manuscript had been rejected by the major gifted education journals and, on the advice of E. Paul Torrance, Renzulli did "an end run around" the field and submitted to a journal outside the field, *Phi Delta Kappan* (Conceptual Foundations Network, 2009; Reis, 2016; Renzulli, 1999). This journal's audience included mainstream educators and policy makers, not one specifically aimed at gifted education scholars and/or practitioners. The header of the article, "What Makes Giftedness? Reexamining a Definition," begins: "Mr. Renzulli offers a new research-based definition of the gifted and talented. It is an operational definition intended to help the practitioner" (Renzulli, 1978, p. 181). After all, the majority of gifted children did and do spend the majority of their school day in non-specialized classrooms. His definition focused on the interaction of three features—above-average general abilities, task commitment, and creativity—and signified above-average as the top 15–20% of any domain. In summarizing his Three Ring Definition, Renzulli (1978, p. 261) wrote:

> Giftedness consists of an interaction among three basic clusters of human traits—these clusters being above-average general abilities, high levels of task commitment, and high levels of creativity. Gifted and talented children are those possessing or capable of developing this composite set of traits and applying them to any potentially valuable area of human performance. Children who manifest or are capable of developing an interaction among the three clusters require a wide variety of educational opportunities and services that are not ordinarily provided through regular instructional programs.

Renzulli believed his definition provided an operational alternative based on research, which also allowed for development of identification processes, programming, and for the first time included creative production as an indicator of giftedness (Plucker & Callahan, 2014; Renzulli, 1978). "What Makes Giftedness?" is "now the most widely cited publication in the field" (Renzulli, 2006, p. 236), with over 3,000 citations of the original manuscript and follow-up articles (Reis, 2016) providing just one indicator of its impact on the field.

In 1983, Howard Gardner developed the Theory of Multiple Intelligences (MI) based on "hierarchically related abilities that contribute[d] to intellectual gifts" (Kaufman & Sternberg, 2008, p. 74), which asked educators to expand their traditionally held views of intelligence and "to identify what maybe unique about an individual's proclivities and capabilities in a number of spheres"

(Von Károlyi, Ramos-Ford, & Gardner, 2003, p. 101). These intelligences relied heavily on cultural setting and could be expressed in the following categories: linguistic, logical-mathematical, musical, spatial, bodily-kinesthetic, interpersonal, intrapersonal, and naturalist (Gardner, 1983, 1995). Gardner believed that MIs could assist teachers' response to students' specific needs (Gardner, 1995; Von Károlyi et al., 2003). Many educators did expand their view of intelligence based on the introduction of Gardner's MIs; as Gardner and his colleagues explained, "One impact of MI theory on the field of giftedness has been to broaden the construct from traditional giftedness to one that is more *intelligence fair*—one that values a wider range of culturally meaningful human potentials" (Von Károlyi et al., 2003, p. 110). However, the theory has not been without criticism, particularly in relation to the lack of empirical evidence available to test the overall theory (Kaufman & Sternberg, 2008).

Robert Sternberg introduced his Triarchic Theory of Successful Intelligence in 1988, which provided an alternative approach to intelligence as a multifaceted concept (Sternberg, 1985) and is "a balance of analytical, creative, and practical abilities" (Sternberg, 2003, p. 89) considered through the lens of one's sociocultural context. Success would be achieved when these abilities were capitalized upon and limitations offset. Sternberg (2003) posited that giftedness had too long been treated as a unidimensional construct and could not be captured by singular scores produced by IQ or achievement test outcomes. These three theories have been critical in extending practitioners' conceptions of giftedness and have also underscored the function of the sociocultural perspective in the identification and development of giftedness (Plucker & Callahan, 2014).

Additional conceptions of giftedness were introduced involving developmental models to incorporate greater environmental factors. Tannenbaum's Sea Star Developmental Model of Giftedness is an attempt to explain the relationship between ability and achievement (Reis, 2005). The internal (general ability, special ability, and non-intellective factors) and external variables (environmental factors and chance) coalesce together to produce superior performance (Tannenbaum, 1983). Gagné's, Differentiated Model of Gifted and Talented (DMGT) specifically distinguished between gifts and talents. Prior to this the terms "gifted" and "talented" were often used interchangeably. Gagné highlighted those factors that could support or detract from talent development (Plucker & Callahan, 2014). However, for Gagné, "talent development corresponds to the progressive transformation of gifts into talents" (Gagné, 2008, p. 1). Giftedness for Gagné designated "competence which is distinctly above average in one or more domains in human aptitude. Talent corresponds to performance that is distinctly above average in one or more fields of human activity" (Gagné, 1985, p. 108). Gifts are to be developed into talents with the interaction of catalysts such as chance, environmental factors, the developmental process, and interpersonal characteristics (Gagné, 1985).

In 2011, Subotnik, Olszewski-Kubilius, and Worrell (p. 7) offered a comprehensive definition of giftedness in relation to a renewed discussion involving talent development, noting that

> Giftedness is the manifestation of performance or production that is clearly at the upper end of the distribution in a talent domain even relative to that of other high-functioning individuals in that domain. Further, giftedness can be viewed as developmental, in that in the beginning stages, potential is the key variable; in later stages, achievement is the measure of giftedness; and in fully developed talents, eminence is the basis on which this label is granted. Psychological variables play an essential role in the manifestation of giftedness at every developmental stage. Both cognitive and psychosocial variables are malleable and need to be deliberately cultivated.

The conceptions and definitions presented here are just a sampling of the confounding range that have been offered by scholars in the field (Coleman & Cross, 2005). As the conception of giftedness broadened, scholars and researchers developed nuanced and novel ideas in regard to the qualities and assumptions as to what giftedness represented and how it was expressed. These broadened conceptions challenge scholars, practitioners, and policy makers to consider the nature of giftedness and its development, including the types of identification instruments and to capture various qualities, skill, and abilities and the programming and services matched to identified needs (Plucker & Callahan, 2014).

Expansion of Scope and Influence

Research centers often offer environments that allow for research, training, and career development. The 1970s witnessed the establishment of a number of centers devoted to research in gifted education and talent development. These centers also provided an additional type of infrastructure from that established by the N/S-LTI-G/T, OGT, and leadership programs (Tash, 2006). Geographically diverse, leading figures in both research and advocacy provided central bases for graduate student development, research, resource building, community engagement, and advocacy. Many of these centers remain vital to the local, state, and national gifted communities they serve. The first of these centers was the Gifted Education Resource Institute (GERI) founded by John Feldhusen at Purdue University in 1974, which provides a range of services and programs, including research and graduate studies, enrichment programs for talented youth, and professional learning for educators (GERI, n.d.).

Some centers were initially established to serve high-ability students, like the Early Entrance Program (EEP) at the University of Washington, which eventually became the Robinson Center for Young Scholars. Established in 1977 under the leadership of Halbert Robinson, the program provided middle school students of advanced abilities who were ready for postsecondary education a pathway to university study. The center also came to produce research and offer resources (Robinson Center for Young Scholars, n.d.). In 1979, both the Center for Talented Youth (CTY) at Johns Hopkins University and The Center for Gifted Studies at the University of Southern Mississippi were founded. In collaboration with Johns Hopkins University, Julian Stanley had established CTY. The idea initially grew from helping one young man who needed access to more advanced mathematics classes and soon blossomed into a greater mission to "recognize and develop the world's brightest minds" (Center for Talented Youth, n.d., para. 2). CTY included research and service as part of the center's mission and work. The Center for Gifted Studies, headed by Frances Karnes, was one of the first centers serving the gifted education community in the southeast region of the United States. Joyce VanTassel-Baska followed in 1982 at Northwestern University with the founding of the Center for Talent Development with the mission of talent identification, talent development, research, and advocacy (Center for Talent Development, n.d.). Six years later, VanTassel-Baska would open her next center at the College of William and Mary, the Center for Gifted Education, with a focus on curriculum and leadership development (Center for Gifted Education, n.d.). The Torrance Center for Creative, Gifted, and Future Studies (today known as the Torrance Center for Creativity and Talent Development) was established at the University of Georgia in 1984 by Dr. Mary Frasier as a living tribute to E. Paul Torrance (Hébert, 2014). The federally funded National Research Center on the Gifted and Talented (NRC/GT) was established in 1991 with Javits Act funding, with the first consortia comprised of universities including the University of Georgia, Yale University, the University of Virginia, and at the University of Connecticut, where the actual center was housed (Harrington, Harrington, & Karns, 1991), in order to "provide a platform for a national program of systematic research"; NRC/GT members were also committed to translating the research produced for use by practitioners (Renzulli et al., 2014, p. 341).

Throughout the 1980s and 1990s, centers across the United States would continue to be established, each making their own unique contribution to the field through summer and Saturday programming for gifted students, professional development for educators, and/or research associated with gifted education and talent development. Similar to the N/S-LTI-G/T, these centers provide a vital network for the field in the continuing absence of a central federal system to support gifted education.

Summary

With the establishment of a critical mass of research centers across the United States, which also included instances of intentional and purposeful efforts to train the next generation of researchers, the field of gifted education fulfilled the last of Fensham's criteria to signify the development of a fully formed field of inquiry

(Fensham, 2004). Moving into the last decade of the 20th century, the field continued to grapple with contextual issues such as legislative mandates set by the federal government. No Child Left Behind (NCLB) proved to be one of the most stunting for gifted children. NCLB, the reauthorization of the Elementary and Secondary Education Act (ESEA) in 2001, resulted in one of the most fallow periods in gifted education and for gifted children in schools. With the focus of the legislation on children reaching levels of minimum proficiency, teachers and schools concentrated their efforts on students who were struggling to attain these goals of mastery. The accountability system created under NCLB jeopardized the educational progress of high-ability students, especially for students from low-income backgrounds, groups who lacked English language proficiency, and other underserved gifted students (Loveless, 2008; Plucker, Burroughs, & Song, 2010). However frustrating and disappointing, this cycle of obstruction followed by growth should not come as a surprise. The structures put in place during the 1970s and 1980s have ensured that even depressed periods such as these research, professional development, advocacy, and services for gifted students continues.

EPILOGUE

Nearly 150 years after Galton began his studies of eminence and 100 years since the founding of the contemporary field of gifted education, what does gifted education's future hold? The journey of gifted education since late 1800s to the present day has been one of consistent expansion and contraction. Fensham's six indicators of a developed field, presented in the Introduction, are useful in understanding the progress the field has made over the past 150 years. These include (1) academic recognition by other fields of study, (2) the establishment of research journals specific to the discipline, (3) professional associations devoted to the advancement of the field, (4) research conferences focused on the advancement of empirical knowledge, (5) the creation of research centers, and (6) the concerted effort to train new researchers. The formal field of gifted education has met each of these indicators with varying degrees of success, leaving a number of questions still to be answered and work to be done in understanding giftedness and gifted education.

In 2006, several scholars (Coleman, 2006; Robinson, 2006; Subotnik, 2006; VanTassel-Baska, 2006) were asked to comment on the state of research in the field of gifted and talented. Three of the four assigned the field a grade of C, not exactly a ringing endorsement of a field of study nearly 100 years after its establishment. In addition to this rather middling grade the field received, the scholars were also generally in agreement as to the field's strengths and challenges. The most influential persons and research that dominated the field had been led by psychologists, which aligned to the field's foundational origins (Coleman, 2006; Robinson, 2006). There were also bodies of research which can be viewed with positivity. These include those that address acceleration (Assouline, Colangelo, VanTassel-Baska, & Lupkowski-Shoplik, 2015; Colangelo, Assouline, & Gross, 2004) and investigations into highly and profoundly gifted students (Gross, 2006; Lubinski, 2016). Investigations of highly and profoundly gifted individuals have been especially important as "major longitudinal findings on large samples of intellectually precocious students have fulfilled their promise by solidifying empirical generalizations that replicate throughout the educational and psychological science" (Lubinski, 2016, p. 935) and underscore the impact outcomes that well-designed longitudinal studies can produce.

Apart from these solid bodies of empirical research, Robinson (2006, p. 342) noted, "I think we will all have to admit that our imaginations exceed our empiricism." So why hasn't the field made greater gains and progress given that 100 years have passed since its inception as a formal field of study and nearly 150 since Galton began his empiricist investigations into eminence? Suggestions to address the field's challenges include the lack of theories to direct research, the inability to come to consensus over a definition of giftedness, issues over disproportionality with underserved minority students, and a lack of funding to conduct research, which has resulted in studies conducted with an overreliance on the use of convenience samples and an absence of collaboration with other disciplines (Robinson, 2006). Coleman (2006, p. 348) echoed these concerns, lamenting that "our field is not theory driven, but rather is theory associated. Theory provides a rationale for research, but rarely does the research develop a warrant for the theory." Greater use of longitudinal, replication, and intervention studies were also suggested, but the scholars also noted that the lack of research funding prohibited more of this work from taking place (Robinson, 2006; Subotnik, 2006; VanTassel-Baska, 2006).

Despite the ways in which the field has come into being with the establishment of several research journals in the field—*Roeper Review,* the *Journal for the Education of the Gifted,* and the *Journal for Advanced Academics,* in addition to *Gifted Child Quarterly*—the founding of gifted education research centers located across the United States, academic recognition by other fields of study, and a commitment to the training of graduate students, the research trajectory for the field remains rather tepid and the concerns raised by Coleman, Subotnik, Robinson, and VanTassel-Baska are nearly identical on reflection five (Dai, Swanson, & Cheng, 2011) and ten (Plucker & Callahan, 2014) years later.

The status of the field remains hampered by many of the same issues that were raised in 2006. Others have characterized the field as being "fractured, contested, porous rather than unified, insular, and firmly policed" (Dai, Swanson, & Cheng, 2011, p. 126). Dai and his colleagues (2011) conducted a review of empirical studies between 1998 and 2010 and offered recommendations in hopes of improving the empirical trajectory of the field. These recommendations echoed those offered by Coleman, Subotnik, VanTassel-Baska, and Robinson in 2006. These include (1) continued efforts to connect with fields outside of gifted education, (2) research published in journals outside the field of gifted education, (3) awareness and acceptance of research advances that can inform the field, and (4) research conducted that addresses theoretical debates and policy issues. In Plucker and Callahan's (2014) review of research on giftedness and gifted education, they too, provided recommendations for consideration, which included: (1) a greater number of third-party and replication studies, (2) increased efforts to close the excellence gaps, so that underachieving groups attain higher levels of achievement, (3) greater data mining of already existing large data sets that include gifted students, and (4) research that addresses the definition of giftedness, talent development, curriculum, and programming to better inform policy makers.

Even the lure of global competition has not created the traction gifted education has needed in the past to sustain a research agenda, obtain appropriate and adequate funding sources for research and classroom services, and respond to the matching of programming and services to student need at the district and school level. The approach taken during the heights of the Cold War targeted talented youth in the STEM fields to battle the spread of communism and compete with the then-Soviet Union and its allies. Today the United States competes on a global stage, and talented youth are measured by their performance on assessments such as the Trends in Math and Science Study (TIMSS), the Program for International Student Assessment (PISA), and Progress in Internal Reading Literacy (PIRLS). However, the United States lags behind other peer countries when comparing the performance of other high-achieving students, especially those from low-income students. Plucker and Peters (2016) have recommended interventions to address these deficiencies, which include (1) the provision of authentic and achievable opportunities for advanced learning, (2) the use of universal testing and local norms in the identification process, (3) the use of ability grouping and differentiation as part of the advanced learning process, (4) the creation of accountability systems that take into account schools that close the excellence gaps, (5) offering comprehensive teacher development and ongoing support, and (6) interventions that support psychosocial development. Addressing these *excellence gaps*, with the ultimate goal of eliminating them, can also help improve the United States' performance on these international measures of achievement (Plucker, Burroughs, & Song, 2010; Plucker, Peters, & Schmalensee, 2017).

The renewed conversation regarding talent development in Subotnik, Olszewski-Kubilius, and Worrell's 2011 monograph "Rethinking Giftedness and Gifted Education: A Proposed Direction Forward Based on Psychological Science" (p. 3) argued that "the abilities of individuals do matter, particularly their abilities in specific talent domains; different talent domains have different talent trajectories that vary as to when they start, peak, and end; and opportunities provided by society are crucial at every point in the talent development process." Even though the entirety of the gifted education community did not embrace these ideas, they have pushed the field to respond and examine its current definitions, modes of identification, models, and programming (Worrell, Olszewski-Kubilius, & Subotnik, 2012).

Over the course of the past decade, there have been a number of recommendations made and discussions initiated to help further the field of gifted education. Even with the NRC/GT, reviews of literature, and missives by scholars in the field, there remains the absence of another galvanizing event, equal to the Soviet launch of Sputnik I, to marshal the scholars, practitioners, policy makers, and advocates to guide the field forward. What the next 150 years hold for the field of gifted education will depend on its ability to address these recommendations and provide greater relevance and application to practitioners and to other academic fields.

REFERENCES

AAGC (American Association for Gifted Children.) (n.d.). *Realizing the promise of gifted children*. Unpublished manuscript.

Abraham, W. (1957). Administrators look at gifted children. *Educational Administration and Supervision, 43*, 280–284.

American Association for Gifted Children. (1999). *A historical perspective: Chronology of special events—1946–1996*. Retrieved from https://aagc.ssri.duke.edu/history-aagc/

Anderson, K. W. (2015). *The Los Angeles State Normal School: UCLA's forgotten past: 1881–1919)*. Morrisville, NC: Lulu.com

Anderson, L. (2007). *Congress and the classroom: From the Cold War to "No Child Left Behind."* University Park, PA: Penn State University Press.

Anonymous. (2001). Calvin W. Taylor (1915–2000). *American Psychologist, 56*, 519.

Assouline, S. G., Colangelo, N., VanTassel-Baska, J., & Lupkowski-Shoplik, A. (2015). *A nation empowered: Evidence trumps the excuses holding back America's brightest students*. Iowa City, IA: Connie Belin & Jacqueline N. Blank International Center for Gifted Education and Talent Development, University of Iowa.

Autobiography by John Stuart Mill (1873). (n.d.). Retrieved from www.utilitarianism.com/millauto/

Bagley, W. C. (1922). Educational determinism; or democracy and the IQ. *School and Society, 15*, 373–384.

Baldwin, B. T. (1910). Communication and discussions: Sir Francis Galton. *Journal of Educational Psychology, 2*, 149–150.

Baldwin, B. T. (1911). William James' contributions to education. *Journal of Educational Psychology, 2*, 369–382.

Barbe, W. (1958). President's message. *Gifted Child Quarterly, 2*, 55.

Barbe, W. (1959). President's message. *Gifted Child Quarterly, 3*, 72.

Bartlett, P. D. (1983). *Biographical memoir of James Bryant Conant: 1893–1978*. Retrieved from www.nasonline.org/publications/biographical-memoirs/memoir-pdfs/conant-james-b-1893-1978.pdf

Beauvais, C. (2016). California genius: Lewis Terman's gifted child in regional perspective. *Paedagogica Historica, 52*, 748–765.

Becker, K. A. (2003). *History of the Stanford-Binet intelligence scales: Content and psychometrics.* (Stanford-Binet Intelligence Scales, Fifth Edition Assessment Service Bulletin No. 1). Itasca, IL: Riverside Publishing.

Beineke, J. (1987). Sir Francis Galton: Pioneer in gifted education. *Vitae Scholasticae, 6*, 45–58.

Bell, E. T. (1937). *Men of mathematics.* New York, NY: Simon & Schuster.

Benbow, C. (n.d.). In appreciation, Julian Stanley: A powerful American intellect. *Observer.* Retrieved from www.psychologicalscience.org/index.php/uncategorized/in-appreciation-julian-stanley.html

Benjamin, L. T., Jr. (1975). The pioneering work of Leta Hollingworth in the psychology of women. *Nebraska History, 56*, 493–505.

Benjamin, L. T., Jr. (2004). Meet me at the fair. *Observer, 17.* Retrieved from www.psychologicalscience.org/index.php/uncategorized/meet-me-at-the-fair.html

Benjamin, L. T., Jr. (2006). *A brief history of modern psychology.* New York, NY: Wiley-Blackwell.

Benjamin, L. T., Jr. (2009). The birth of American intelligence testing. *Monitor on Psychology, 40*, Retrieved from www.apa.org/monitor/2009/01/assessment.aspx

Benjamin, L. T., Jr. (2013). Introduction. In L. T. Benjamin, Jr. & L. R. Barton (Eds.), *From Coca-Cola to chewing gum: The applied psychology of Harry Hollingworth* (Vol. 2, pp. ix–xx). Akron, OH: The University of Akron Press.

Benjamin, L. T., Jr., Durkin, M., Link, M., Vestal, M., & Acord, J. (1992). Wundt's American doctoral students. *American Psychologist, 47*, 123–131.

Benjamin, L. T., Jr., Rogers, A. M., & Rosenbaum, A. (1991). Coca-Cola, caffeine, and mental deficiency: Harry Hollingworth and the Chattanooga trial of 1911. *Journal of the History of the Behavioral Sciences, 27*, 42–55.

Berliner, D. C. (1993). The 100-year journey of educational psychology. *Exploring applied psychology: Origins and critical analyses*, 37–78.

Bernstein, J. L. (1958). Midwood High School's Advanced Placement program. *NASSP Bulletin, 42*, 22–23.

Berube, M. R. (1994). *American school reform: Progressive, equity, and excellence moments: 1883–1993.* Westport, CT: Praeger Publishers.

Boake, C. (2002). From Binet-Simon to the Wechsler-Bellevue: Tracing the history of intelligence testing. *Journal of Clinical and Experimental Neuropsychology, 24*, 383–405.

Board of Education. (1965). *The quest for racial equality in the Pittsburgh public schools: The annual report.* Pittsburgh, PA: Board of Public Education.

Boring, E. G. (1959). *A biographical memoir: Lewis Madison Terman (1877–1956).* Retrieved from www.nasonline.org/publications/biographical-memoirs/memoir-pdfs/terman-lewis.pdf

Bound, J., & Turner, S. (2002). Going to war and going to college: Did World War II and the G.I. Bill increase educational attainment for returning war veterans? *Journal of Labor Economics, 20*, 784–815.

Bray, J. (1991). The governor's school of North Carolina (West). *Gifted Child Today, 14*, 52–53.

Bredo, E. (2003). The development of Dewey's psychology. In B. J. Zimmerman & D. H. Schunk (Eds.), *Educational psychology: A century of contributions* (pp. 81–111). Washington, DC: American Psychological Association.

Brickman, W. W. (1958). Educational developments in the United States during 1956. *International Review of Education, 4*, 124–126.

Briggs, J. (2013). *Human Betterment Foundation (1928–1942)*. Retrieved from https://embryo.asu.edu/pages/human-betterment-foundation-1928-1942

Bristol, M. (2006, January/February). Born of controversy: The GI Bill of Rights. *Vanguard*, p. 23.

Bristow, W. H., Craig, M. L., Hallock. G. T., & Laycock, S. R. (1951). Identifying gifted children. In P. Witty (Ed.), *The gifted child* (pp. 10–19). Boston, MA: D. C. Heath.

Brooklyn Daily Eagle. (1910, March 20). Cultured Boston has new infant prodigy, p. 11. Retrieved from https://bklyn.newspapers.com/image/59747275/?terms=William+Sidis+genius

Bruce, H. A. (1910). Bending the twig: The education of the eleven-year-old boy who lectured before the Harvard professors on the fourth dimension. *American Magazine*, *69*, 690–695.

Bruner, H. B. (1941). Education's role in developing leadership. *Teachers College Record*, *42*, 375–377.

Bryan, A., & Boring, E. G. (1944). Women in American psychology: Prolegomenon. *Psychological Bulletin*, *5*, 447–454.

Burgess, C. (1971). Ruth Strang: A biographical sketch. In R. J. Havinghurst (Ed.), *Seventeenth yearbook of the National Society for the Study of Education: Vol. 2. Leaders in American Education* (pp. 398–411). Chicago, IL: University of Chicago Press.

Burk, F. (1913). *Lock-step schooling and a remedy; the fundamental evils and handicaps of class instruction; and a report of progress in the construction of an individual system*. Sacramento, CA: Superintendent of State Printing.

Burks, B. S., Jensen, D. W., & Terman, L. S. (1930). *Genetic studies of genius, Vol. III: The promise of youth*. Palo Alto, CA: Stanford University Press.

Burt, C. (1961). Gifted children: The latest report of the Terman studies. *The Eugenics Review*, *53*, 17–20.

Burt, C. (1962). Francis Galton and his contributions to psychology. *The British Journal of Statistical Psychology*, *15*, 1–49.

Butz, W., Kelly, T. K., Adamson, D. M., Bloom, G. A., Fossum, D., & Gross, M. E. (2004). *Will the scientific and technology workforce meet the requirements of the federal government?* Pittsburgh, PA: RAND Corporation.

Bycroft, M. (2012). Psychology, psychologists, and the creativity movement: The lives of method inside and outside the Cold War. In M. Solovey & H. Cravens (Eds.), *Cold War social science* (pp. 197–214). New York, NY: Palgrave.

Capshew, J. H. (1992). A reconnaissance of the historiography of the laboratory. *American Psychologist*, *47*, 132–142.

Caraley, D., & Schlussel, Y. R. (1986). Congress and Reagan's new federalism. *Publius*, *16*, 49–79.

Cattell, J. M. (1888). The psychological laboratory at Leipsic. *Mind*, *13*, 37–51.

Cattell, J. M. (1890). Mental tests and measurements. *Mind*, *51*, 373–381.

Cattell, J. M. (1903). A statistical study of eminent men. *The Popular Science Monthly*, *62*, 359–377.

Cattell, R. B. (1963). Theory of fluid and crystallized intelligence: A critical experiment. *Journal of Educational Psychology*, *54*, 1–22.

CEC-TAG. (n.d.). About. Retrieved from http://cectag.com

Center for Gifted Education. (n.d.). *About the center*. Retrieved from http://education.wm.edu/centers/cfge/about/index.php

Center for Talent Development. (n.d.) *History*. Retrieved from www.ctd.northwestern.edu/history/

Center for Talented Youth. (n.d.). *Mission and history*. Retrieved http://cty.jhu.edu/about/mission/
Chapman, P. D. (1988). *Schools as sorters: Lewis M. Terman, applied psychology, and the intelligence testing movement, 1890–1930*. New York, NY: New York University Press.
Chauncey, H. (1958). Measurement and prediction—Test of academic ability. In J. B. Conant (Ed.), *The identification and education of the academically talented student in the American secondary school* (pp. 27–34). Washington, DC: NEA.
Civil Rights Act of 1964 §6, 42 U. S. C. §2000e et seq. (1964).
Clark, H. F., & Williamson, P. (1951). Foreword. In P. Witty (Ed.), *The gifted child*. (pp. v–vi). Boston, MA: D. C. Heath.
Clynes, T. (2016). How to raise a genius: Lessons from a 45-year study of super-smart children. *Nature, 537*, Retrieved from www.nature.com/news/how-to-raise-a-genius-lessons-from-a-45-year-study-of-super-smart-children-1.20537
Cobb, M. V., Hollingworth, L. S., Monahan, J. E., Taylor, G. A., & Theobald, J. S. (1923). The special opportunity class for gifted children at Public School 165 Manhattan. *Ungraded, 8*, 121–128.
Coffey, K., Ginsberg, G., Lockhart, C., McCartney, D., Nathan, C., & Wood, K. (1976). *Parentspeak*. Ventura, CA: Office of the Ventura County Superintendent of Schools.
Cohen, L. M., Austin, K. D., & Odoardi, R. H. (2014). Calvin W. Taylor: A man of many talents (1915–2000). In A. Robinson & J. L. Jolly (Eds.), *A century of contributions to gifted education: Illuminating lives* (pp. 144–162). New York, NY: Routledge.
Colangelo, N., Assouline, S. G., & Gross, M. U. M. (2004). *A nation deceived: How schools hold back America's brightest students*. Iowa City, IA: Connie Belin & Jacqueline N. Blank International Center for Gifted Education and Talent Development, University of Iowa.
Colangelo, N., & Davis, G. A. (2003). Introduction and overview. In N. Colangelo & G. A. Davis (Eds.), *Handbook of gifted education* (3rd ed., pp. 3–23). Boston, MA: Allyn & Bacon.
Coleman, L. J. (2006). A report card on the state of research on the talented and gifted. *Gifted Child Quarterly, 50*, 346–350.
Coleman, L. J., & Cross, T. C. (2005). *Being gifted in school: An introduction to development, guidance, and teaching* (2nd ed.). Waco, TX: Prufrock Press.
Committee No. 4. (1947). The discovery of outstanding talent in youth. *Teachers College Record, 48*, 260–268.
Conant, J. B. (1943). Wanted: American radicals. *The Atlantic*. Retrieved from www.theatlantic.com/past/docs/issues/95sep/ets/radical.htm
Conant, J. B. (1948). Public schools and the talented. *Understanding the Child, 17*(2), 52.
Conant, J. B. (Ed.) (1958a). *The identification and education of the academically talented student in the American secondary school*. Washington, DC: National Education Association.
Conant, J. B. (1958b). Conference report. In *The identification and education of the academically talented student in the American secondary school* (pp. 135–140). Washington, DC: National Education Association.
Conceptual Foundations Network. (2009). *A conversation with Joe Renzulli: Portraits in gifted education—The legacy series*. Washington, DC: NAGC.
Conceptual Foundations Network. (2011). *An afternoon with Alexinia Y. Baldwin: Portraits in gifted education—The legacy series*. Washington, DC: NAGC.
Cooke, G. J., & Baldwin, A. Y. (1979). Unique needs of a special population. In A. Passow (Ed.), *The gifted and the talented: Their education and development—The seventy-eighth Yearbook of the National Society for the Study of Education, Part 1* (pp. 388–394). Chicago, IL: The University of Chicago Press.

Corn, A. L. (1999). Missed opportunities—but a new century is starting. *Gifted Child Today, 22*(6), 19–21.

Cox, C. M. (1926). *The early mental traits of 300 geniuses: Genetic studies of genius, Vol. 2.* Stanford, CA: Stanford University Press.

Crabtree, D. (1993). *The importance of history.* Retrieved from http://msc.gutenberg.edu/2001/02/the-importance-of-history/

Cravens, H. (1978). *The triumph of evolution: American scientists and the heredity-environment controversy, 1900–1941.* Philadelphia, PA: University of Pennsylvania Press.

Cravens, H. (1992). A scientific project locked in time: The Terman Genetic Studies of Genius, 1920s–1950s. *American Psychologist, 47,* 183–189.

Cremin, L. A. (1959). John Dewey and the Progressive-education movement: 1915–1952. *The School Review, 67,* 160–173.

Crissey, M. S. (1990). Beth Lucy Wellman (1895–1952). In A. N. O'Connell & N. F. Russo (Eds.), *Women in psychology: A bio-bibliographic sourcebook* (pp. 350–360). Westport, CT: Greenwood Publishing.

Cross, T. L. (1999). Top ten list for the 20th century (plus or minus two). *Gifted Child Today, 22*(6), 22–25.

Cutts, N. E., & Moseley, N. (1957). *Teaching the bright and gifted.* Englewood Cliffs, NJ: Prentice-Hall.

Da Costa, M. P., Zenasi, F., Nicolas, S., & Lubart, T. (2014). Alfred Binet: A creative life in measurement and pedagogy. In A. Robinson & J. L. Jolly (Eds.), *A century of contributions to gifted education: Illuminating lives* (pp. 23–40). New York, NY: Routledge.

Dahlstrom, W. G. (1985). The development of psychological testing. In G. A. Kimble & K. Schlesinger (Eds.), *Topics in the history of psychology* (Vol. 2). New York, NY: Psychology Press.

Dai, D. Y., Swanson, J. A., & Cheng, H. (2011). State of research on giftedness and gifted education: A survey of empirical studies published during 1998–2010. *Gifted Child Quarterly, 55,* 126–138.

Darwin, C. (1859). *On the origin of species.* Retrieved from http://darwin-online.org.uk/content/frameset?itemID=F373&viewtype=text&pageseq=1

Davis, G. A., & Rimm, S. B. (1989). *Education of the gifted and talented* (2nd ed.). Englewood Cliffs, NJ: Prentice-Hall.

Davis, G. A., & Rimm, S. B. (1994). *Education of the gifted and talented* (3rd ed.). Boston, MA: Allyn & Bacon.

Davis, J. L. (2014). Dr. Martin D. Jenkins: A voice to be heard (1904–1978). In A. Robinson & J. L. Jolly (Eds.), *A century of contributions to gifted education: Illuminating lives* (pp. 130–143). New York, NY: Routledge.

Davis, N. (1954). Teachers for the gifted. *Journal for Teacher Education, 5,* 221–224.

Davis, O. L., Jr., (2011). The NDEA and American education: Reflections on review of Wayne Urban's *More Than Science and Sputnik. Education and Review, 16.* Retrieved from www.edrev.info/essays/v16n6.pdf

Davis, P. I. (1978). *Community-based efforts to increase the identification of the number of gifted minority children.* (ED 176487).

Davis, W. (1951). Search for talent in science. In P. Witty (Ed.), *The gifted child* (pp. 235–242). Boston, MA: D. C. Heath.

D. C. Heath. (1946). *A Heath portrait of Paul Witty: The man who knows children.* Boston, MA: Author.

DeHaan, R. F., & Havighurst, R. J. (1957). *Educating gifted children.* Chicago, IL: University of Chicago Press.

DeHaan, R. F. (1959). Identifying gifted children. In J. L. French (Ed.), *Educating the gifted child: A book of readings* (pp. 74–81). New York, NY: Henry Holt.

Department of Veterans Affairs. (n.d.). *VA history in brief*. Retrieved from www.va.gov/opa/publications/archives/docs/history_in_brief.pdf

Derthick, L. G. (1959). *Soviet commitment to education: Report of the first official U.S. education mission to the U.S.S.R.* Washington, DC: Department of Health, Education, and Welfare.

Dewey, J. (1900). Psychology and social practice. *The Psychology Review, 7*, 105–124.

Dewey, J. (1916). *Democracy and education*. Retrieved from www.gutenberg.org/files/852/852-h/852-h.htm

Douglas, E. C. (1959). The Advanced Placement Program of the CEEB. *NASSP Bulletin, 43*(247), 92–95.

Dreier, P. (2012). *The 100 greatest Americans of the 20th century: A social justice hall of fame*. New York, NY: Nation Books.

DuBois, W. E. B. (1903). The talented tenth. In B. T. Washington (Ed.), *The Negro problem: A series of articles by representative American Negros of today* (pp. 33–75). New York, NY: James Pott.

DuBois, W. E. B. (1910). Editorial. *The Crisis, 1*, 10. Retrieved from http://library.brown.edu/pdfs/127470517978125.pdf

Dudley, D. A. (1958). The Advanced Placement Program. *NASSP Bulletin, 42*(242), 1–5.

DuPont, L. (1941). The place of the gifted in industry and business. *Teachers College Record, 42*, 382–385.

E. B. T. (1925). Edmund Clark Sanford 1859–1924. *The American Journal of Psychology, 36*, 157–170.

Edgerton, H. A., & Britt, S. W. (1946). The third annual Science Talent Search. *Science, 99*, 319–320.

Editorial: Understanding the gifted child. (1948). *Understanding the Child, 17*(2), 33–34.

Educational Policies Commission. (1950). *Education of the gifted*. Washington, DC: National Education Association.

Elliott, C. (1958). America's backlog of bight boys and girls—Her underdeveloped resource. In J. B. Conant (Ed.), *The identification and education of the academically talented student in the American secondary school*, 141–148. Washington, DC: National Education Association.

Engelstein, S. S., & Miller, H. H. (1958). Advanced work for gifted students at Senn High School: Special history classes permit students to earn college credit. *NASSP Bulletin, 42*, 32–38.

Ericson, S. C. (1985). *Education of the gifted and talented in American public schools: A retrospective view*. Unpublished doctoral dissertation, Washington State University.

Fancher, R. (1985). *The intelligence men: Makers of the IQ controversy*. New York, NY: W. W. Norton.

Fass, P. A. (1980). The IQ: A cultural and historical framework. *American Journal of Education, 88*, 431–458.

Feldhusen, J. F. (2003). Lewis M. Terman: A pioneer in the development of ability tests. In B. J. Zimmerman & D. H. Schunk (Eds.), *Educational psychology: A century of contributions* (pp. 155–169). Washington, DC: American Psychological Association.

Fensham, P. J. (2004). *Defining an identity: The evolution of science education as a field of research*. Dordrecht, Netherlands: Klewer Academic Publishers.

Fernberger, S. W. (1932). The American Association: A historical summary, 1892–1930. *Psychological Bulletin, 29*, 1–89.

Finn, C., Jr. (2008). *Troublemaker*. Princeton, NJ: Princeton University Press.

Fiske, E. B. (1986, April 27). Effort to improve U.S. schools entering a new phase. *New York Times*. Retrieved from www.nytimes.com/1986/04/27/us/effort-to-improve-us-schools-entering-a-new-phase.html

Flattau, E., Bracken, J., Van Atta, R., Bandeh-Ahmadi, A., de la Cruz, R., & Sullivan, K. (2006). *The National Defense Education Act of 1958: Selected outcomes*. Washington, DC: Institute for Defense Analyses Science and Technology Policy Institute.

Fleming, A. S. (1960). The philosophy and objectives of the National Defense Education Act. *Annals of the American Academy of Political and Social Science, 327*, 132–138.

Fliegler, L. A., & Bish, C. E. (1959). The gifted and talented. *Review of Educational Research, 29*, 408–450.

Ford, D. Y. (1995). Desegregating gifted education: A need unmet. *Journal of Negro Education, 64*, 52–62.

Ford, D. Y. (2011). *Reversing underachievement among gifted Black students*. Waco, TX: Prufrock Press.

Fox, L. (1978). Report for the USOE Task Force on Gifted and Talented Education. *Gifted Child Quarterly, 23*, 284–289.

French, J. L. (Ed.). (1959). *Educating the gifted*. New York, NY: Henry Holt.

From Correspondent. (1921). The study of gifted children. *School and Society, 8*, 338–339.

Fund for the Advancement of Education, The. (1957). *They went to college early: Evaluation report number 2*. New York, NY: Author.

Gaddis, J. L. (2006). *The Cold War: A new history*. New York, NY: Penguin Books.

Gagné, F. (1985). Giftedness and talent: Reexamining a reexamination of the definitions. *Gifted Child Quarterly, 29*, 103–112.

Gagné, F. (2008). *Building gifts into talents: Overview of the DMGT*. Retrieved from www.templetonfellows.org/program/francoysgagne.pdf

Gallagher, J. J. (1966). The gifted. *Review of Educational Research, 36*, 37–55.

Gallagher, J. J. (1994). *Current and historical thinking on education for gifted and talented students*. Washington, DC: Office of Educational Research and Improvement (ED 372584).

Gallagher, J. J., & Weiss, P. (1979). *The education of gifted and talented students: A history and prospectus*. Washington, DC: Council for Exceptional Children.

Galton, F. (1865). Hereditary talent and character. *Macmillan's Magazine, 12*, 157–166, 318–327. Retrieved from http://galton.org/essays/1860-1869/galton-1865-hereditary-talent.pdf

Galton, F. (1874). *English men of science: Their nature and nurture*. London, UK: Macmillan. Retrieved from http://galton.org/books/men-science/pdf/galton-men-science-1up.pdf

Galton, F. (1883). *Inquiries into human faculty and its development*. London, UK: Macmillan. Retrieved from http://galton.org/books/human-faculty/text/human-faculty.pdf

Gamson, D. (2009). District Progressivism: Rethinking reform in urban school systems, 1900–1928. *Paedagogica Historica, 39*, 417–434.

Gan, H. (2008). Chinese education tradition—Imperial examination system in feudal China. *Journal of Management and Social Science, 4*, 115–133.

Gardner, D. P. (2005). *Earning my degree: Memoirs of an American university president*. Berkeley, CA: University of California Press.

Gardner, H. (1983). *Frames of mind: The theory of multiple intelligences*. New York, NY: Basic Books.

Gardner, H. (1995). Reflections on multiple intelligences myths and messages. *Phi Delta Kappan, 77*, 200–203, 206–209.

Garrison, C. G., Burke, A., & Hollingworth, L. S. (1917). The psychology of a prodigious child. *The Journal of Applied Psychology, 1*, 101–110.

Gear, G. H. (1974). *Teaching the talented program: A progress report.* Storrs, CT: School of Education, University of Connecticut (ED102765).

George, M. (2012). *Profile of Beth Wellman.* In A. Rutherford (Ed.), *Psychology's feminist voices multimedia internet archive.* Retrieved from www.feministvoices.com/beth-wellman/

George Meany Center for Labor Studies. (2000). *Child labor in the United States.* Retrieved from www.georgemeany.org/archives/labor.html#section1

GERI. (n.d.). *Advocating for high ability students.* Retrieved from www.education.purdue.edu/geri/

Getzels, J. W., & Jackson, P. W. (1958). The meaning of "giftedness"—An examination of an expanding concept. *The Phi Delta Kappan, 40,* 75–77.

Gifted and Talented Children Educational Assistance Act: Hearing before the Subcommittee on Education, Senate 91st Congress. (1969a) (testimony of Jacob Javits).

Gifted and Talented Children Educational Assistance Act: Hearing before the Subcommittee on Education, House of Representatives, 91st Congress. (1969b) (testimony of John Ashbrook, John Erlenborn, James J. Gallagher, & Albert Quie).

Gillham, N. W. (2001). Sir Francis Galton and the birth of eugenics. *Annual Review of Genetics, 35,* 83–101.

Goddard, H. H. (n.d.). *The Ohio State University: News bureau.* Retrieved from https://library.osu.edu/documents/university-archives/biographical_files/Goddard_Henry.pdf

Goddard, H. H. (1912). *The Kallikak family: A study in the heredity of feeble-mindedness.* New York, NY: Macmillan.

Gold, S. (1984). Sixty years of programming for the gifted in Cleveland. *Phi Delta Kappan, 65,* 497–499.

Goldberg, M. L. (1958). Recent research on the talented. *Teachers College Record, 60,* 150–163.

Gottfredson, L., & Saklofske, D. H. (2009). Intelligence: Foundations and issues in assessment. *Canadian Psychology, 50,* 183–195.

Governor's Program for Gifted Children. (n.d.). *History and mission of GPGC.* Retrieved from www.gpgc.org/history-and-mission-of-the-gpgc/

Gowan, J. C. (1969, December). The education of disadvantaged gifted youth. *California Journal for Instructional Improvement,* 239–251.

Gray, H. A., & Hollingworth, L. S. (1931). The achievement of gifted children enrolled and not enrolled in special opportunity classes. *The Journal of Educational Research, 24,* 255–261.

Green, C. D., Shore, M., & Teo, T. (2001). *The transformation of psychology: Influence of 19th-century philosophy, technology, and natural science.* Washington, DC: American Psychological Association.

Gross, M. U. M. (2006). Exceptionally gifted children: Long-term outcomes of academic acceleration and nonacceleration. *Journal for the Education of the Gifted, 29,* 404–429.

Guilford, J. P. (1950). Creativity. *American Psychologist, 5,* 444–454.

Guilford, J. P. (1967). Creativity: Yesterday, today, and tomorrow. *Journal of Creative Behavior, 1,* 3–14.

Guilford, J. P. (1972). Intellect and the gifted. *Gifted Child Quarterly, 16,* 175–184.

Hall, G. S. (1888–1920). Graduate student correspondence. Dr. G. Stanley Hall Collection (B1-6-12). Clark University Archives and Special Collections, Worcester, MA.

Hall, V. C. (2003). Educational psychology from 1890 to 1920. In B. J. Zimmerman & D. H. Schunk (Eds.), *Educational psychology: A century of contributions* (pp. 3–40). Washington, DC: American Psychological Association.

Hankins, F. H. (1925). Individual differences: The Galton-Pearson approach. *Social Forces, 4*, 272–281.

Hardesty, L. (2011). *The original absent-minded professor.* Retrieved from www.technologyreview.com/s/424363/the-original-absent-minded-professor/

Harmon, L. R., & Soldz, H. (1963). *Doctorate production in U.S. universities 1920–1962.* Washington, DC: National Academy of Sciences.

Harrington, J., Harrington, C., & Karns, E. (1991). The Marland Report: Twenty years later. *Journal for the Education of the Gifted, 15*, 31–43.

Hastorf, A. (2011, April). *History of the psychology department.* Retrieved from https://psychology.stanford.edu/historyofdepartment

Hearst, E., & Capshew, J. H. (Eds.). (1988). *Psychology at Indiana University: A centennial review and compendium.* Bloomington, IN: Indiana University Department of Psychology. Retrieved from http://psych.indiana.edu/tradition/Hearst_and_Capshew_1988.pdf

Heck, A. O. (1953). *The education of exceptional children: Its challenge to teachers, parents, and laymen* (2nd ed.). New York, NY: Macmillan.

Herbers, J. (1970, September 23). Nixon nominates Marland as U.S. education chief. *The New York Times.* Retrieved from www.nytimes.com/1970/09/23/archives/nixon-nominates-marland-as-us-education-chief-president-nominates.html?_r=0

Hébert, T. P. (2014). Illuminating our lives with creativity: The life and legacy of E. Paul Torrance (1915–2003). In A. Robinson & J. L. Jolly (Eds.), *A century of contributions to gifted education: Illuminating lives* (pp. 161–180). New York, NY: Routledge.

Hébert, T. P., Cramond, B., Speirs Neumeister, K. L., Millar, G., & Silvian, A. F. (2002). *E. P. Torrance: His life, accomplishments, and legacy.* Retrieved from http://files.eric.ed.gov/fulltext/ED505439.pdf

Henry, T. S. (1920). *Classroom problems in the education of gifted children. The nineteenth yearbook of the National Society for the Study of Education (Part II).* Chicago, IL: University of Chicago Press.

Henshon, S. E. (2014). Virgil S. Ward: An Axiomatic approach to work and life (1916–2003). In A. Robinson & J. L. Jolly (Eds.) (2014). *A century of contributions to gifted education: Illuminating lives* (pp. 232–240). New York, NY: Routledge.

Herbold, H. (1994–1995). Never a level playing field: Blacks and GI Bill. *The Journal of Blacks in Higher Education, 6*, 104–108.

Hertberg-Davis, H. (2014). Leta Stetter Hollingworth: A life in schools (1886–1939). In A. Robinson & J. L. Jolly (Eds.), *A century of contributions to gifted education: Illuminating lives* (pp. 79–100). New York, NY: Routledge.

Hildebrand, S. (1981). *Democracy's aristocrat: The gifted child in America, 1910–1960.* Unpublished doctoral dissertation, University of California, Berkeley.

Hilgard, E. R. (1957). Lewis Madison Terman: 1877–1956. *American Journal of Psychology, 70*, 472–479.

Hilgard, E. R. (1965). *Biographical memoir of Robert Means Yerkes: 1876–1956.* Retrieved from www.nasonline.org/publications/biographical-memoirs/memoir-pdfs/yerkes-robert-m.pdf

Hilgard, E. R. (1987). *Psychology in America: A historical survey.* Fort Worth, TX: Harcourt Brace Jovanovich College Publishers.

Hilliard, A. G. (1976). *Alternative to IQ testing: An approach to the identification of gifted "minority" children.* Sacramento, CA: California State Department of Education (ED 147009).

Hindley, M. (2014, July/August). How the GI Bill become law in spite of some veterans' groups. *National Endowment for the Humanities.* Retrieved from www.neh.gov/print/21906

Hogan, J. D., & Sexton, V. S. (1991). Women and the American Psychological Association. *Psychology of Women Quarterly, 15,* 623–634.

Holland, J. L., & Stalnaker, R. C. (1958). A descriptive study of talented high school seniors: National Merit Scholars. *NASSP Bulletin, 42*(236), 9–21.

Hollingworth, H. L. (1990). *Leta Stetter Hollingworth: A biography.* Bolton, MA: Anker Publishing.

Hollingworth, L. S. (1922). Subsequent history of E—; Five years after the initial report. *Journal of Applied Psychology, 6,* 205–210.

Hollingworth, L. S. (1924a). Provisions for intellectually superior children. In M. V. O'Shea (Ed.), *The child: His nature and needs* (pp. 277–299). New York, NY: The Children Foundation.

Hollingworth, L. S. (1924b). An introduction to biography for young children who test above 150 IQ. *Teachers College Record, 26,* 277–287.

Hollingworth, L. S. (1926). *Gifted children: Their nature and nurture.* New York, NY: Macmillan.

Hollingworth, L. S. (1929). The production of gifted children from the parental point of view. *Eugenics, 2,* 3–7.

Hollingworth, L. S. (1936a). The Terman classes at Public School 500. *Journal of Educational Sociology, 10,* 86–90.

Hollingworth, L. S. (1936b). The founding of Public School 500: Speyer School. *Teachers College Record, 38,* 119–128.

Hollingworth, L. S. (1938). An enrichment curriculum for rapid learners at Public School 500: Speyer School. *Teachers College Record, 39,* 296–306.

Hollingworth, L. S. (1939). What we know about the early selection and training of leaders. *Teachers College Record, 40,* 575–592.

Hollingworth, L. S. (1942). *Children above 180 IQ.* Yonkers-on-Hudson, NY: World Book.

Howard, R. (2009). Alfred Binet: A truly applied psychologist. *The Psychologist, 22,* 278–279.

Isaacs, A. F. (1957). President's message. *Gifted Child Newsletter, 1,* 2, 6.

Isaacs, A. F. (1968, May). Find the gifted children. *The Wonderful World of Ohio,* 30–33.

Isaacs, A. F. (1974). XVIII. Biographical background. *Gifted Child Quarterly, 18,* 75–81.

Jacob K. Javits Gifted and Talented Students Education Act of 1988, 20 USC §3065.

Jackson, D. M. (1979). The emerging national and state concern. In A. H. Passow (Ed.), *The gifted and the talented: Their education and development: The seventy-eighth yearbook of the National Society for the Study of Education, Pt. 1* (pp. 55–74). Chicago, IL: University of Chicago Press.

James, W. (1899/1962). *Talks to teachers on psychology and to students on some of life's ideals.* Mineola, NY: Dover Publications.

Jarvin, L., & Sternberg, R. J. (2003). Alfred Binet's contributions to educational psychology. In B. J. Zimmerman & D. H. Schunk (Eds.), *Educational psychology: A century of contributions* (pp. 65–79). Washington, DC: American Psychological Association.

Javits, J. K. (1981). *Javits.* Boston, MA: Houghton Mifflin.

Jefferson, T. (1801). *Notes on the State of Virginia.* Boston, MA: David Carlisle. Retrieved from https://books.google.com.au/books?id=NDo_AAAAYAAJ&pg=PA217&dq=most+promising+genius+and+disposition+notes+on+virgina+jefferson&hl=en&sa=X&ved=0ahUKEwjauo_Ci9jSAhUC12MKHTVNC7sQ6AEILTAD

Jenkins, M. D. (1943). Case studies of Negro children of Binet IQ 160 and above. *The Journal of Negro Education, 12,* 159–166.

Jenkins, M. D. (1948). The upper limit of ability among American Negroes. *The Scientific Monthly, 66,* 399–401.

Johnson, L. B. (1964). *Remarks at the University of Michigan*. Retrieved from http://www.presidency.ucsb.edu/ws/?pid=26262

Johnson, B. (1977). What can you do for the gifted on Monday morning? *Educational Leadership, 35*, 35–41.

Jolly, J. L. (2004). *A conceptual history of gifted education: 1910–1940*. (Unpublished doctoral dissertation). Baylor University, Waco, TX.

Jolly, J. L. (2005). Foundations of the field of gifted education. *Gifted Child Today, 28*(2), 14–18, 65.

Jolly, J. L. (2006a). Curriculum for the gifted student: Lulu Stedman's contributions. *Gifted Child Today, 29*(1), 49–53.

Jolly, J. L. (2006b). Leta S. Hollingworth: P. S. 165 & 500: Lessons learned. *Gifted Child Today, 29*(3), 28–34.

Jolly, J. L. (2007a). Guy M. Whipple. *Gifted Child Today, 30*(1), 55–57.

Jolly, J. L. (2007b). The research legacy of Leta S. Hollingworth. *Gifted Child Today, 30*(3), 57–64.

Jolly, J. L. (2008a). Lewis Terman: Genetic study of genius—elementary school students. *Gifted Child Today, 31*(1), 27–33.

Jolly, J. L. (2008b). A paradoxical point of view: Lewis M. Terman. *Gifted Child Today, 31*(2), 36–37.

Jolly, J. L. (2009a). A resuscitation of gifted education. *American Educational History Journal, 36*(1), 37–52.

Jolly, J. L. (2009b). Sidney P. Marland, Jr. *Gifted Child Today, 32*(4), 40–43, 65.

Jolly, J. L. (2010). Florence L. Goodenough: Portrait of a psychologist. *Roeper Review, 32*, 98–105.

Jolly, J. L. (2013). The Servicemen's Readjustment Act of 1944. *Gifted Child Today, 36*, 266–268.

Jolly, J. L. (2014). Building gifted education one state at a time. *Gifted Child Today, 37*(4), 258–260.

Jolly, J. L. (2015). The gifted at risk. *Gifted Child Today, 38*(2), 124–127.

Jolly, J. L., & Bruno, J. (2010). The public's fascination with prodigious youth. *Gifted Child Today, 32*(2), 61–65.

Jolly, J. L., & Kettler, T. (2008). Gifted education research 1994–2003: A disconnect between priorities and practice. *Journal for the Education of the Gifted, 31*, 427–446.

Jolly, J. L., & Makel, M. (2010). No Child Left Behind: The inadvertent costs for high-achieving and gifted students. *Childhood Education, 87*, 34–40.

Jolly, J. L., & Matthews, M. S. (2014). Sidney P. Marland: The commissioner. In A. Robinson & J. L. Jolly (Eds.), *A century of contributions to gifted education: Illuminating lives* (pp. 289–301). New York, NY: Routledge.

Jolly, J. L., & Robins, J. H. (2014). Paul Witty: A gentleman scholar (1898–1976). In A. Robinson & J. L. Jolly (Eds.), *A century of contributions to gifted education: Illuminating lives* (pp. 118–129). New York, NY: Routledge.

Jolly, J. L., & Robins, J. H. (2016). After the Marland Report: Four decades of progress? *Journal for the Education of the Gifted, 39*, 132–150.

Jolly, J. L., & Robinson, A. (2014). James J. Gallagher: Man in the white hat. *Journal for Advanced Academics, 25*, 445–455.

Journal of Blacks in Higher Education, The. (2015). National Merit Scholarship Corporation ends its program for Black students entering college. Retrieved from www.jbhe.com/2015/09/national-merit-scholarship-corporation-ends-its-program-for-black-students-entering-college/

Kaestle, C. (n.d.). *Testing policy in the United States: A historical perspective.* Retrieved from www.gordoncommission.org/rsc/pdfs/kaestle_testing_policy_united_states.pdf

Kantor, H. (1991). Social reform and the state: ESEA and federal education policy in the 1960s. *American Journal of Education, 100,* 47–83.

Kaplan, S. N. (1975). *Providing programs for the gifted and talented: A handbook.* Ventura, CA: Office of the Ventura County Superintendent of Schools.

Kaufman, J. C., Kaufman, S. B., & Plucker, J. A. (2013). Contemporary theories of intelligence. In D. Reisberg (Ed.), *Oxford handbook of cognitive of psychology* (pp. 811–822). New York, NY: Oxford University Press.

Kaufman, S., & Sternberg, R. (2008). Conceptions of giftedness. In S. I. Pfeiffer (Ed.), *Handbook of giftedness in children* (pp. 71–91). New York, NY: Springer.

Kaye, G. T. (2001). *Celebrating 60 years of science.* Washington, DC: Science Service.

Kearney, K., & LeBlanc, J. (1993). Forgotten pioneers in the study of gifted African Americans. *Roeper Review, 15,* 192–199.

Keller, C. R. (1958). The Advanced Placement program now has a history. *NASSP Bulletin, 42,* 6–12.

Kevles, L. J. (1985). *In the name of eugenics: Genetics and the uses of human heredity.* New York, NY: Knopf.

Kennedy, J. F. (1961). *Special message to Congress on education.* Retrieved from www.presidency.ucsb.edu/ws/?pid=8433

Keys, N. (1942). Should we accelerate the bright? *Exceptional Children, 8,* 248–269.

Kirschenbaum, R. T. (1998). Interview with Dr. A. Harry Passow. *Gifted Child Quarterly, 42*(4), 194–199.

Klein, A. (2002). *A forgotten voice: The biography of Leta Stetter Hollingworth.* Scottsdale, AZ: Great Potential Press.

Kliebard, H. M. (1995). *The struggle for the American curriculum* (2nd ed.). New York, NY: Routledge.

Knight, E. W. (1952). *Fifty years of American education—A historical review and appraisal.* New York, NY: The Ronald Press.

Kode, K. (2002). *Elizabeth Farrell and the history of special education.* Arlington, VA: Council for Exceptional Children. Retrieved from http://files.eric.ed.gov/fulltext/ED474364.pdf

Kronborg, L. (2014). Ruth May Strang: Leading advocacy for the gifted (1895–1971). In A. Robinson & J. L. Jolly (Eds.), *A century of contributions to gifted education: Illuminating lives* (pp. 241–255). New York, NY: Routledge.

Kuhn, T. S. (1996). *The structure of scientific revolutions* (3rd ed.). Chicago, IL: University of Chicago Press.

Kuo, J. (1998). Excluded, segregated and forgotten: A historical view of the discrimination of Chinese Americans in public schools. *Asian American Law Review, 5,* 181–212.

Labaree, D. F. (2005). Progressivism, schools, and schools of education: An American romance. *Paedagogica Historica, 41,* 275–288.

Lagemann, E. C. (1989). The plural worlds of educational research. *History of Education Quarterly, 29,* 185–214.

Lagemann, E. C. (2000). *An elusive science: The troubling history of education research.* Chicago, IL: The University of Chicago Press.

Landrum, M. S., Katsiyannis, A., & DeWaard, J. (1998). A national survey of current legislative and policy trends in gifted education: Life after the *National Excellent* report. *Journal for the Education of the Gifted, 21,* 352–371.

Lemann, N. (2000). *The big test: The secret history of the American meritocracy.* New York, NY: Farrar, Straus & Giroux.

Leonard, T. C. (2005). Eugenics and economics in the progressive era. *Journal of Economic Perspectives*, *19*, 207–224.

Lepore, J. (2011, March). Twilight: Growing old and even older. *The New Yorker*. Retrieved from www.newyorker.com/magazine/2011/03/14/twilight-jill-lepore

Leslie, M. (2000). The vexing legacy of Lewis Terman. *Stanford Magazine*. Retrieved from https://alumni.stanford.edu/get/page/magazine/article/?article_id=40678

Lewis, D. L. (2009). *W.E.B. DuBois: A biography 1868–1963*. New York, NY: Holt.

Lippmann, W. (1922, November 15). The mental age of Americans. *The New Republic*, *33*, 297–298.

Lippmann, W. (1923, January 3). The great confusion. *The New Republic*, *33*, 146.

Lombroso, C. (1901). *The man of genius*. New York, NY: Scribner.

Loveless, T. (2008). *An analysis of NAEP data*. Washington, DC: Thomas B. Fordham Institute.

Lubinski, D. (2016). From Terman to today: A century of findings on intellectual precocity. *Review of Educational Research*, *86*, 900–944.

Lubinski, D., & Benbow, C. P. (2006). Study of mathematically precocious youth after 35 years. *Perspectives on Psychological Science*, *1*, 316–345.

Margolin, L. (1993). Goodness personified: The emergence of gifted children. *Social Problems*, *40*, 510–532.

Marland, S. P., Jr. (1972a). *Education of the gifted and talented: Report to the Congress of the United States by the U.S. Commissioner of Education and background papers submitted to the U.S. Office of Education* (2 vols.). Washington, DC: U.S. Government Printing Office. (Government Documents, Y4.L 11/2: G36)

Marland, S. P., Jr. (1972b). Interview by J. B. Frantz [Tape recording]. Lyndon Baines Johnson Library, Austin, TX.

Martin, P. L., & Duignan, P. (2003). *Making and remaking America: Immigration into the United States*. Retrieved from www.hoover.org/sites/default/files/uploads/documents/he_25.pdf

Martinson, R. A. (1960). The California study of programs for gifted pupils. *Exceptional Children*, *26*, 339–343.

Martinson, R. A. (1974). *The identification of the gifted and talented*. Ventura, CA: National/State Leadership Training Institute on the Gifted and Talented. (ED 104904).

Matthews, M. S. (2004). Leadership education for gifted and talented youth: A review of the literature. *Journal for the Education of the Gifted*, *28*, 77–113.

Matthews, M. S., Ritchotte, J. A., & Jolly, J. L. (2014). What's wrong with giftedness? Parents' perceptions of the gifted label. *International Studies in Sociology of Education*, *24*, 372–393.

Mayer, G. (2013). *Child labor in America: History, policy, and legislative issues*. Washington, DC: Congressional Research Service. Retrieved from https://fas.org/sgp/crs/misc/RL31501.pdf

Mayer, R. E. (2003). E. L. Thorndike's enduring contributions to educational psychology. In B. J. Zimmerman & D. H. Schunk (Eds.), *Educational psychology: A century of contributions* (pp. 113–154). Washington, DC: American Psychological Association.

Mayhew, K. C., & Edwards, A. C. (1936). *The Dewey School: The laboratory school of the University of Chicago*. New York, NY: Appleton-Century.

Mazuzan, G. T. (1994). *The National Science Foundation: A brief history*. Retrieved from www.nsf.gov/about/history/nsf50/nsf8816.jsp

McCann, C. (2014). *Federal funding for students with disabilities*. Washington, DC: New American Education Policy Program.

McDermid, D. (n.d.). *William James studies.* Retrieved from http://williamjamesstudies.org/brazil-through-the-eyes-of-william-james-diaries-letters-and-drawings-1865-1866-edited-by-maria-helena-p-t-machado/

McNutt, S. (2013). A dangerous man: Lewis Terman and George Stoddard, their debates on intelligence testing and the legacy of the Iowa Child Welfare Research Station. *Annals of Iowa, 72,* 1–30.

Meister, M. (1956). Co-operation of secondary school and colleges in acceleration of gifted students. *Journal of Educational Sociology, 29,* 220–227.

Melnik, A. (1960). The writings of Ruth Strang. *Teachers College Record, 61,* 464–476.

Mettler, S. (2012). *How the G.I. Bill built the middle class and enhanced democracy.* Retrieved from www.scholarsstrategynetwork.org/sites/default/files/ssn_key_findings_mettler_on_gi_bill.pdf

Miley, J. F. (1975). *Promising practices: Teaching the disadvantaged gifted.* Ventura, CA: Office of the Ventura County Superintendent of Schools.

Minton, H. L. (1984). The Iowa Child Welfare Research Station and 1940 debate on intelligence: Carrying on the legacy of a concerned mother. *Journal of the History of the Behavioral Sciences, 20,* 160–176.

Minton, H. L. (1988). *Lewis M. Terman: Pioneer in psychological testing.* New York, NY: New York University Press.

Mitchell, R. W., & Jenkins, R. (2010). The Talented Tenth. In K. Lomotey (Ed.), *Encyclopedia of African American education* (Vol. 1, pp. 613–617). Thousand Oaks, CA: Sage.

Montour, K. (1977). William James Sidis: The broken twig. *American Psychologist, 32,* 265–279.

Morehouse, H. L. (1896). The talented tenth. *The American Missionary, 50*(6), 182–183. Retrieved from www.gutenberg.org/files/19890/19890-pdf.pdf?session_id=aa6a3b2ff7cc1c226cdace2ae8c58422b046bc06

Munson, G. (1944). Adjusting the reading program for the gifted child. *Exceptional Children, 11,* 45–48.

National Association for Gifted Children. (n.d.). *Questions and answers about the Every Student Succeeds Act (ESSA).* Retrieved from www.nagc.org/sites/default/files/Advocacy/Q%2BA%20on%20ESSA%20(web).pdf

NCES (National Center for Education Statistics). (1993). *120 years of American education: A statistical portrait.* Washington, DC: U.S. Department of Education.

NCES (National Center for Education Statistics). (2016). *Children and youth with disabilities.* Retrieved from https://nces.ed.gov/programs/coe/indicator_cgg.asp

National Conference of Governor's Schools. (n.d.). *Governor's Schools FAQs.* Retrieved from www.ncogs.org/index.php/faqs/governor-s-school-faqs

National Education Association. (1918). *Cardinal principles of secondary education.* Washington, DC: Department of the Interior/Bureau of Education. Retrieved from http://files.eric.ed.gov/fulltext/ED541063.pdf

National Merit Scholarship Corporation. (2008). *About us.* Retrieved from www.nationalmerit.org/s/1758/interior.aspx

National Science Foundation. (n.d.). *About the National Science Foundation.* Retrieved from www.nsf.gov/about/

Needs of Elementary and Secondary Education for the Seventies. Hearing before the Subcommittee on Education, House of Representative, 91st Congress. (1969) (testimony of James J. Gallagher). Retrieved from http://congressional.proquest.com.libezp.lib.lsu.edu/congressional/docview/t9.d30.hrg-1968-edl-0026?accountid=12154

Newland, T. E. (1955). Essential research directions on the gifted. *Exceptional Children, 21,* 292–296, 310.

New York State Department of Education. (n.d.). *Reagan years: A nation at risk.* Retrieved from www.nysa.nysed.gov/edpolicy/research/res_essay_reagan_outline.shtml

New York Times. (1917, October 4). Dismissal illegal, Cattell declares. Retrieved from https://brocku.ca/MeadProject/NYT/NYT_1917_10_04.html

New York Times. (1922, February 8). Columbia settles Dr. Cattell's suits. Retrieved from https://brocku.ca/MeadProject/NYT/NYT_1922_02_09b.html

No author. (1911). Communications and discussions: Sir Francis Galton. *Journal of Educational Psychology, 2,* 149–150.

O'Connor, S. M. (1999). Mothering in public: The division of organized child care in the kindergarten and day nursery, St. Louis, 1886–1920. *Early Childhood Research Quarterly,* 1063–80.

Office of Civil Rights. (2012). *2011–2012 gifted and talented enrollment estimations.* Retrieved from http://ocrdata.ed.gov/StateNationalEstimations/Estimations_2011_12#

O'Shea, M. V. (1911). Popular misconceptions concerning precocity in children. *Science, 34,* 666–674.

Pajares, F. (2003). William James: Our father who begat us. In B. J. Zimmerman & D. H. Schunk (Eds.), *Educational psychology: A century of contributions* (pp. 41–64). Washington, DC: American Psychological Association.

Passow, A. H. (1957). The Talented Youth Project: A report on research under way. *Educational Research Bulletin, 36,* 199–216.

Passow, A. H. (1960). Educating the gifted in the U.S.A. *International Review of Education, 60,* 141–153.

Passow, A. H., & Goldberg, M. (1962). Talented Youth Project: A progress report 1962. *Exceptional Children, 28,* 223–231.

Passow, A. H., & Tannenbaum, A. J. (1954). What of the talented in today's high schools? *Educational Leadership, 12,* 148–155.

Pastore, N. (1978). The army intelligence tests and Walter Lippmann. *The Journal of the History of the Behavioral Sciences, 14,* 316–327.

PBS. (1999). *History of the SAT: A timeline.* Retrieved from www.pbs.org/wgbh/pages/frontline/shows/sats/where/timeline.html

Peters, S. J., Kaufman, S. B., Matthews, M. S., McBee, M. T., & McCoach, B. (2014, April). *Gifted education is crucial, but the label isn't.* Retrieved from www.edweek.org/ew/articles/2014/04/16/28peters_ep.h33.html

Peterson, J. (1925). *Early conceptions and tests of intelligence.* Yonkers-on-Hudson, NY: World Book.

Pillsbury, W. B. (1947). *Biographical memoir of James McKeen Cattell: 1860–1944.* Retrieved from www.nasonline.org/publications/biographical-memoirs/memoir-pdfs/cattell-james-m.pdf

Pillsbury, W. B. (1957). *Biographical memoir of John Dewey: 1859–1952.* Retrieved from www.nasonline.org/publications/biographical-memoirs/memoir-pdfs/dewey-john.pdf

Pitner, R. (1941). Superior ability. *Teachers College Record, 42,* 407–419.

Plantec, P., & Hospodar, J. (1973). *Evaluation of the National/State Leadership Training Institute on the Gifted and Talented: Final report.* Silver Springs, MD: Operations Research.

Plucker, J. A., Burroughs, N., & Song, R. (2010). *Minding the other gap! The growing excellence gap in K–12 education.* Bloomington, IN: Center for Evaluation and Education Policy. Retrieved from www.jkcf.org/assets/1/7/ExcellenceGapBrief_-_Plucker.pdf

Plucker, J. A., & Callahan, C. M. (2014). Research on giftedness and gifted education: Status of the field and considerations for the future. *Exceptional Children, 80,* 390–406.

Plucker, J. A., & Peters, S. J. (2016). *Excellence gaps in education: Expanding opportunities for talented youth*. Cambridge, MA: Harvard Education Press.

Plucker, J. A., Peters, S. J., & Schmalensee, S. (2017). Reducing excellence gaps: A research-based model. *Gifted Child Today, 40*, 245–250.

Poffenberger, A. T. (1957). Harry Levi Hollingworth: 1880–1956. *The American Journal of Psychology, 70*, 136–140.

Pritchard, M. C. (1951). The contributions of Leta S. Hollingworth to the study of gifted children. In P. Witty (Ed.), *The gifted child* (pp. 47–85). Boston, MA: D. C. Heath.

Reed, A. L. (1997). *W. E. B. DuBois and American political thought: Fabianism and the color line*. New York, NY: Oxford University Press.

Reis, S. M. (2005). Feminist perspectives on talent development. In R. J. Sternberg & J. E. Davidson (Eds.), *Conceptions of giftedness* (2nd ed.) (pp. 217–245). New York, NY: Cambridge University Press.

Reis, S. M. (Ed.) (2016). *Reflections on gifted education: Critical works by Joseph S. Renzulli and colleagues*. Waco, TX: Prufrock Press.

Reis, S. M., & Renzulli, J. S. (2010). Is there still a need for gifted education? An examination of current research. *Learning and Individual Differences, 20*, 308–317.

Renzulli, J. S. (1973). Talent potential in minority group students. *Exceptional Children, 39*, 437–444.

Renzulli, J. S. (1978). What makes giftedness: Reexamining a definition. *Phi Delta Kappan, 60*, 180–184, 261.

Renzulli, J. S. (1999). What is this thing called giftedness, and how do we develop it? A twenty-five-year perspective. *Journal for the Education of the Gifted, 23*, 3–54.

Renzulli, J. S. (2006). Swimming upstream in a small river: Changing conceptions and practices about the development of giftedness. In M. A. Constas & R. J. Sternberg (Eds.), *Translating theory and research into educational practice* (pp. 223–254). New York, NY: Routledge.

Renzulli, J. S., Callahan, C. M., & Gubbins, E. J. (2014). Laying the base for the future: One cornerstone for the Javits Act. *Journal for Advanced Academics, 25*, 338–348.

Revelle, W. (2015). Cattell, Raymond B. (1905–98). In R. L. Cautin & S. O. Lilienfeld (Eds.), *The encyclopedia of clinical psychology* (Vol. II, Cli–E, pp. 460–462). New York, NY: Wiley Blackwell.

Richardson, J. G. (1980). Variation in date of enactment of compulsory school attendance laws: An empirical inquiry. *Sociology of Education, 53*, 153–163.

Richardson, T., & Johanningmeiera, E. V. (1998). Intelligence testing: The legitimation of meritocratic educational science. *International Journal of Educational Research, 27*, 699–714.

Richards-Nash, A. A. (1924). The psychology of superior children. *The Pedagogical Seminary, 31*, 209–246.

Rickover, H. G. (1959). *Education and freedom*. New York, NY: Dutton.

Rhodes, M. (1961). An analysis of creativity. *Phi Delta Kappan, 42*, 305–310.

Roback, A. A. (1952). *History of American psychology*. New York, NY: Library Publishers.

Robinson Center for Young Scholars. (n.d.). *History*. Retrieved from https://robinsoncenter.uw.edu/about-us/history/

Roberts, R. J., & Nichols, R. C. (1967). *Participants in the National Achievement Scholarship Program for Negroes*. Washington, DC: U.S. Department of Health, Education, and Welfare (ED011527).

Robins, J. H. (2010). *An explanatory history of gifted education: 1940–1960*. (Unpublished doctoral dissertation). Baylor University, Waco, TX.

Robinson, N. M. (2006). A report card on the state of research in the field of gifted education. *Gifted Child Quarterly, 50,* 342–345.
Robinson, A., & Jolly, J. L. (Eds.). (2014). *A century of contributions to gifted education: Illuminating lives.* New York, NY: Routledge.
Rogers, K. B. (2014). Ann Fabe Isaacs: She made our garden grow. In A. Robinson & J. L. Jolly (Eds.), *A century of contributions to gifted education: Illuminating lives* (pp. 256–276). New York, NY: Routledge.
Roosevelt, F. D. (1943). *Draft statement of the President on signing S. 1767.* Retrieved from https://fdrlibrary.wordpress.com/tag/g-i-bill-of-rights/
Root, W. T. (1921). A socio-psychological study of fifty-three supernormal children. *Psychological Monographs, 29*(4), i–85.
Ruckmich, C. A. (1912). The history and status of psychology in the United States. *The American Journal of Psychology, 23,* 517-531.
Rudnitski, R. A. (1994). A generation of leaders for gifted education. *Roeper Review, 16,* 265–270.
Rudnitski, R. A. (1996). Leta Stetter Hollingworth and the Speyer School, 1934–1940: Historical roots of the contradictions in progressive education for gifted children. *Education and Culture, 13,* 1–6.
Runco, M. A. (2000–2001). Introduction to the special issue: Commemorating Guilford's 1950 Presidential address. *Creativity Research Journal, 13,* 245.
Rury, J. L. (2015). *Education and social change: Contours in the history of American schooling.* New York, NY: Routledge.
Russell, J. E. (1900). The function of the university in the training of teachers. *Teachers College Record, 1,* 1–11.
Russell, W. F. (1941). The importance of social capillarity. *Teachers College Record, 42,* 389–391.
Sanchez, G. J. (1993). *Mexican American: Ethnicity, culture and identity in Chicano Los Angeles, 1900–1945.* New York, NY: Oxford University Press.
Salisbury, E. I., & Stedman. L. M. (1935). *Our ancestors in the ancient world: How they lived.* Boston, MA: Little, Brown, & Co.
Santayana, S. G. (1947). The intellectually gifted child. *The Clearing House: A Journal of Educational Strategies, Issues, and Ideas, 47,* 259–267.
Sato, I. S., Birnbaum, M., & LoCicero, J. E. (1974). *Developing a written plan for the education of the gifted and talented.* Ventura, CA: Office of the Ventura County Superintendent of Schools.
Scheifele, M. (1953). *The gifted child in the regular classroom.* New York, NY: Teachers College, Columbia University.
Scot's Magazine. (1780). Child of Lubeck. *42,* 8–11.
Seagoe, M. V. (1975). *Terman and the gifted.* Los Altos, CA: William Kaufmann.
Seevers, R., & Shaughnessy, M. F. (2003). Reflective conversation with Dorothy Sisk. *Gifted Education International, 17,* 16–41.
Selden, S. (1994). Early twentieth-century biological determinism and the classification of exceptional students. *Evaluation and Research in Education, 8,* 21–39.
Selden, S. (1999). *Inheriting shame: The story of eugenics and racism in America.* New York, NY: Teachers College Press.
Selden, S. (2000). Eugenics and the social construction of merit, race and disability. *Journal of Curriculum Studies, 32,* 235–252.

Selden, S. (2005). Transforming better babies into fitter families: Archival resources and the history of the American Eugenics Movement, 1908–1930. Proceedings of the American Philosophical Society, *149*, 199–225.

Sherman, T. (2007). *Why gifted children act out.* Retrieved from www.helium.com/items/744627-why-gifted-chidren-act-out

Sherman, W. L., & Theobald, P. (2001). Progressive Era rural reform: Creating standard schools in the Midwest. *Journal of Research in Rural Education, 17,* 84–91.

Sidis, B. (1911). *Philistine and genius.* New York, NY: Moffat, Yard, & Co. Retrieved from https://archive.org/details/philistineandge03sidigoog

Sinatra, M. (2006). The birth of experimental psychology in Germany between psychophysical methods and physiological theories. *Physis; Rivista Internazionale di Storia della Scienza, 43,* 91–131.

Smith, R. J. (1994). *China's cultural heritage: The Qing Dynasty, 1644–1912.* Boulder, CO: Westview Press.

Smurro, C. C. (2011). Against the root of privilege. *The Harvard Crimson.* Retrieved from www.thecrimson.com/article/2011/10/21/conant-375-profile/?page=1

Sokal, M. M. (1971). The unpublished autobiography of James McKeen Cattell. *American Psychologist, 26,* 626–635.

Spencer, L. (1958). Implementation—The effective use of identification techniques. In J. B. Conant (Ed.), *The identification and education of academically talented students in the American secondary school* (pp. 39–45). Washington, DC: NEA.

Spring, J. H. (1972). Psychologists and the war: The meaning of intelligence in the Alpha and Beta tests. *History of Education Quarterly, 12,* 3–15.

Stalnaker, J. M. (1957). National program for discovering students of exceptional ability. *Exceptional Children, 23,* 234–266.

Stalnaker, J. M. (1958). Methods of identification—The complexity of the problem. In J. B. Conant (Ed.), *The identification and education of the academically talented student in the American secondary school* (pp. 18–26). Washington, DC: NEA.

Stanley, J. C. (1959). Enriching high-school subjects for intellectually gifted students. *School and Society, 87,* 170–171.

Stanley, J. C. (1975). Intellectual precocity. *The Journal of Special Education, 9,* 29–44.

Stanley, J. C. (1976). Concern for intellectually talented youths: How it originated and fluctuated. *Journal of Clinical Child Psychology, 5,* 38–42.

Stanley, J. C. (1980). On educating the gifted. *Educational Researcher, 9,* 8–12.

Stanley, J. C. (1996). *In the beginning: The Study of Mathematically Precocious Youth (SMPY).* Baltimore, MD: Johns Hopkins University.

Stedman, L. M. (1924). *Education of the gifted.* Yonkers-On-Hudson, NY: World Book Company.

Sternberg, R. (1985). *Beyond IQ: A triarchic theory of human intelligence.* New York, NY: Cambridge University Press.

Sternberg, R. (1991). Death, taxes, and bad intelligence tests. *Intelligence, 15,* 257–269.

Sternberg, R. (2003). Giftedness according to the theory of successful intelligence. In N. Colangelo & G. Davis (Eds.), *Handbook of gifted education* (3rd ed., pp. 88–99). Boston, MA: Allyn & Bacon.

Sternberg, R. J., & Lubart, T. I. (1999). The concept of creativity: Prospects and paradigms. In R. J. Sternberg (Ed.), *Handbook of creativity* (pp. 1–14). New York, NY: Cambridge University Press.

Stewart, E. D. (1999). An American century of roots and signposts in gifted and talented education. *Gifted Child Today, 22*(6), 56–57.

Stoner, W. S. (1914). *Natural education*. Indianapolis, IN: The Bobbs-Merrill Company.
Stoskopf, A. (2002). Echoes of a forgotten past: Eugenics, testing, and educational reform. *Educational Forum, 66*, 126–133.
Strang, R. (1954). Introduction. *Journal of Teacher Education, 5*, 210.
Subotnik, R. F. (2006). A report card on the state of research in the field of gifted education. *Gifted Child Quarterly, 50*, 354–355.
Subotnik, R. F., Olszewski-Kubilius, P., & Worrell, F. C. (2011). Rethinking giftedness and gifted education: A proposed direction forward based on psychological science. *Psychological Science in the Public Interest, 12*, 3–54.
Sumpton, M. R., & Luecking, F. M. (1960). *Education of the gifted*. New York, NY: Ronald Press.
Tannenbaum, A. J. (1983). *Gifted children: Psychological and educational perspectives*. New York, NY: Macmillan.
Tannenbaum, A. J. (2000). A history of giftedness in school and society. In K. A. Heller, F. J. Mönks, R. Subotnik, & R. J. Sternberg (Eds.), *International handbook of giftedness and talent* (pp. 23–53). New York, NY: Pergamon.
Tash, W. R. (2006). *Evaluating research centers and institutes for success!* Fredericksburg, VA: WT & Associates.
Taylor, C. W. (1960). The creative individual: A new portrait in giftedness. *Educational Leadership, 18*, 7–12.
Taylor, C. W. (1986). Cultivating simultaneous student growth in both multiple creative talents and knowledge. In J. S. Renzulli (Ed.), *Systems and models for developing programs for the gifted and talented* (pp. 307–350). Mansfield Center, CT: Creative Learning Press.
Terizan, S. G. (2008). "Adventures in science": Casting scientifically talented youth as national resources on American radio, 1942–1958. *Paedagogica Historica, 44*, 309–325.
Terman, L. M. (1906). Genius and stupidity. *Pedagogical Seminary, 31*, 307–373.
Terman, L. M. (1910–1992). Correspondence. Lewis Madison Terman papers (Box 14, Folder 19), Department of Special Collections and University Archives, Palo Alto, CA.
Terman, L. M. (1913). Psychological principles underlying the Binet-Simon Scale and some practical considerations for its use. *Journal of Psycho-Asthenics, 18*, 93–104.
Terman, L. M. (1915). The mental hygiene of exceptional children. *The Pedagogical Seminary, 22*, 529–537.
Terman, L. M. (1916a). *The measurement of intelligence: An explanation of and a complete guide for the use of the Stanford revision and extension of the Binet-Simon Intelligence Scale*. Cambridge, MA: The Riverside Press.
Terman, L. M. (1916b). *The uses of intelligence tests*. Boston, MA: Houghton Mifflin.
Terman, L. M. (1917). The intelligence quotient of Francis Galton in childhood. *The American Journal of Psychology, 28*, 209–215.
Terman, L. M. (1919). *The intelligence of school children*. Boston, MA: Houghton Mifflin.
Terman, L. M. (1921a). Intelligence and measurement. *Journal of Educational Psychology, 11*, 127–133.
Terman, L. M. (1921b). Mental growth and IQ. *Journal of Educational Psychology, 11*, 325–341.
Terman, L. M. (1924a). The conservation of talent. *School and Society, 19*, 359–364.
Terman, L. M. (1924b). Tests and measurements of gifted children. *Washington Education Journal, 3*, 172–190.
Terman, L. M. (1925). *Genetic studies of genius: Volume I*. Palo Alto, CA: Stanford University Press.
Terman, L. M. (1930a). Autobiography of Lewis M. Terman. In C. Murchison (Ed.), *History of psychology in autobiography* (Vol. 2, pp. 297–331). Worcester, MA: Clark University Press.

Terman, L. M. (1930b). Talent and genius in children. In V. F. Calverton & S. D. Schmalhausen (Eds.), *The new generation* (pp. 405–423). New York, NY: The Macaulay Company.

Terman, L. M. (1939). Educational suggestions from follow-up studies of intellectually gifted children. *The Journal of Educational Sociology, 13*, 82–89.

Terman, L. M., & Merrill, M. A. (1937). *Measuring intelligence: A guide to the administration of the new revised Stanford-Binet Tests of Intelligence*. Boston, MA: Hougton Mifflin.

Terman, L. M., & Oden, M. (1947). *The gifted child grows up: Twenty-five years' follow-up of a superior group: Genetic studies of genius, Vol. 4*. Stanford, CA: Stanford University Press.

Terman, L. M., & Oden, M. (1959). *The gifted group at mid-life: Thirty-five years' follow-up of the superior child: Genetic studies of genius, Vol. 5*. Stanford, CA: Stanford University Press.

The Galileo Project (n.d.). *Science*. Retrieved from http://galileo.rice.edu/science.html

Theman, V., & Witty, P. (1943). Case studies and genetic records of two gifted Negroes. *The Journal of Psychology, 15*, 165–181.

Thomas, J. Y., & Brady, K. P. (2005). The Elementary and Secondary Education Act at 40: Equity, accountability, and the evolving federal role in public education. *Review of Research in Education, 29*, 51–67.

Thorndike, E. L. (1906). *Principles of teaching based on psychology*. New York, NY: Seiler. Retrieved from https://archive.org/stream/principlesofteac00thor#page/237/mode/1up

Thorndike, E. L. (1910). The contribution of psychology to education. *Journal of Educational Psychology, 1*, 5–12.

Thorndike, E. L. (1914). Professor Cattell's relation to the study of individual differences. In R. S. Woodworth (Ed.), *The psychological researches of James McKeen Cattell: A review of some of his pupils* (pp. 92–101). New York, NY: The Science Press.

Thorndike, E. L. (1918). The nature, purposes, and general methods of measurement of educational products. In S. A. Courtis (Ed.), *The measurement of educational products* (17th Yearbook of the National Society for the Study of Education, Pt. 2., pp. 16–24). Bloomington, IL: Public School.

Thorndike, E. L. (1925). *Biographical memoir of Granville Stanley Hall: 1846–1924*. Retrieved from www.nasonline.org/publications/biographical-memoirs/memoir-pdfs/hall-g-stanley.pdf

Thut, I. N. (1947). By way of comment: 4. The discovery and development of talent in youth. *Educational Administration and Supervision, 33*, 223–226.

Time. (1937, September 6). The strange case of Winifred Sackville Stoner Jr. *30*, 52, 54, 56.

Titchener, E. B. (1921). Wilhelm Wundt. *The American Journal of Psychology, 32*, 161–178.

Tomlinson, S. (1997). Edward Lee Thorndike and John Dewey on the science of education. *Oxford Review of Education, 23*, 365–383.

Torrance, E. P. (1959). Research notes from here and there: Current research on the nature of creative talent. *Journal of Creative Talent, 6*, 309–316.

Torrance, E. P. (1971). Creativity and its education implications for the gifted. In J. C. Gowan & E. P. Torrance (Eds.), *Educating the ablest* (pp. 208–221). Itasca, IL: F. E. Peacock Publishers.

Torrance, E. P. (1972). Predictive validity of the Torrance Tests of Creative Thinking. *Journal of Creative Behavior, 6*, 236–262.

Torrance, E. P. (1977). *Discovery and nurturance of giftedness in the culturally different*. Reston, VA: Council for Exceptional Children.

Torrance, E. P. (1979). Unique needs of the creative child and adult. In A. H. Passow (Ed.), *The gifted and talented: Their education and development, The seventy-eighth yearbook of the National Society for the Study of Education: Part I* (pp. 352–371). Chicago, IL: University of Chicago Press.

Truman, H. S. (1950). *Statement by the President upon signing bill creating the National Science Foundation.* Retrieved from http://trumanlibrary.org/publicpapers/index.php?pid=743&st=&st1=

Tyack, D. (1976). Ways of seeing: An essay on the history of compulsory schooling. *Harvard Educational Review, 46,* 355–389.

Urban, W. J. (2010). *More than science and Sputnik.* Tuscaloosa, AL: University of Alabama Press.

U. S. Citizenship and Immigration Service. (2012). *Overview of INS history.* Retrieved from www.uscis.gov/sites/default/files/USCIS/History%20and%20Genealogy/Our%20History/INS%20History/INSHistory.pdf

U. S. Department of Education. (1983). *A nation at risk: An imperative for educational reform.* Washington, DC: Author.

U. S. Department of Education. (2006). *10 facts about K–12 education funding.* Retrieved from www2.ed.gov/about/overview/fed/10facts/index.html

U. S. Department of Education, Office of Educational Research and Improvement. (1993). *National excellence: A case for developing America's talent.* Washington, DC: U. S. Government Printing Office.

U. S. Department of Health, Education, and Welfare Social and Rehabilitation Service. (1967). *The story of White House Conferences on children and youth.* Washington, DC; Children's Bureau (DHEW).

Valencia, R. R., & Suzuki, L. A. (2001). *Intelligence testing and minority students: Foundations, performance, factors, and assessment issues.* Thousand Oaks, CA: Sage.

Van Sickle, J. H. (1910). Provision for gifted children in public schools. *The Elementary School Teacher, 10,* 357–366.

VanTassel-Baska, J. (2006). NAGC Symposium: A report card on the state of research in the field of gifted education. *Gifted Child Quarterly, 50,* 339–341.

VanTassel-Baska, J. (2014). Sir Francis Galton: The Victorian polymath (1822–1911). In A. Robinson & J. L. Jolly (Eds.), *A century of contributions to gifted education: Illuminating lives* (pp. 8–22). New York, NY: Routledge.

Von Károlyi, C., Ramos-Ford, V., & Gardner, H. (2003). Multiple Intelligences: A perspective on giftedness. In N. Colangelo & G. Davis (Eds.), *Handbook of gifted education* (3rd ed., pp. 100–112). Boston, MA: Allyn & Bacon.

Walsh, R. T. G., Teo, T., & Baydala, A. (2014). *A critical history and philosophy: Diversity of context, thought, and practice.* New York, NY: Cambridge University Press.

Ward, V. (1961). *Educating the gifted: An axiomatic approach.* Columbus, OH: Charles Merrill.

Ward, V. (1979). The governor's school of North Carolina. In A. H. Passow (Ed.), *The gifted and talented: Their education and development, The seventy-eighth yearbook of the National Society for the Study of Education: Part I* (pp. 209–217). Chicago, IL: University of Chicago Press.

Washburne, C. W. (1918). The lock step in our schools. *School and Society, 8,* 391–402.

Washburne, C. W. (1924). The attainments of gifted children under individual instruction. In G. M. Whipple (Ed.), *The twenty-third yearbook of the National Society for the Study of Education: Part I* (pp. 247–261). Bloomington, IL: Public School Publishing Company.

Washburne, C. W., & Marland, S. P. (1963). *Winnetka: The history and significance of an educational experiment.* Englewood Cliffs, NJ: Prentice-Hall.

Watson, R. I. (1961). A brief history of educational psychology. *The Psychological Record, 11,* 209–242.

Wellman, B. L. (1940). Iowa studies on the effects of schooling. In G. M. Whipple (Ed.), *The thirty-ninth yearbook of the National Society for the Study of Education: Part I* (pp. 377–399). Bloomington, IL: Public School Publishing Company.

Wertheimer, M. (1970). *A brief history of psychology*. New York, NY: Holt, Rinehart, & Winston.

Whipple, F. H. (1958). Memorial High School's Advanced Placement Program. *NASSP Bulletin, 42*(242), 24–26.

Whipple, G. M. (1919a). *Classes for gifted children*. Bloomington, IL: Public School Publishing Company.

Whipple, G. M. (1919b). Experiments in the education of gifted children. *Journal of the Michigan Schoolmaster's Club, 53*, 8–23.

Whipple, G. M. (1924). Historical and introductory. In G. M. Whipple (Ed.), *The twenty-third yearbook of the National Society for the Study of Education: Part I* (pp. 1–24). Bloomington, IL: Public School Publishing Company.

Williamson, P. B. (1948). The American Association for Gifted Children: A progress report. *Understanding the Child, 17*, 53–55.

Williamson, P. B. (1953). Preparation for teachers of the gifted pupil. *Education Administration and Supervision, 37*, 65–79.

Wilson, F. T. (1951). The evidence about acceleration of gifted youth. *School and Society, 73*, 3–19.

Wilson, F. T. (1953). Preparation for teachers of gifted children in the United States. *Exceptional Children, 20*, 78–80.

Wineburg, S. (2001). *Historical thinking and other unnatural acts: Charting the future of teaching the past*. Philadelphia, PA: Temple University Press.

Winkler, D. L., & Jolly, J. L. (2011). The Javits Act: 1988–2011. *Gifted Child Today, 34*(4), 61–63.

Winkler, D. L., & Jolly, J. L. (2014). Lewis M. Terman: A misunderstood legacy. In A. Robinson & J. L. Jolly (Eds.) *A century of contributions to gifted education: Illuminating lives* (pp. 64–78). New York, NY: Routledge.

Winkler, D. L., Stephenson, S., & Jolly, J. L. (2012). Governor's schools: An alternative for gifted children. *Gifted Child Today, 35*, 292–294.

Witty, P. A. (1953). What is special about special education? The gifted child. *Exceptional Children, 19*, 255–259.

Witty, P. A. (1930). A study of one hundred gifted children. *University of Kansas Bulletin of Education, 2*(7), 3–44.

Witty, P. A. (1949). The gifted child in secondary school. *NASSP Bulletin, 33*(162), 259–264.

Witty, P. A. (Ed.). (1951). *The gifted child*. Boston, MA: D. C. Heath.

Witty, P. A. (1954). Programs and procedures for the education of gifted children. *Journal of Teacher Education, 5*, 225–229.

Witty, P. A., Conant, J. B., & Strang, R. (1959). *Creativity of gifted and talented children*. New York, NY: Teachers College, Columbia University.

Witty, P. A., & Jenkins, M. D. (1934). The educational achievement of a group of gifted Negro children. *Journal of Educational Psychology, 25*, 585–597.

Witty, P. A., & Jenkins, M. D. (1935). The case of "B"—A gifted Negro girl. *The Journal of Social Psychology, 6*, 117–124.

Witty, P. A., & Lehman, H. C. (1927). Drive: A neglected trait in the study of the gifted. *Psychological Review, 34*, 364–376.

Witty, P. A., & Theman, V. (1943). A follow-up study of educational attainment of gifted Negros. *Journal of Educational Psychology, 34*, 35–47.

Wolf, T. (1964). Alfred Binet: A time of crisis. *American Psychologist, 19*, 762–771.

Wolters, R. (2008). *Race and education (1954–2007)*. Columbia, MO: University of Missouri Press.

Woodworth, R. S. (1952). *Biographical memoir of Edward Lee Thorndike: 1874–1949.* Retrieved from www.nasonline.org/publications/biographical-memoirs/memoir-pdfs/thorndike-edward-1.pdf

Worcester, D. A. (1956). *The education of children above-average mentality.* Lincoln, NE: University of Nebraska Press.

Worrell, F. C. (2013). Nonverbal assessment. In C. M. Callahan & H. L. Hertberg-Davis (Eds.), *Fundamentals of gifted education: Considering multiple perspectives* (pp. 135–147). New York, NY: Routledge.

Worrell, F. C. (2014). William Edward Burghardt DuBois. In A. Robinson & J. L. Jolly (Eds.), *A century of contributions to gifted education: Illuminating lives* (pp. 41–60). New York, NY: Routledge.

Yerkes, R. M. (1918). Psychology in relation to the war. *The Psychological Review, 25,* 85–115.

Yerkes, R. M. (Ed.). (1921). *Psychological examining in the United States Army.* Washington, DC: National Academy of Science. Retrieved from https://ia601408.us.archive.org/20/items/psychologicalexa00yerkuoft/psychologicalexa00yerkuoft.pdf

Yoakum, C. S., & Yerkes, R. M. (1920). Methods and results. In C. S. Yoakum & R. M. Yerkes (Eds.), *Army mental tests* (pp. 12–40). New York, NY: Henry Holt and Company.

Yockelson, M. (1998). They answered the call: Military service in the United States Army during World War I, 1917–1919. *Prologue Magazine, 30*(3), Retrieved from www.archives.gov/publications/prologue/1998/fall/military-service-in-world-war-one.html

Yoder, A. H. (1894). The study of the boyhood of great men. *Pedagogical Seminary, 3,* 134–156.

York, C. (Producer). (2011). *A school of their own* (Part 2) [Video file]. Retrieved from www.youtube.com/watch?v=q7sIc8RXspk

Young, K. (1924). The history of mental testing. *Pedagogical Seminary, 31,* 1–48.

Zangwill, I. (1909). *The melting pot.* Baltimore, MD: Lord Baltimore Press. Retrieved from https://archive.org/details/themeltingpot23893gut

Zenderland, L. (1998). *Measuring minds: Henry Herbert Goddard and the origins of American intelligence testing.* New York, NY: Cambridge University Press.

Zettel, J. J. (1982). The education of gifted and talented children from a federal perspective. In J. Ballard, B. A. Ramirez, & F. J. Weintraub (Eds.), *Special education in America: Its legal and governmental foundations* (pp. 51–64). Reston, VA: Council for Exceptional Children.

INDEX

A Nation at Risk 164, 166, 167, 168, 199, 205
acceleration 52, 53, 54, 57, 76, 79, 81, 113, 114, 118–120, 148, 181, 192, 198, 206
American Association for Gifted Children (AAGC) 122, 126, 131, 185, 206
Army Alpha and Army Beta 31, 32, 64, 101

Binet, Alfred 22–24

capacity building 3, 147, 155, 156–161
Cattell, James McKeen 16–20, 24–31, 63, 65, 73

Dewey, John 20, 34, 35, 127
DuBois, W. E. B. 49–50

enrichment 57, 76, 87, 107, 102, 104, 117, 118–120, 143, 177
eugenics 13, 14, 82–83

father of gifted education 61–72

Galton, Francis 3, 11–13, 46–47, 82,
giftedness: conceptions 103, 116, 176; definitions 54, 65, 67, 86, 87, 103, 104, 115, 141, 142, 174–175
Goddard, H. H. 20, 23, 26–27, 30–31, 37
Governor's Schools 143–144

Hall, Stanley 16, 17, 19, 26, 35, 62, 127, 192
Hollingworth, Leta S. 13, 15, 16, 26, 28, 56, 68, 80

Jacob K. Javits Gifted Children and Youth Education Act 161
James, William 15, 16, 18, 43, 127
Jenkins, Martin 128, 129
Lombroso, Cesare 46–48

Marland Report, The 105, 145–157, 160, 162, 163, 170, 174
mother of gifted education 13, 15, 16, 26, 28, 56, 68, 80

National Association for Gifted Children (NAGC) 104, 122, 124, 126, 168, 198
National Defense Education Act (NDEA) 100–104, 137, 154
National Education Association (NEA) 53, 103, 123
National Excellence: A Case for Developing America's Talent 168
National Science Foundation (NSF) 98–99, 156
National/State Leadership Training Institute on the Gifted and Talented (N/S-LTI-G/T) 156–162, 177, 178

Office of Gifted and Talented, The (OGT) 153, 155

Progressive Era of Education 34–38
P. S. 165 55, 75–78
P. S. 500 (The Speyer School) 55, 77–79

Serviceman's Readjustment Act of 1944, The 96
Speyer School, The 55, 77–79
Stedman, Lulu 56
Strang, Ruth 101, 123, 127, 129, 130

Terman, Lewis 11, 13, 16, 30, 56, 58, 80, 82, 134
Thorndike, E. L. 16, 20–21, 24, 26, 27–29, 34, 63, 64, 74, 83, 86, 127

Whipple, Guy M 24, 30, 42, 46, 48–49, 52, 53, 55, 86, 109
Witty, Paul 91, 101, 114, 123–129
Wundt, Wilhelm 15, 16

Yoder, Alfred 48

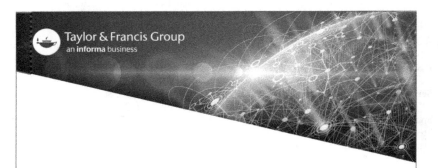